CONSUMER BEHAVIOUR

EXCLUSIVE PARTNER

Paradox
PUBLICATIONS GUIDE HOUSE
+91 8848074612 \ +91 7907367147

CONSUMER BEHAVIOUR

Dr. R. Jayanthi
B. Anjanee Kumar
Dr. A. John William
Abhishek Duttagupta
Dr. S. Saravanan

red'shine
PUBLICATION
INDIA | UNITED KINGDOM | SWEDEN

CONSUMER BEHAVIOUR

by: Dr. R. Jayanthi, B. Anjanee Kumar, Dr. A. John William, Abhishek Duttagupta, Dr. S. Saravanan

■

RED'SHINE PUBLICATION PVT. LTD.
Headquarters (India): 88-90 REDMAC, Navamuvada,
Lunawada, India-389 230
Contact: +91 76988 26988
Registration no. GJ31D0000034

In Association with,
RED'MAC INTERNATIONAL PRESS & MEDIA. INC
India | Sweden | UK

■

■

■

ISBN: 978-81-960634-1-2
ISBN-10: 81-96063-41-5
DIP: 18.10.8196063415
DOI: 10.25215/8196063415
Price: ₹ 500
January, 2023 (First Edition)

■

■

www.redshine.co.in | info@redshine.in
Printed in India | Title ID: 8196063415

PREFACE

Consumer behaviour is the study of how individuals make decisions about what they need and want, and how they go about obtaining those things. It is a field of study that encompasses both psychological and sociological factors that influence the way people shop, purchase, and consume goods and services. Understanding consumer behaviour is essential for businesses and marketers as it helps them to identify and target specific segments of the population, design effective marketing strategies, and improve the overall customer experience.

One of the main areas of focus in consumer behaviour is the decision-making process. This includes understanding how people gather information, evaluate options, and make choices. Factors such as motivation, perception, learning, attitude, and personality all play a role in the decision-making process.

Another important aspect of consumer behaviour is the influence of social and cultural factors on purchasing decisions. People are influenced by their family, friends, and social groups, as well as by larger cultural and societal trends. Marketers must understand these influences in order to effectively target and communicate with specific segments of the population.

In addition to these traditional areas of focus, consumer behaviour also encompasses newer areas of study such as digital marketing, e-commerce, and the impact of technology on consumer behaviour. As technology continues to advance, it is becoming increasingly important for businesses to understand how consumers use digital platforms and devices in their shopping and purchasing decisions.

Despite the many complexities involved in understanding consumer behaviour, the field is constantly evolving and improving. With the advent of big data, businesses can now access vast amounts of information on consumer behaviour that can be used to improve marketing strategies and optimize the customer experience. Additionally, advances in technology such as artificial intelligence and machine learning are allowing businesses to better predict and understand consumer behaviour in real-time.

In conclusion, consumer behaviour is a fascinating and constantly evolving field that plays a critical role in the success of businesses and marketers. Understanding consumer behaviour can help businesses to identify and target specific segments of the population, design effective marketing strategies, and improve the overall customer experience. In this book, we will delve deeper into the various factors that influence consumer behaviour and explore the latest trends and innovations in the field.

- Authors

SYLLABUS

UNIT NO.	CONTENTS
1	**INTRODUCTION TO CONSUMER BEHAVIOUR:** • Introduction • Market Strategy and Consumer Behaviour • Market Analysis. • Consumer Decision Process.
2	**CULTURE AND CONSUMER BEHAVIOUR:** • Meaning of Culture • Characteristics of Culture • Function of Culture • Types of Culture • Cross-cultural Consumer Analysis • Cross cultural Marketing Objective • Basic areas for Cross-Cultural Marketing • Problem in Cross Cultural Marketing • Motivation and Consumer Behaviour • Motives and Motivation • Positive or Negative Motivation • Consumer Motives: Personal, Social motives • Involvement: Types of Involvement • Measuring Involvement Values • Values and Attitudes • Means and End Chain Model.
3	**REFERENCE GROUP AND CONSUMER BEHAVIOUR:** • Introduction of Groups • Advantages and Disadvantage of Group • Reference Group • Types of Reference Group • Social class and Consumer Behaviour • Introduction Social class Categorization • Social class lifestyle and buying behaviour • Social class and Market Segmentation • Social factors, Social class and Consumer Behaviour.

UNIT NO.	CONTENTS
4	**PERCEPTION AND CONSUMER BEHAVIOUR:** • Introduction • Meaning. Nature, Importance and limitation of Perception • Barriers to Accurate Perception • Sensation • Perception of Values • Perception of Process • Determining Consumer Buying Behaviour • Consumer Purchase Decision • Types of Decision • Types of Decision Behaviour • Buying stage and Situational influence • Models of Consumer Behaviour • Economic Model • Teaming Model • Sociological Model • Howard Sheth Model of Buying.
5	**ATTITUDE AND CONSUMER BEHAVIOUR:** • Meaning of Attitude • Nature and Characteristics of Attitude • Types of Attitude • Learning of Attitude • Sources of influence on Attitude formation • Model of Attitude • Tricomponent Attitude Model • Multi-Attribute Attitude Model • Consumer Decision Making Process • Levels of Consumer Decision • Consumer Information Processing Model • Hierarchy of Effects Model.

CONTENTS

1

INTRODUCTION TO CONSUMER BEHAVIOUR

Introduction and concept of Consumer Behaviour

The study of consumer behavior is a relatively recent academic discipline, having emerged just after World War II. It is now a buyer's market rather than a seller's. Because of this, businesses have shifted their emphasis from making products to caring about their customers and, more specifically, their habits. Buyer behavior has developed into its own field as a consequence of the evolution of marketing theory from the traditional "selling idea" to the more recent "consumer-oriented marketing." The rise of consumer culture and protection laws shows how seriously consumers are taken. Individuals' choices about the allocation of their resources (time, money, and effort) in the context of consumption are the focus of consumer behavior research.

Because individuals are so different from one another, it's hard for marketers to predict how they'll behave. As a result, business owners felt compelled to learn as much as they could about customers' purchasing habits. In the end, this information served as a crucial resource for marketers in their efforts to foresee clients' future purchasing habits and develop four marketing tactics aimed at establishing a lasting connection with them.

Consumer Behavior: Definition

Consumer behavior research examines how people find, evaluate, and ultimately get rid of goods, services, experiences, and ideas in pursuit of satisfying their wants and requirements.

Customers versus Consumers

The word "customer" refers to a very particular kind of person who patronizes a certain business. A brand loyalist is someone who consistently buys a certain brand of goods from a specific retailer shop. One who frequents Bata Stores or wears Raymond's garments is, thus, a client of these businesses. A 'consumer,' on the other hand, is someone who does things like shop for, evaluate, utilize, and get rid of goods, services, experiences, and ideas.

The Importance of Researching Consumer Habits

Since everyone uses products and services, understanding customer behavior is beneficial. For marketers to thrive in today's cutthroat industry, they must have a deep familiarity with their target demographic. The following arguments show why consumer behavior research is so vital.

Relevance to Everyday Activities

The point of learning a subject area is to increase one's appreciation of the value it brings to society. Considering the significance of consumer behavior to everyday life, it's no surprise that researchers devote time and energy to the topic. Markets are where people spend the majority of their leisure time, whether shopping or doing other activities. The time is generally spent learning about new things, thinking about existing ones, talking about them with friends, and watching commercials for those items. Our utilization of them says a lot about the kinds of people we are. Due to these factors, research is warranted. However, it's possible that the goal is to address pressing, material concerns. Imperative for the Process of Determination

Since consumers' behaviors and preferences may have a significant impact on businesses' choices, studying consumer behavior is considered an applied field of study. Micro and macro viewpoints are interested in applying its findings.

The goal of studying the customer from a micro viewpoint is to aid the macro goal of a business. Understanding customers is a priority for those working in this area, who do so in an effort to improve their performance.

Whereas the aggregate-level problems encountered by the mass or society as a whole may be addressed using consumer insight gained from a macro viewpoint. Consumers' actions have a major impact on the standard of life.

Buyer Organization vs. Buyer Person

Unlike consumer markets, where goods are purchased for personal use, those in industrial or institutional markets are used for commercial purposes. Consumer markets and consumer purchasing behaviour vary from business markets and business purchasing behaviour in a number of important ways. Those things that set them apart are primarily:

1) Structure of the market and consumer needs
2) Buyer Characteristics
3) Considerations in making choices and purchasing behaviour

1) Structure of the market and consumer needs

- Differentiating elements of market supply and demand include:
- Unlike consumer markets, where customers may be found all over the place, business markets have a far smaller global footprint.
- The number of organizations that purchase is less than the number of individuals who do so, but these organizations purchase in greater quantities.
- To put it simply, there are two types of buyer marketplaces in organizations: vertical and horizontal. Vertical buildings only serve one or two industries, whereas the potential customer pool for horizontal structures is too large.
- The need for a product or service is driven by the market and then translated into a need inside an organization. Demand is unpredictable and rather inelastic.

2) Buyer Characteristics The following are some of the unique features of purchasers:

- The decision-making process involves a large number of people or groups.
- Customers from corporations often have a high level of expertise and professionalism.
- The majority of shoppers are driven by logic rather than emotion when making purchases.

3) Considerations in making choices and purchasing behaviour

The key distinctions are as follows.

- In contrast to individual consumers, businesses have stricter guidelines to adhere to while making purchases, such as proposals, quotes, and processes.
- The decision-making process is very difficult because of the enormous stakes involved, the technical details, the number of variables, etc.
- When making purchases for an organization, it is necessary to engage in more thorough negotiation over a longer time period than when making purchases as an individual.

Participatory Marketing

One kind of shopper is often portrayed as being more engaged with items and stores than another. An enthusiastic buyer wants to learn as much as possible about the product before making a purchase. Thus, he researches extensively by reading product literature, comparing brands and models at various stores, consulting experts, and asking for advice. An informed consumer is one who actively seeks out, pays attention to, and considers product information before making a purchase.

Reasons Why Customers Get Involved

Consumer participation is affected by a variety of elements, including the individual, the product, and the setting.

Reasons unique to the individual

The degree to which a customer invests in a product or service is largely determined by the individual's sense of self-worth, their wants, and their values. To the extent that the customer's self-image, their values, and the requirements that the product fulfills are consistent with those of the product, the more invested the consumer will feel in the product. The world of celebrities, for instance, has a common sense of identity, set of values, and set of requirements. People with this lifestyle are more likely to buy items and services that are designed with them in mind. They invest a lot of time and energy into shopping for luxury items such as name-brand clothing, foreign automobiles, high-end medical equipment, etc.

Various Aspects of the Product

When there is more at stake for the customer in the purchase of a product or service, they are more likely to get actively involved in the decision-making process. Consumers will likely feel more invested in the purchase of their home than in the purchase of tooth paste due to the higher perceived risk associated with the former.

The level of participation is influenced by how the product is differentiated. The more options people are presented with, the more invested they get in making a decision.

➢ One's enthusiasm for an endeavor might also be affected by how much they like utilizing the product or service. For consumers, certain goods and services just provide more satisfaction than others. When compared to, example, home cleansers, beverages like tea and coffee have a far higher hedonic value. As a result, people are really invested.

➢ When people start talking about a product, more people want to become involved with it. Public consumption or production of any good requires extensive participation. One's level of participation increases, for instance, when one buys a vehicle as opposed to when one buys a television.

Constraints of the Circumstances

➢The context in which a product is purchased or utilized may evoke strong feelings. The level of investment is affected by the context in which the purchase is made. Consider the difference in effort required when shopping for socks for yourself vs socks for a close friend.

➢A lot of people are more involved when they feel social pressure to be. In comparison to when one is shopping alone, when one is with friends, one is more likely to feel self-conscious about the things and brands that one considers.

➢The time pressure associated with making a choice also plays a role. A customer in dire need of a new refrigerator who happens across a "today only offer" at an appliance store will not have the luxury of time to research other stores and models. The stakes of the choice inspire more participation.

➢In cases when there is no turning back, such as when a store does not allow returns or exchanges on clearance products, a lot of people need to be involved.

Therefore, participation might come from the outside, as in the case of situational involvement, or from the inside, as in the case of persistent involvement. Numerous individual and contextual elements, many of which are within the marketer's sphere of influence, might trigger this emotion. Consumers' perception, thought processes, and communication styles are all influenced.

Types of Involvement

One might be involved in a situation or in a way that lasts for a long time.

The two types of involvement are:

A) Situation

B) Enduring

A) Situational involvement

"Situational involvement" refers to the fleeting emotional connection a customer has to a brand whenever they are reminded of a specific occasion in which they use that brand's products.

B) Enduring Involvement

The term "enduring participation" is used to describe the experience of consistently positive emotions for a product category throughout time and across contexts. Vacationers, for instance, who hire a resort for their vacation, have a significant but fleeting interest in the facility they choose. Alternatively, a person's pre-buy, purchase, and post-purchase reactions to sport motorcycles are all influenced by the level of interest that he has in his activity. It has been seen that whereas vacationers' participation is prompted by unique circumstances, the engagement in the second example originates from and is an integral component of the customer.

There is a significant difference between engagement in a single incident and commitment to a cause over time. In order to quantify engagement, businesses look at how much it may be prompted by the offering at hand. When marketers become aware of the level of participation they're up against, they take action to gain command of the items or sales environments they're tasked with moving.

Outcomes of Consumer Participation

Consumers are better able to easily comprehend information linked to the product when they have a personal investment in the product. This data undergoes extensive processing, which ensures its long-term storage. As a result, users experience an increase in positive emotions and are more likely to participate in prolonged problem solving and informal conversation with others. You may classify the outcomes into three groups: information discovery, information processing, and communication.

Engaged consumers are more likely to do extensive research before making a purchase, as well as to look at alternatives to the original vendor. The consumer who is really interested in vehicles and is considering purchasing one is likely to do research. He looks at competing theories to weigh their merits and drawbacks. As they get more invested, they gain exposure to other options within that class. They employ a wide variety of resources to compile the data. One such action is window shopping, the practice of going to many stores and asking about prices and products before making a final purchase decision. Retailers should encourage clients of this kind to visit stores in order to learn about and compare different models in order to satisfy their informational requirements.

Processing of Data

Understanding, cognitive elaboration, and emotional arousal are all aspects of information processing that will be addressed in greater detail below.

Strength of Understanding

Customers who are more invested in the process have a greater tendency to comprehend product information at a more in-depth level. The involvement of urban parents with higher levels of education in the selection of baby food is higher than that of rural parents with lower levels of education. They remember that for a very long time as well. In such a scenario, it is the marketer's responsibility to supply customers with memory jogging aids in the form of information cues. However, since the audience consists mostly of "low involvement" shoppers, it is essential that all relevant details be easily available throughout the decision-making process.

Complexity of Thought

Consumers who are highly engaged in the decision-making process give more consideration to the products they purchase than those who are less so. They have a comprehensive grasp that includes reasons in favour of and against their position. What this means is that highly engaged customers often develop cognitive reactions that are either pro- or anti-marketing.

Using the earlier example of selling infant food items, the product, however beneficial, may have substantial adverse effects, such as obesity. Most intelligent parents will think long and hard about this before giving it to their kids. Marketers need to make a strong case that the product's positives exceed any potential drawbacks in order to encourage the parents to have a favourable impression of it. An adverse disposition toward the product is more likely to emerge if the arguments are poorly researched and fail to persuade.

Measure of Emotional Reactivity

Customers who actively participate in a brand's marketing efforts tend to have stronger emotional responses.

Active consumers have stronger reactions to product-related information, which may work for or against marketers. This is because clients are more likely to reject a product if its negative connotation is amplified.

Message Transfer

Information transmission refers to the rate at which highly engaged consumers tell their peers about their experiences with the product. The most common method for doing this is via informal word-of-mouth. The study participants also discussed the product more often than the control group. Customers who are happy with the goods will likely spread positive reviews, while those who are unhappy will spread negative ones. As a result, businesses aiming to please active customers should work to reduce complaints and boost gratification. A satisfied ONIDA TV viewer could, for instance, spread the word about their positive experience to others.

Customer Participation Schemes

Marketers might benefit from considering four key involvement-based customer behavior models when making strategic decisions, especially those concerning marketing communication tactics. Here is a rundown of the four different types.

1. Low Involvement Learning Model
2. Learn-Feel-Do Hierarchy model
3. Level of Message Processing Model
4. Product versus Brand Involvement Model

1. Low Involvement Learning Model

Products with a low involvement level are ones that customers often use but seldom have to worry about any negative consequences. Those in charge of marketing do their best to move merchandise without attempting to alter buyers' opinions. The old brand's reputation is supplanted by the new product's reputation. By strategically situating their products, marketers may provide low-effort education. New customers are attracted to products like "uninterrupted flow" pens and "mouth wash" toothpastes.

2. Learn-Feel-Do Hierarchy model

The manner in which a purchase choice is made might affect its outcome. Thoughtful deliberation is not always the driving force behind the judgments we make. Some decisions are made automatically out of habit, while others are deliberate. Consumers' decisions are explained by their levels of ignorance (learn), apathy (feel), and inaction (do) according to the learn-feel-do matrix. Each of the four quadrants of this matrix represents a distinct objective of marketing communication: to educate, to persuade, to develop a habit, or to boost consumer pleasure. We see that there is a continuum between rational thought and emotional reaction, with some choices requiring more of one than the other and others including components of both. As a continuum, the range between high and low significance is also shown.

(i) High Involvement / High Thinking

More information is needed for purchases in the first quadrant because of the higher perceived value of the goods and the higher cognitive load associated with the purchase. Automobiles, homes, and other large, infrequent purchases fall under this group. This technique is based on the learn-feel-do framework. Marketers must provide comprehensive data if they want to win over consumers.

(ii) Deep Emotional Investment

The second quadrant's buyers rely more on gut instinct than logic when making purchases. Jewellery, clothes, makeup, and accessories are all examples of common purchases associated with self-esteem. The paradigm of strategy is "feel, learn, do." Marketers that want to increase sales should appeal to consumers' emotions.

(iii) Lack of Engagement/Emotion

In this section, consumers shop to indulge their own unique preferences, many of which are sha7ped by their perception of themselves. This class includes items like newspapers, soft drinks, alcoholic beverages, etc. The decision to buy is often influenced by peer pressure. The strategy model is do-feel-learn. It aids product promotion by using social networks and word-of-mouth.

(iv) A Lack of Engagement and Logical Deliberation

It requires less deliberate deliberation and more mechanical habitual purchasing. Common examples include meals, groceries, office supplies, and more. Any product, throughout time, may be classified here. When attempting to set yourself apart from the competition, knowledge plays a crucial role. Habitual use may be all that's needed to instill brand loyalty. The strategy model is do-learn-feel. It argues that marketers generate trial using different sales promotion strategies.

3. Level of Message Processing Model

Customer attention to commercials or any other marketing communication relies on four degrees of consumer involvement: Pre-attention, focused attention, understanding and elaboration. Phone calls are made by everyone for varying degree of message processing. With pre-attention, the customer has to do little more than recognize the brand before moving on to the purchasing process. Focal attention includes fundamental information like product name or usefulness. In comprehension level, the message is studied and the substance of the message is merged with other information, via elaboration, which helps to establish attitude towards the product. It is proposed that marketers produce commercials which may stimulate elaboration.

4. Product versus Brand Involvement Model

An individual may have an interest in a product category but not a specific brand, or vice versa. Housewives, for instance, tend to be experts on kitchen supplies, but they could be confused by the differences between different brands. There are four distinct sorts of consumers that may be identified based on their level of investment in a certain product or label.

i. Brand loyalists are very invested in both the product category as a whole and the brand in question. For example, cigarette smokers and paper readers fit in this group.

ii. Information Seekers: These shoppers are engaged more with product category but may not have favorite brand. They are likely to see information to chose a certain brand. For instances, air- conditioning and washing machine purchasers belong into this group.

iii. Routine Brand Buyers: These customers are not strongly concerned with the product category but may be involved with the specific brand within that category. They don't feel strongly about the category as a whole and are more loyal to their specific brand. People in this group have been loyal to one service or establishment for an extended period of time, such as long-time consumers of one brand of soap or frequent diners at one restaurant.

iv. Those who easily switch brands have little loyalty to either the category or any specific brand within it. Price is usually what gets their attention. For example stationery goods, fashion things fall under this category.

Market strategy and consumer behaviour

Marketing Implications of Consumer Behavior

Any organization with a strong marketing focus will tell you that the client is the center of their universe. Therefore, it is crucial to your company's success to know what motivates people to purchase in general and what motivates your consumer to buy specifically. Simply said, the market is the client, and they are the focus of all marketing efforts. Managers in charge of marketing are using a wide variety of strategies aimed at improving the quality of the end product customers get. This trend indicates that, as the marketing landscape evolves, more and more professionals recognize the need of basing their strategies on a thorough understanding of customer behavior. Among the many consequences of customer behavior for marketers are the ones listed below.

Marketing Strategies and Consumer Behaviour

The foundation of every successful marketing plan is a firm grasp of customer psychology. Organizational fortunes rise and fall based on how customers respond to a plan. To thrive in today's market, businesses must provide customers with more value (the positive difference between the entire benefits of a product and its acquisition costs) than their rivals. In order to outperform the competition and provide higher customer value, businesses must be more adept at predicting and responding to consumer requirements. To put it simply, a firm's marketing strategy is the response to the question, "How will the company supply its target market with higher customer value?" Solving this conundrum calls for the development of marketing mix tactics that take into account product, pricing, placement, and promotion. An optimal mix of these factors delivers value to the consumer and satisfies their expectations. To give exceptional customer value, a bike retailer, for instance, has to understand the buyer's performance expectations, desired service, price willingness to pay, information sought, and after-sales service.

Market Segmentation and Consumer Behaviour

A company's marketing strategy hinges on the choice of which market segment(s) to target. To be more precise, marketers don't construct segments, but rather identify existing ones in the marketplace. The goal of market segmentation is to identify distinct groups of customers who have similar preferences and buying habits so that those groups may be targeted with tailored marketing strategies. Inasmuch as each market segment has its own set of requirements, a company that caters to the demands of a specific segment in its product development will more effectively satisfy the desires of its target demographic and provide more value to its customers. Femina magazine, for instance, should target smart city ladies. Getting a handle on the urban lady is crucial to the success of this publication.

The Role of Consumer Behaviour in Strategic Product Positioning

Positioning a product, service, firm, or retail establishment in the minds of its intended audience is known as product positioning. With the use of positioning, businesses try to find the sweet spot between product features and consumer needs. For a firm to successfully position its product in the market, it must first have an in-depth familiarity with how its target demographic thinks about the company and its offerings. For example, Samsung brand is viewed as luxury brand by few consumers and value-driven brand by others in the market, but marketer must figure out what causes their target market to perceive differently and position it appropriately.

Consumer Behavior and Marketing Research

Studying consumer behavior helps marketing analysts to forecast how customers will respond to promotional communications and to understand why they make the purchasing choice they do. The marketing industry has come to recognize that influencing customers' purchasing decisions requires an in-depth understanding of the factors that go into shaping such decisions. As a result of the critical importance of understanding customer behaviour, the marketing industry developed a subfield called consumer research. The current trend in consumer research is to investigate the factors that influence consumers' learning and attitude development, as well as the demands and motivations that drive their purchasing choices.

Consumer Behavior and Non-Profit and Societal Marketing

A thorough grasp of consumer behavior may benefit the organizations that market ideas and concepts of social importance. Family planning organizations, AIDS prevention groups, government agencies, religious orders, and educational institutions all ask for public funding to help them provide services that people desire and need. Organizations that engage in such pursuits benefit from understanding their prospective donors, what inspires their giving, and how to successfully appeal to those motivations.

Political Determinants of Consumer Behaviour

Policy making on different services and the creation of consumer protection laws are two significant areas where government may benefit from research on consumer behaviour. Understanding customers requires familiarity with their values, norms, normatives, and practices.

Market Analysis

Market analysis is the process of evaluating the attractiveness and competitiveness of a market, as well as the potential for a new product or service to succeed in that market. This process involves researching and analyzing various market conditions, including the size and growth of the market, the key market segments, the major players and their market share, the distribution channels, and the overall economic and regulatory environment. It also includes identifying the target customer, their needs and preferences, and how they currently satisfy those needs. This information can be used to identify opportunities and threats, and to develop a marketing strategy that takes into account the unique characteristics of the market.

One important aspect of market analysis is understanding the size and growth of the market. This includes evaluating the current market size, as well as projections for future growth. This information can help a company determine if the market is large enough to support their product or service, and if it is expected to grow in the future, which can indicate a potential for increased sales and revenue.

Another important aspect is identifying key market segments, which are groups of customers with similar characteristics or needs. By understanding these segments, a company can tailor their product or service to better meet the needs of specific customers and potentially increase their market share.

It's also important to understand the major players in the market and their market share. This can provide insight into the level of competition, and whether it is possible for a new player to enter the market and be successful.

Distribution channels, such as retail stores, online marketplaces, and direct-to-consumer sales, are also important to consider. Understanding how products or services are sold in a market can help a company determine the best way to reach their target customers.

Finally, the overall economic and regulatory environment can also play a role in the success of a product or service. This includes factors such as economic conditions, government regulations, and cultural norms. A company should consider how these factors may impact their ability to sell their product or service in a market.

Overall, market analysis is a crucial step in the development of a marketing strategy and can help a company understand the opportunities and challenges they may face in a particular market.

Consumer decision process

The Buying Decision Procedure

Due to the fundamental idea of a marketing-oriented corporation — that the customer is the center around which the business revolves — the customer environment is the most significant environment in which enterprises function. This means that those working in marketing have a vested interest in learning about the decision-making processes their target demographic uses.

The consumer decision making process comprises number of connected and sequential phases of activity. The process starts with the identification and acknowledgement of an unmet need or desire. It turns becomes an impetus. The shopper initiates an inquiry. After considering all of the results, a buyer makes a final choice. The customer then does an after-purchase survey to gauge satisfaction. See the diagrammatic explanation of the procedure that follows.

1. Indicating a Desired Change

When a consumer has a want that must be met, they are more likely to make a purchase. The urge may be aroused by internal or external stimuli. A person's rate of action toward obtaining what they want is proportional to the degree of their desire. The priorities are set based on the level of need and the timeframe involved. Marketers should supply essential details regarding selling points.

2. A Quest for Data

Only when the product is both well-known and widely accessible can unrecognized requirements be addressed. There are many options for consumers to choose from, but it is up to them to choose which product or brand would provide them with the most happiness. And they'll need to do some digging to uncover specifics about the product, brand, or place. Those shopping for a product or service have several options, including talking to their neighbors, friends, and family. Advertisements, merchants, dealers, packaging and sales promotion, and storefront window displays are all channels via which marketers provide useful information to consumers. Mass media including news sheets, radio, and television deliver information. The internet has evolved into a significant and trustworthy information resource in recent years. Marketers are obliged to supply newest, dependable and appropriate information.

3. Consideration of Possible Courses of Action

This is a vital step in the process of purchasing. The following are crucial components of the alternatives assessment process.

a) Characteristics are grouped together to form a product. Products and brands may be evaluated based on these characteristics. For example, in washing machine customer evaluates price, capacity, technology, quality, model and size.

b) Distribution network and after-sales service, as well as the firm and brand's reputation in the target market, become crucial assessment factors.

c) When creating and promoting their goods, businesses should keep this in mind.

4. Reasons to Buy

The evaluation's findings shape customers' opinions of competing items and brands. One's purchase choice is affected by one's feelings about the brand. Buyer is moving closer to making a final decision. In addition to all the foregoing variables, situational considerations like credit alternatives, dealer conditions, lowering prices etc., are also evaluated.

5. Post- Purchase Behavior

Post-purchase behavior of customer is more crucial as far as marketing is concerned. Consumer gains brand preference only when that brand lives up to his expectation. This brand affinity automatically replicates sales of marketer. Someone who has purchased from you and been pleased is the best kind of silent salesman. If the brand is utilized and does not provide the expected benefits, unfavorable emotions and thoughts will develop, and a negative brand attitude will emerge. Cognitive dissonance describes this experience. In an effort to win over customers of competing businesses, marketers have begun capitalizing on this trend. Marketers may improve client retention and acquisition with the aid of many components of the promotional-mix strategy.

The Laws of Buying and Selling

These methods are often known as "data processing techniques." Consumers benefit from these processes because they provide a framework for weighing their alternatives and minimizing the uncertainty inherent in decision-making. There are two main types of decision rules that have been identified:

Consumers use the compensatory decision rules to rank brands by a weighted score based on how well they perform in each criterion. Indicative of the brand's potential value to you as a consumer is the score you just saw. It is presumed that consumers would go with the highest-rated product when given a choice. The distinctive characteristic of this rule is that it balances the good rating of a brand on one attribute to balance off a poor evaluation on some other trait. For example, good characteristic like great fuel economy is balanced with the negative rating of high maintenance cost.

In contrast to the aforementioned rule, non-compensatory decision rules do not let customers to counteract a favorable rating of one brand characteristic with a less favorable evaluation of another attribute. There are three sorts of non-compensatory norms.

Consumers using the conjunctive decision rule set a distinct, least acceptable amount as a threshold for each characteristic. In this the choice is excluded for further consideration if a given brand or model falls below the cutoff mark on any characteristic.

As its name implies, disjunctive rule is the inverse of conjunctive rule. In this scenario, the buyer sets a unique floor for each criterion. In this scenario, the choice is allowed if it satisfies or surpasses the threshold set for any one of the criteria.

Lexicographic Decision Rule: In this rule the customer first rates the qualities in terms of perceived relevance or significance. Later he examines several possibilities in terms of the one feature that is judged most essential. If one choice ranks well enough based on this criterion, regardless of how it fares on the other attributes, it is chosen and the process is completed.

Consumers' Determination-Making Processes on a Scale

The customer choice making process is complicated with different degree. It's not necessary to put in a lot of time and thought into every buying choice. On continuum of effort ranging from extremely high to very low, it may be differentiated into three unique categories of consumer choice making:

1. Solving Complex Problems (EPS)
2. Limited Problem Solving (LPS) (LPS)
3. Routine Problem Solving (RPS) (RPS)

1) Extensive Problem Solving (EPS): When customers purchase a new or unfamiliar product, they often need to gather extensive information and spend considerable time making a decision.

They must establish the concept of a new product category and identify the criteria to be utilized in picking the product or brand.

2) Second, customers may exhibit Limited Problem Solving (LPS) when they are well-versed in a product category and its numerous brands but have yet to settle on a favourite. They look for more details to assist them choose between brands.

3) Routine Problem Solving (RPS): When customers have previously bought a product or brand, they need little or no information to pick the product. Consumers engage in habitual and automatic buying.

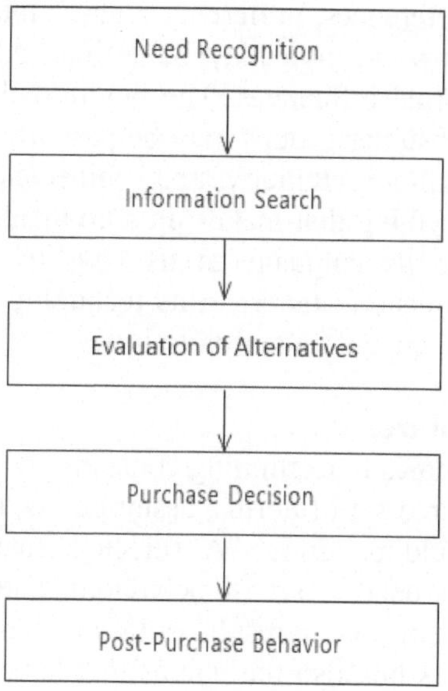

2

CULTURE AND CONSUMER BEHAVIOUR

Culture and consumer behaviour: - Meaning of culture

Everyone on Earth is a devoted shopper. Every day, we purchase and consume a vast array of products and services. However, when it comes to purchasing purchases, everyone of us is unique in our preferences, preferences, and habits. What we purchase, consume, and how we live may be influenced by a wide range of external and internal influences. The buying habits of individuals and the actions of consumer groups may be partially explained by external factors such as culture, ethnicity, and socioeconomic status. Culture is the study of everything that makes up a civilization, from its beliefs to its knowledge to its language to its laws to its conventions to its traditions to its music to its art to its technology to its goods. Culture has a tremendous impact on our daily lives.

Definition of culture:

When it comes to examining consumer behavior, "culture" refers to a society's shared set of norms, assumptions, and expectations about how things should be done. "A selected, manufactured manner of reacting to experience, a set of behavioral pattern," as described by Howard and Sheth. As a result, cultural elements include not just established beliefs but also the values that have evolved around those beliefs through time. All the things that a person picks up as a result of being socialized into a society are part of culture. It is generally agreed that a civilization's culture consists of its members' common set of norms for appropriate social conduct, which are passed down from older to younger members of the same community.

The three methods through which people acquire cultural knowledge are as follows:

1. **Formal learning**: Parents and other adults are the primary educators of children in the first formal learning setting. You may have heard, for example, that education is essential to finding success and fulfilment. What you discover here may change how you react to school as an individual.
2. **Informal learning**: Observing and mimicking the actions of adults, such as parents and peers, or fictional characters in media

serves as a source of inspiration and knowledge for those who engage in informal learning.

3. **Technical learning**: Students acquire technical knowledge by being taught the steps involved in doing a certain activity, such as painting, dancing, singing, etc.

Characteristics of Culture

- A person's cultural norms may be taught.
- The rules, standards of conduct, and rewards and punishments of a society are governed by its culture.
- Culture improves productivity in many aspects of life.
- Everyone adheres to the same standards.
- Culture, as the saying goes, changes with the times.
- The environment is a major contributor to cultural norms.
- There is a hierarchical structure of several cultural layers.

Advertising norms are culturally relative. How individuals dress, eat, live, and vacation are all influenced by their culture. Healthy living, learning, and honoring one's elders are highly prized in Indian culture. However, in today's society, time shortage is an increasing concern, suggesting a shift in dining habits. Some changes in the way we live:

1. **Convenience**: First, it's handy; with more and more women entering the labor field, there's a greater need for items that make it easier to do everyday home tasks. The skyrocketing demand for these items is mirrored in the market for frozen foods, mixer-grinders, food processors, microwaves, pressure cookers, and other kitchen appliances.
2. **Education level**: People in today's culture value education highly since it provides them with opportunities to advance in their chosen fields. So many schools catering to professionals and those seeking to further their careers have opened in recent years, yet they still haven't been able to keep up with demand. You might take the opening of new computer training centers as an example.
3. **Physical appearance**: Thirdly, one's physical appearance is more important in today's society. Weight-loss clinics and spas and salons are proliferating in every major American city. In recent years, there has been a rise in the sales of cosmetics for both sexes. Designer clothing is now sold at even the most elite boutiques.
4. **Materialism** The change from spiritualism to materialism in people's cultural values is extremely clear. Products that improve

our physical comfort and social standing, such as air conditioners, automobile CD players, etc., are commanding a larger share of our disposable income than ever before.

Indicators of cultural identity

Culture has four defining features, as outlined by William Haviland. Culture, first of all, is what unites the members of a given society. Culture may be thought of as a collection of indicators that each individual displays to the world in order to be recognized as an individual. In doing so, it clearly delineates our distinctions from one another.

It's not innate but rather acquired via experience and education after birth. Diverse cultural practices allow us to learn about and appreciate one another and ourselves. Diversity of cultural practices is made possible by urban lifestyles and the apathy that comes with urbanization. When individuals of diverse cultural backgrounds interact in an urban setting, the area in between them is contested territory. According to sociologist George Simmel, therefore, indifference plays just as large a role in contemporary urban society as does diversity.

Culture relies on individuals adhering to the norms and standards connected with it, which are symbolized by things like images, objects of worship, rituals, literature, and artifacts. They pick it up from one another and adopt it as part of their shared culture. These symbols are not representative of the culture as a whole, though. They may serve as a window into a culture's inner workings, but they only have significance when used by a community of people. A sign may be anything from a color to a stone to a hand motion. No one can confidently claim that they have mastered another culture by studying its symbols. We need to see how individuals use and misuse them on a regular basis to get a sense of their significance in society.

It combines aspects of society, the economy, and government. Raymond Williams, a scholar in the field of cultural studies, defines culture as "a full way of existence" or "a framework of emotion." This description is the foundation for the notion that culture is something that an individual absorbs, usually unknowingly, and that then goes on to form his or her whole worldview, including his or her beliefs, values, and behaviors.

Since culture is a set of norms or signals that govern how we behave, it may also influence our openness to others' differences and our ability to get along with rule-breakers. While societies that are less confident in themselves tend to take rule breakers more seriously, those with a stronger sense of self-worth tend to shrug it off. Thus, culture may be exclusive or inclusive, depending on factors such as customs, location, historical context, etc. Ethics and politics, both internal to the culture and external to it, frequently influence the degree to which members of that culture are open to one another. It's because of this that cultural politics and cultural relativism are flourishing nowadays.

Culture gives its members a feeling of who they are, which helps in coping with adversity, and also gives their lives purpose and continuity, two things that are essential in times of stress. In a world where fast political and economic change has undermined the feeling of continuity and where, as Karl Marx put it, "everything that is solid dissolves into air, all that is holy is profaned," the process of cultural production stands as the lone affirmation of one's sense of self and identity.

Cultures that see the economy as a complement to their values sometimes find themselves at odds with the forces that drive a nation's economy.

Culture is neither the work of any one individual or the product of a single event in history. It has been a slow and steady progression through the ages and across history. Culture is the accumulated result of many attempts, failures, and successes that have occurred throughout the course of a civilization's history. This is not something that can be formed or changed in a single generation or age, but rather something that evolves gradually over many decades, if not centuries. The whole of human society's past may be found inside the boundless depths of culture. It chronicles the ebb and flow of ideas and actions, the rise and fall of civilizations, the setbacks to forward development, and the repeated collapse and revival of communities on local, national, and global scales. Any progress done in any field, whether it psychology, art, science, politics, the economics, or even the spiritual world, will be documented in culture.

Thus, one may argue that a society's culture serves as its foundation. The community's culture is influential in many aspects of life, including the arts, customs, festivals, rituals, attire, and cuisine. The very fabric of a society might shift if there is a disruption in the development and dissemination of cultural values. Culture and its outward manifestation, civilization, are inseparable and interdependent pillars of human history. Culture is the foundation and fortification of a civilisation, whereas civilization itself is the product of that culture. In the same way that humans can't live without culture, culture can't exist without human beings. Culture mainly serves as a means of expression, information, and socialization within a society, hence it would not be too far off to say that these social functions are its fundamental meaning. Yet, just as cultural outputs reflect social reality, so too may its meaning be seen as a reflection of a reality that transcends mere factual, pragmatic, and scientific explanations. Culture, in the eyes of these theorists, is a manifestation of a spiritual power that predates human reason and interaction.

The culture in which one lives has an impact on every person. Our life would lose meaning and purpose if we severed ties with our cultural traditions, thus it's crucial that we keep in close touch with our ancestry.

It is only inevitable that there would be racial, geographical, socioeconomic, and temporal differences in cultural practices. On the other hand, when a culture's foundation is built on ideals with broad applicability, that culture grows and endures long after the civilization that gave origin to it has vanished. However, if a culture's foundation is based on avarice or fanatically strict dogma, it will not last.

It is impossible to preserve a culture that refuses to change or evolve. Culture, like a river or stream, may bend and reroute itself to avoid impediments without ever pausing to rest. Over the course of centuries and across varying landscapes, no civilization was able to establish a permanent hegemony. Their success and durability may be attributed to their openness to change and their ability to incorporate new elements into an established totality.

DIFFERENT STYLES OF CULTURE

There is "corporate culture," which refers to the business world, "competitive culture" in schools, which encourages students to do their best, "consumerist culture," which emphasizes status and spending power and is linked to greater material satisfaction, and "emerging culture," which is an index of the attitudes and behavior patterns of a particular group. Because of its loose use, the core concept of culture may have been lost.

The following categories may be used to categorize cultural practices:

1) High culture
2) Low culture.
3) Popular culture.
4) Folk culture.

High culture is a concept that was first used in English by Victorian poet and critic Matthew Arnold in his book Culture and Anarchy. "High culture," in his view, was a motivating factor for social and political progress. He described "high culture" as the "study of perfection" and what this meant was to "know the finest that has been spoken and thought in the world." In Notes towards a Definition of Culture, poet T. S. Eliot argued that both high and popular civilization are necessary for a whole culture.

Much of what we mean when we talk about "high culture" has to do with appreciating "high art," which encompasses fields as diverse as literature, theater, music, and painting. The majority of the works considered to be part of this "high culture" were made during an era when artists had the financial and social support of affluent, cultured, and aesthetically-inclined patrons, allowing them to focus on their craft without distraction. As a result, the Western idea of "high art" originates in the Greco-Roman and Renaissance periods. The ancient civilizations of Egypt, Greece, Rome, India, Byzantium, Persia, China, etc., were not the only ones to have it.

"High Culture" refers to works of art, film, music, dance, and literature that have been deemed to be in the established canons of their respective fields. There have been many attempts to include the general people in exhibits or performances that highlighted "high culture," despite criticism that it is elitist and primarily serves the educated, urban, rich elite. Museums, libraries, and arts organizations in many nations are supported by their respective governments as part of an effort to foster this field.

Courses that emphasize the liberal arts foster this notion, but the name "liberal arts" is seldom used nowadays. This is because, as access to literature and education steadily opened up, academics took up the study of all areas of high culture.

The topic of elite vs populist or mass culture has been explored from many different angles in the disciplines of Cultural Studies, Media Studies, Critical Theory, Sociology, Marxist thinking, and Postmodernism. It's also been a major focus in the study of nationalism's theoretical underpinnings. For example, Ernest Gellner described high culture as "...a literate codified culture which facilitates context- free communication," and held that it was crucial to the development of a unified national identity. He compares 'high culture' with simpler, agriculture-based 'low cultures,' rather than focusing on variations within a single society.

One more sociologically informed, all-encompassing, and social-class-based definition of "high culture" is "taste," which encompasses things like proper table manners, a refined palate, and an appreciation of the arts. It may also allude to elitist social norms that the general populace is not allowed to follow.

A person with low culture

As the antonym of "high culture," this word is used to dismiss some forms of popular entertainment. Theorists of human social behavior have long debated whether or not "high" and "low" cultures are not, in fact, subcultures. It may seem that in the modern age of postmodernism the boundary between the two has blurred. "Low culture" refers to things like "kitsch," "slapstick," "escapist," "pulp," and "popular" art forms including film, music, and dance (as opposed to classical music and dance).

At a period when medieval romances, which had previously been disparaged, started to impact literature, the Romantic Movement was among the first to take another look at the presumed "low culture" and re-value it. The phrase "low culture" may also refer to something that has broad appeal. Popular culture might refer to everything from tabloids and talk programs to popular sports like football and cricket to the most popular songs and novels right now.

In the realm of popular culture

To be popular in law and politics in the fifteenth century was to be low, base, vulgar, and representative of the common people. The term didn't come to denote "widespread" and "well-liked" until the late eighteenth century.

As its name indicates, popular culture (or pop culture) revolves on well-known pastimes and the icons that represent them. The obvious follow-up question is, "How is that decided?" What is popular in the social context, that is, everything that is accepted by the majority of people of a society, is often defined and even dictated by the mass media. When we talk about a society's popular culture, we're also referring to the aspects of that culture that are extensively disseminated via the language used there.

The boundaries of time and place are always pushing against the stability of popular culture. It moves, splitting off into divergent currents that coalesce into new ways of thinking that influence one another. It is possible that certain aspects of popular culture may split off and become their own unique subculture. Whatever it is that we define as "pop culture," it is enjoyed by a sizable percentage of the general population.

Mass culture, another name for popular culture, refers to anything that is commercially driven, mass produced, and intended for widespread consumption. It's the most accurate representation of widespread societal preferences at the time, hence it's often referred to as the "genuine" culture. Having developed from the move to urbanization during the Industrial Revolution, popular culture is frequently considered as being nearly antagonistic to the elite, elitist 'high culture' and a show of resistance by the people.

Everything from mass media and entertainment to food, literature, clothes, sports, fashion, music, and other forms of popular culture are conveyed via mass consumption. It has had a significant impact on the visual arts, particularly on works created in the United Kingdom and the United States after the 1950s. It's often accused, particularly by religious groups, for being shallow, consumerist, corrupt (and corruptible), sensationalist, and pandering to the lowest common denominator. Some people think it's beneath them and irrelevant since it doesn't deal with the serious issues of life and also doesn't appreciate the little things that make life worth living. There are certain works that, for one reason or another, seem to belong in both "high" and "popular" culture.

Aspects of Popular Culture

What makes a group or culture unique is the way of life, which is shaped by generations of tradition and custom. Traditions in folk culture are often passed down orally from one generation to the next, and they have a strong sense of communal identity. It also highlights the transition from the old to the new methods. Folk culture was the equivalent of mass culture before the industrial revolution, therefore it might be considered the popular culture of its day.

Folklore has always been an element of popular culture, spreading from person to person and, more recently, from screen to screen through digital media such as the Internet and text messages.

Traditional cultures have deep roots in their physical communities. When certain parts of a culture are transplanted to another location, as happens during migration, such parts retain strong associations with their original home. When compared to mainstream culture, folk culture is characterized by an internal focus that makes no external references. Folk culture, however, has always had an influence on both "popular" and "high" culture, and many aspects of folk culture have become indistinguishable and inextricable parts of both of these cultures.

Functions of Culture

1. Socialization: Culture plays a crucial role in the process of socialization by providing individuals with the norms, values, and beliefs that are necessary for them to function within a particular society. Through socialization, individuals learn how

to behave, communicate, and think in ways that are appropriate and expected within their culture. For example, in some cultures, it is considered rude to interrupt someone while they are speaking, while in others it is common practice.

2. Identity formation: Culture also helps to shape an individual's sense of self and identity. Culture provides individuals with a sense of belonging and connection to a particular group or community. For example, an individual's culture may include shared traditions, customs, and beliefs that are passed down from generation to generation.
3. Communication: Culture serves as a means of communication among individuals within a group or society. It allows them to share common experiences and understandings. For example, in some cultures, it is customary to bow or to shake hands as a form of greeting, and understanding these customs helps individuals communicate effectively in those cultures.
4. Preservation of tradition: Culture helps to preserve the traditions, customs, and history of a particular group or society. It passed them down from generation to generation. This helps to maintain a sense of continuity and identity for the group or society.
5. Economic and political organization: Culture can also play a role in shaping economic and political systems, influencing how resources are allocated and decisions are made within a society. For example, in some cultures, there is a strong emphasis on collective decision-making, while in others, individual achievement is highly valued.
6. Creative expression: Culture is also a source of creative expression, with art, music, literature, and other forms of creative expression reflecting the values, beliefs, and experiences of a particular group or society. Through creative expression, cultures are able to convey their stories, emotions, and ideas to others.
7. Adaptation and survival: Culture can also play a role in helping individuals and groups adapt to and survive in their environment. It provides knowledge and techniques for obtaining food, shelter, and other necessities of life. For example, the knowledge of how to farm or the technique of building shelter is passed down through culture.
8. Empowerment: Culture provides individuals and groups with a sense of power and agency, allowing them to shape their own lives and the world around them. Culture can empower people by providing them with a sense of identity, community, and

tradition. This sense of empowerment can lead to the development of leaders, activists, and other change agents within a society.

Types of Culture

- National culture
  - The culture prevalent in a nation, common to everyone
- Popular culture
  - The culture of the masses with norms of mass appeal
- Subculture
  - The culture of a group within the larger society
  - Group identification based on nationality of origin, race,region, age, religion, gender, etc.
- Corporate culture
  - The company's values, rituals, customs, myths and heroes

Culture in Hoffstede's Five Dimensions

Consumers' identities, the things they choose to acquire and use, the methods through which they make purchases, and the companies they choose to do business with are all profoundly influenced by cultural norms. However, these days, marketers are paying a lot more attention to the ways in which macro-cultures influence consumer behaviour. Five cultural factors were identified by Hoffstede as being shared by 66 nations. You may use them to find out which parts of the market are more eco-conscious, and use them as a basis for describing and comparing the cultures of other countries.

1) Individualism vs. collectivism (Pursuit of self or group interest): The interaction between an individual and the group mentality that dominates most societies is what is meant by the term "individualism." Table below highlights the mental and behavioural distinctions between individualism and collectivism.
2) Distance of power (Social inequality and submission to authority): The extent to which a culture tolerates power disparities within institutions and organizations may be inferred from the magnitude of this gap. It may modify how individuals with various social standings choose to share power, respond to unfair pay, and collaborate.
3) Uncertainty aversion (ambiguity tolerance/sensitivity): The phenomenon known as "uncertainty avoidance" refers to the many ways in which communities cope with the ambiguity and unpredictability of daily existence. Certain communities thrive

with well established rituals and protocols for social conduct, while others are more accepting of unconventional ideas and actions.

4) Identities of men and women (Segregation of male and female roles in society): The degree to which a culture embraces ideals seen as generally masculine or feminine is largely based on this. For instance, a culture's masculinity is often associated with characteristics like assertiveness, respect for achievement, and the pursuit of wealth and material possessions, while the feminine is often associated with characteristics like nurturing, concern for the environment, and advocacy for the underdog.

5) Differences between abstract and associative thinking: The process of adding value to a product via a chain of events that lacks a logical connection but is still plausible.

Cultural Factors

Knowledge, religion, art, law, morality, conventions, and any other talents and habits gained by members of society are all part of what we call culture. People's lifestyles, purchasing habits, and decision making tendencies are all shaped by their own cultures. Culture is something we pick up as we go through life, and it might be from our parents, our community, or wherever else we've lived. A person's thoughts and actions are constrained by the norms of his or her culture. When a person's thoughts and actions go beyond these norms, he is engaging in cross-cultural conduct and is subject to the impact of several cultures. Unfortunately, it's usually not until after the fact that we realize we've been influenced by another culture. As a member of a culture, one shares attitudes, rituals, and worldview with others who share that culture. It's ubiquitous and it permeates everything. Marketers may better tailor their wares to the preferences of consumers by keeping an eye on how trends in material culture, such as the proliferation of mobile phone usage and the ever-changing patterns of popular clothes, impact technological advancements.

Culture establishes norms as limits on individual conduct. Cultures have norms because people have shared opinions about what is good and bad. It is only natural for people to conform to social conventions. Many accepted practices in business, families, and communities are mapped out by cultural norms. The manner in which we greet others, the appropriate distance at which to stand while doing business, the clothes we choose to wear, and so on.

Cultural norms and practices evolve gradually over time. Rapid technological development causes changes in society. Understand the current culture and the evolving culture and culture of the nation where the commodities are to be sold is essential for marketers and managers in times of emergency, war, or natural tragedies. The world's largest corporations have successfully adapted to local cultures across the world.

Coca-Cola is a global beverage brand. Companies like Procter & Gamble and others provide cross-cultural training for its staff. Companies sometimes have trouble pushing items due of cultural misunderstandings, such as when I Coca-Cola pulled its 2-liter bottle from Spain because it wouldn't fit in local refrigerators and (ii) many nations are highly traditional and don't want women represented on the products. In a nutshell, this is bad for trade with those nations.

Cross-cultural consumer analysis

As can be seen in the accompanying diagram, there are essentially three distinct types of cultural values.

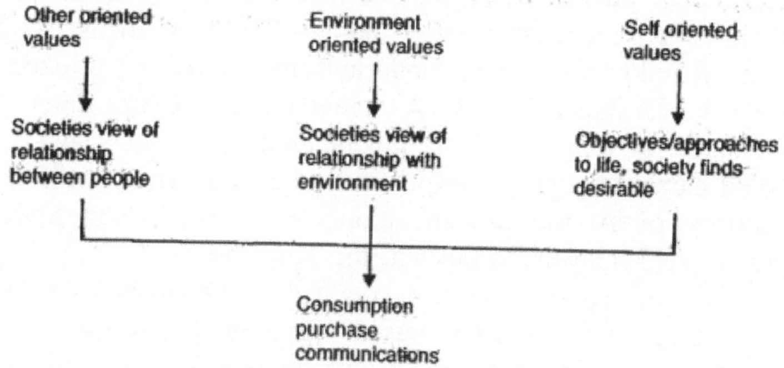

Values Orientation influencing Behavior

i) Values With a Different Direction

This exemplifies the interdependence of people and their community. As a result of the connection, marketing strategies have changed. Decisions are more likely to be made collectively in societies that place a premium on doing things together. It gives rise to following questions which impact customer behavior.

The question of whether or not an individual's initiative is more valuable than group effort.

Whether or whether a message is more persuasive if it stresses courting depends on its romantic orientation. A love plotline has greater universal appeal and performs better in many nations.

Adult/ kid theme: Is it the kids or the grownups that take center stage in your family? In what ways do kids have input on adult decision-making?

Masculine/Feminine: Whether men or women have more power in the culture.

To what extent competition and cooperation are complementary to one another.

This is accomplished through building alliances with others.

Do more prestigious jobs tend to go to those who are younger or older in age? Korean culture places more value on senior citizens than does American society. Decisions are decided by adult individuals in Korea.

ii) Values in Respect to the Environment

If a society places an abnormally high value on tidiness, it may be overly concerned with this value. Beauty products, soaps, deodorants, pesticides, laundry detergents, vacuum cleaners, and so on all have a market. In western nations, a lot of focus is put on this element and perfumes and deodorants are extensively utilized.

Performance/ status: A status driven culture cares for better standards of existence, and favors quality products and established brand names and premium priced things. The same holds true for the majority of Arabic nations, along with the United States, Japan, Singapore, Malaysia, Indonesia, and Thailand.

Brand names have less weight in civilizations where people are recognized and rewarded based on their performance. Non-name brands that perform the same or similar functions are preferred. Brand names are not as significant to Germans. That's why the marketers change their tactics to fit the situation.

Societies with a strong emphasis on tradition tend to reject new ideas and technologies in favor of tried-and-true methods. Compared to more modern civilizations, traditional societies have a smaller market for new items and a higher desire for traditional goods. Consumers in several rising-middle-class cultures are on the lookout for cutting-edge practices, innovations, and models.

Taking risks while feeling safe might be seen as brave or foolish, depending on the circumstances. That's up to the culture at large. Taking risks is essential for training future business leaders. It inspires brand-new manufacturing processes, marketing ploys, and distribution hubs. There is limited room for progress and creativity in cultures that prioritize security.

Both optimistic and problem-solving societies exist, as do fatalist ones that do nothing and accept whatever happens. There are repercussions for the company's bottom line when customers express dissatisfaction with their purchases by filing formal complaints. To a large degree, these uncertainties are dispelled by the advertising that plays an essential role by providing direction to the buyer.

Differences of opinion exist about the conservation of natural resources. Eco-friendly and easily recyclable packaging is highly valued by shoppers. Some nations attach high emphasis to preventing environmental degradation and to recycling of items.

Companies like Procter & Gamble and Colgate-Palmolive have cornered a sizable portion of the market with eco-friendlier options. In addition, the goods only employ safe substances.

iii) Values Focused on One's Own Interests

Whether or whether one places greater importance on leading an active lifestyle than one does on leading a sedentary one. An aggressive strategy causes one to always do something rather than nothing at all. In many nations, women are now taking an active role in all activities. This results in an extremely productive society in which everyone works.

Many cultures place a premium on material possessions and place more value on those who are financially successful than those who are not. While in many civilizations things like comfort, leisure and relationships have priority over being materialistic. Materialism may be of two sorts.

What we mean by "instrumental materialism" is the practice of accumulating resources for the express purpose of using them to accomplish one's goals. Transportation relies on automobiles. In general, people like acquiring goods that may be put to practical use.

Terminal materialism: the acquisition of material possessions for the purpose of ownership rather than use; the acquisition of art for the sake of ownership. One of the key factors in this kind of materialism is cultural differences. The United States of America is rife with instrumental materialism, whereas Japan's advertising industry is dominated by terminal materialism.

Hard work/leisure: This has marketing ramifications on labor saving items and quick meals. Some communities respect hard labor and regard it as a richer life. Many people nowadays use time-saving tools and quick meals to free up more time for themselves.

Is it better to put money down for a rainy day or to enjoy oneself in the present? Sacrifice the now for the future, or live solely for the day? Others nations like The Netherlands and Germany see purchasing against credit cards as living above one's means, but credit cards are quite popular in America and other countries having a different cultural orientation, some prefer cash to debt. While some cultures prioritize long-term security, others live in the now and lavishly squander their money.

Gluttony/Abstinence: People in certain traditional communities don't indulge in sexual activity unless absolutely necessary. Since it is taboo in many Muslim societies to expose women in any way, shape, or form, the Polaroid camera, with its ability to produce instant shots, is a boon to families who otherwise would have to send their female members to a photo lab to have their pictures developed.

Humor/ serious: Should we treat life lightly and laugh it off on some difficulties or, take things seriously? Another facet of culture is this. These ideas and the appropriate manner to make an appeal for a product in different cultures may be at the center of advertising, personnel selling strategies, and marketing.

Subcultures and Consumer Behavior

Subcultures are a subset of the larger cultural whole. The term "subculture" refers to a cultural group that is easily distinguishable from others within the same community, although sharing many of the same beliefs and practices as the larger society at large.

The following are examples of subcultures:

- Indian, Sri Lankan, and Pakistani
- Spirituality: Hinduism, Islam
- Asian, Black, and Caucasian
- Old, Young, and in Between
- Sex: Male, Female
- Farmer, educator, or entrepreneur
- Upper, medium, and lowest class
- Geographic regions: South India, North-eastern India

1. Regional, Ethnic, and Religious Influences on Consumer Behavior

Regional, ethnic, and religious variations are the three most significant cultural factors that influence consumers' actions. First, there may be regional variations in India and worldwide in terms of consumption habits, necessitating the need for a more nuanced approach to marketing in some parts of the globe.

Second, there are many distinct ethnic groups in the United States, and demographic shifts over the next half-century will have a significant impact on our nation's makeup. Despite the group's variety, marketing tactics may be designed for them.

Lastly, one's religious convictions and principles may influence their purchasing decisions. Increasingly, businesses are attempting to broaden their customer base by appealing to consumers of different cultural backgrounds. While the cultural variety of India is indeed remarkable, there are many other significant ethnic groups throughout the globe as well.

2. Age, Gender, and Household Influences on Consumer Behavior

Teenagers, one of the four primary age groups, are the consumers of the future and a rising effect on family choices because of their urge to find their own unique voice. The members of the somewhat disillusioned Generation X are savvy shoppers who are able to see through blatant advertising. The baby boomer generation places a premium on independence and autonomy as a result of having grown up in a world that was constantly shifting and evolving. The 50+ demographic breaks down into two distinct subsets: the youthful at heart and the gray market. Neither demographic appreciates being stereotyped as senile. Next, we look at how gender plays a role in shaping consumer habits. Gender norms are shifting. The gender roles are shifting, with women becoming more career-focused and self-reliant while males opening up emotionally. There may be distinctions between the sexes in terms of personality, the way they take in data, the way they make choices, and the way they spend their money.

An individual's gender consistently influences their values and preferences throughout their lives. Both men and women exhibit distinct purchasing habits and perspectives on consumer issues. As in, the wedding service.

To understand consumer behavior, it is important to understand the role that households play. Factors including (1) later marriage ages, (2) cohabitation, (3) dual-career families, (4) greater divorce rates, and (5) fewer children have contributed to the rise in the percentage of non-traditional households.

The household unit also has a significant role in shaping consumer behavior. For starters, various members of the home might play key roles in making decisions (gatekeeper, influencer, decider, buyer, and user). Second, the decision-making dynamics between men and wives range from husband-dominant to wife-dominant to autonomic and syncretic, depending on the context.

3. Values, personalities, and lifestyles; psychographics

Below, we'll examine how certain psychographics may have an impact on business outcomes and customer decisions.

Values are long-held convictions about what really matters in life. Acculturation and socialization are the means through which these norms are acquired. The values we hold are structured within a larger value system, with certain values being given more weight than others. Some are considered final values and represent intended final states that govern behavior across numerous contexts. These values are the "instrumental" ones since they are what will bring about the desired outcomes. In contrast to universal values, which apply across all fields, domain-specific values are those that only matter in one particular area. Western societies often put a premium on material possessions, youth, the family, domesticity, children, leisure, health, hedonism, and technology. Value segmentation is a technique used by marketers to classify customers into groups based on their shared beliefs and priorities.

People's personalities are made up of their unique combinations of traits, characteristics, and orientations. Some methods used in personality research are:

1. The psychoanalytic viewpoint, which holds that one's character is the result of hidden mental battles fought unconsciously at formative years;
2. Trait theories, which seek to define a collection of traits (such introversion, extroversion, and stability) that characterize and distinguish people;
3. Phenomenological strategies contend that one's character develops in response to the experiences they have had.
4. Behavioral views, which see an individual's character through the lens of prior reinforcement and punishment.
5. Socio-psychological theories, which center on how people behave in social circumstances (e.g., compliant, distant, or aggressive), rank fifth.

Lifestyle metrics, which describe consumers' typical daily routines, are frequently tracked by marketers (or activities, interests, and opinions). These ways of living might provide light on consumers' purchasing habits. Finally, some academics in the field of marketing apply psychographic methods, which take into account all of these aspects in order to forecast buyers' actions. The Values and Lifestyle Survey is one of the most widely used psychographic instruments (VALS).

To compare and contrast the buying habits of customers in two or more countries is a major part of cross-cultural marketing. This will assist marketers to comprehend the psychological, social and cultural characteristics of foreign customers they desire to target, so as to build successful marketing strategies for each of the individual national markets involved."

Challenges of International Marketing

1. Difficulties in deciding which items to provide Customers and markets in a cross-cultural marketing strategy cannot be narrowed down based on demographic information alone; instead, the marketer must consider the underlying elements that influence consumers' decisions to buy or pass on a product.
2. Ariel in the Middle East and Pepsi both have issues with their marketing and promotion.
3. Problems relating to pricing: the marketer needs to change his pricing strategies according to the local economic circumstances and traditions.
4. Problems relating to selection of distribution channels: in Japan, P & G utilized this to market soap

Cross-Cultural Consumer Analysis

In order to decide whether or not to join a foreign market, and if so, how to go about doing so, we need to undertake a cross-cultural consumer study.

Cross-cultural consumer analysis may be described as the endeavor to identify to what degree the customers of two or more countries are similar or distinct. Marketers may benefit from this kind of research by learning more about the demographics, socioeconomic status, and cultural norms of the international customers they want to reach. This knowledge can then be used to develop targeted promotional campaigns.

Japanese Culture Traits	American Culture traits
➢ Homogenous ➢ Harmony to be valid and ➢ preserved ➢ Group, not individual, ➢ important ➢ Ambiguous ➢ General ➢ Hold back emotions in public ➢ Process-oriented ➢ Make a long story short ➢ Nonverbal communication ➢ important ➢ Interested in who is speaking	➢ Diverse ➢ Fight for one's ➢ beliefs/positions ➢ Individualistic ➢ Clear-cut ➢ Specific ➢ Display emotions in public ➢ Result oriented ➢ Make a short story long ➢ Verbal communication ➢ important ➢ Interested in what is spoken

Japanese and American cultural traits difference

People's similarities and differences

One of the main goals of cross-cultural consumer research is to identify the commonalities and distinctions between consumer behavior in at least two different cultural contexts.

Alternate Multinational Tactics

It may be argued that as markets become more similar, it will be easier to implement generic advertising campaigns. One counterargument is that there are too many variations among international customers to use a globalized approach to advertising. Which segmentation technique, common needs and values or national boundaries, is more effective? If you want to reach customers in other nations, you should focus on what they have in common, such as their wants, values, and aspirations. Using geographical boundaries to divide markets would entail tailoring marketing efforts to the preferences of people from various nations or ethnic groups.

Product Strategy	Standardized Communications	Localized Communications
Standardized Product	**Global strategy:** Uniform product/ Uniform Message	**Mixed strategy:** Uniform Product/ Customized message
Localized Product	**Mixed Strategy:** Customized Product/ Uniform Message	**Local strategy:** Customized Product/ Customized Message

Alternative Global Marketing Strategies

One trend in marketing is the rise of "global brands," or items that are produced, packaged, and marketed in the same manner in every market across the globe. Sony, for one, markets the Walkman in this manner.

In contrast to the first approach, "adaptive global marketing" involves a company's adoption of a method that modifies its marketing messaging in accordance with the cultural norms of its target audience. An excellent case in point would be McDonald's, which makes an effort to adapt its marketing to customers in each of the many different cultural contexts in which it operates.

Differences in Culture and the Role of Body Language

Cultures have numerous different ways of communicating nonverbally. Meanings are placed on the non-verbal signals used by each culture. Nonverbal communication may be impacted by a number of factors. Included in this group are:

- Use of Time
- Space
- Friendship
- Etiquette
- Possessions
- Agreements
- Symbols

1) Time

Everyone has the same amount of time available to them. It's the same for everyone: everyone has the same 24 hours. What distinguishes one culture from another is its conception of time. Cultures may be categorized as either monochromic or polychromic based on the number of colors they use. In the table below, we compare monochrome and polychrome societies and highlight some of the key distinctions between the two.

Monochromic culture	Polychromic culture
Do one thing at a time.	Do many things at once.
Concentrate on the job.	Highly distractible and subject to interruption.
Take deadlines and schedules seriously.	Consider deadlines and schedules secondary.
Committed to job.	Committed to people and relationships.
Adhere religiously to plans.	Change plan often and easily.
Emphasize promptness.	Base promptness on relationship.
Accustomed to short term relationships.	Prefer long term relationships

Differences between Monochromic and Polychromic Culture

Time may have a varying significance in various societies. When it comes to making choices, some individuals take their time depending on how crucial it is. When doing business, some people insist on cutting to the chase. Others keep patients waiting for hours despite having appointments set down to the minute.

2) Space

A lack of space may be more indicative of pride than actual need. The higher up an office is, the more room there is for employees, etc. Executive offices in American companies are usually located on a different floor from those of lower-level employees. The Japanese dollar shops are always on the second level. While members of certain communities keep their distance while doing business with one another, members of others mix freely. When dealing with others, Americans often keep their distance. Middle Easterners tend to cluster closely together.

3) Friendship

When doing business, friendship is crucial. In a binding contract, it is the quality of the human connection between the parties that matters most. Social relationships created by parties have significance over technological criteria. Americans make friends readily, yet abandon them easily as well, because of both social and geographical mobility. Relationships and businesses in cultures like India's and Latin America's tend to be long-lasting. When people know and trust one another, they are more likely to work together and engage in business. For some, generating money is secondary to having a good time while doing business.

4) Agreements

All commercial activity is conducted in accordance with a set of agreements. This kind of arrangement might be documented formally or maintained via mutual agreement. While agreements are the norm, individuals also place a premium on the bonds formed through friendship and blood. In certain societies, a written contract is only a formality, and verbal promises have the same weight.

5) Possession

Things might signify various things depending on your cultural background. Products and presents delivered in social or commercial contexts are both examples of things. Gifts should be thoughtfully selected from a wide range of relevant items. It doesn't matter how large or tiny the presents are. You may hand them out publicly or gift them secretly. The answer to this question is determined by the customs of the nation in question. Some people like to give gifts publicly as a sign of appreciation. However, some people are being rather covert about it.

6) Etiquette

These guidelines represent the recognized standards of conduct. Sitting with one's legs crossed or in a way that exposes the sole of one's shoe, for example, may be considered disrespectful or abusive in certain cultures but perfectly normal in others. It is considered rude to decline a business offer outright in Japan. They expressed it another way, claiming it's really tough, which is code for "no." Exchange of business cards is mandatory in Japan and serves as a symbol of one's professional standing.

The same is true for the production of advertisements, which are influenced by a wide range of cultural norms and practices. While it is customary in the United States to eat with the fork in the right hand and the left hand hidden beneath the table, this is the opposite of the European way of eating, where the fork is used with the left hand.

These forms of nonverbal communication in many nations and languages have an impact on marketing efforts and must be addressed.

Individuals do action in accordance with the spoken languages they understand. To the same end, it's important to learn to read and comprehend people's non-verbal cues. It's important that the message we're trying to spread be presented in a way that's respectful of the local customs and values.

7) Colors and Symbols

Symbols, numbers, and colors may all have vastly different connotations depending on where you are in the world. Flowers, triangles, portraits, animals, etc., are all examples of symbols. There are fortunate numbers, and there are numbers like 13, 4, etc., that are thought to be bad luck. There are several meanings attached to certain hues. In the United States, the color pink is associated with a woman and the color blue with a man, however in the Netherlands, the roles are reversed.

The meanings of various hues are detailed here.

- In the Far East, the color white is associated with sadness and death, whereas in the West it is associated with joy, innocence, and serenity.
- In many Latin American cultures, the color purple represents death.
- In the Netherlands, the color blue is associated with femininity, but in the United States, Sweden, India, etc., it is more associated with masculine.
- The Indian wedding party traditionally wears red, and so do Indian children. In the UK and France, this is seen as a sign of masculinity, whereas in Nigeria and Germany it is seen as a negative.
- As a universal symbol, yellow has various meanings across the world.
- The white lily is the traditional funeral flower in England.
- Numeral Symbol
- A lucky seven: India, the United States, Morocco, Nicaragua, and the Czech Republic. Many cultures, like India's, consider the number 13 to be unlucky.
- In Japanese culture, number four represents the idea of death. There is no need to pack in multiples of four.
- Hong Kong and Taiwan are negative, whereas Columbia is favorable.

- The owl is a symbol of knowledge in America but misfortune in India.
- An American white-tailed deer symbolizes swiftness and elegance, whereas in Brazil it represents homosexuality.

Basic areas for cross-cultural marketing

Some basic areas for cross cultural marketing include:

1. Cultural awareness and understanding: This involves researching and understanding the culture, customs, and values of the target market.
2. Language and communication: Translating marketing materials and ensuring effective communication with the target market.
3. Product and pricing: Adapting products and pricing strategies to meet the needs and preferences of the target market.
4. Promotion and advertising: Creating culturally relevant and sensitive advertising and promotion campaigns.
5. Distribution and logistics: Adapting distribution and logistics strategies to the local market.
6. Legal and regulatory compliance: Ensuring compliance with local laws and regulations.
7. Sales and customer service: Training sales and customer service teams to effectively interact with customers from different cultural backgrounds.

Problem in cross cultural marketing

Cross-cultural marketing can present a number of challenges, such as:

1. Language barriers: It can be difficult to effectively communicate with consumers who speak a different language. This is especially true if the marketing materials are not translated accurately.
2. Cultural differences: Marketing messages and campaigns that are effective in one culture may not be well-received in another culture. For example, what is considered polite or respectful in one culture may be considered rude or offensive in another culture.
3. Different communication styles: Different cultures may have different communication styles and expectations. For example, some cultures may be more direct and assertive, while others may be more indirect and polite.
4. Different consumer needs and preferences: Consumers in different cultures may have different needs and preferences when

it comes to products and services. Marketers need to be aware of these differences and tailor their marketing efforts accordingly.

5. Stereotypes and cultural appropriation: Using stereotypes or cultural appropriation can be offensive and alienate potential customers. Marketers must be careful not to perpetuate negative stereotypes or exploit cultural symbols in their campaigns.
6. Legal and regulatory compliance: Different countries have different laws and regulations regarding advertising and marketing. Marketers must be aware of these laws and regulations and ensure that their marketing efforts comply with them.

Motivation and consumer behaviour – Introduction

Motivation

That which motivates us is:

What every living thing must have in order to survive

How these requirements are met is described by what we call "drives," and the outcomes that these actions are intended to accomplish are described by "goals."

Different Needs

a) Physiological requirements, often known as basic or fundamental wants, are those that are essential to maintaining life and are either genetically predetermined or evolved from an organism. Example: food and air

b) In terms of psychological requirements, Confidence in one's own abilities

c) Academic/cultural requirements: Constraints we've become used to

Requires Stimuli

There are four separate triggers that cause needs to be activated:

- Physiological
- Cognitive
- Environmental
- Emotional

What Factors Influence Client Preferences?

1.One's own unique personality traits

- As an example, food allergies are a product of genetics, the scientific discipline that studies the relationship between inheritance and chemical and biological traits.

- Biogenics are a person's innate qualities, such as their gender or ethnicity.
- Moods and emotions, for example, are examples of psychogenic states and features, which are brought about by the way a person's brain processes information.
- Climate, altitude, and precipitation are all examples of environmental physical properties.

What Factors Influence Client Preferences?

1. One, the specific situation

Individual's net worth or access to capital; examples include pricey vs inexpensive automobiles.

Institutional context: a person's social and professional networks (including, for instance, how they dress)

Cultural factors, such as a customer's background and morals (which might affect their preferences for things like ethnic cuisine),

2. The Nature of the Environment

Economy | Technology | Government Policy

Maslow's Needs Hierarchy

Every person, according to the theory of Abraham Maslow's "hierarchy of needs," has the following five requirements:

1. Physiological
2. Safety
3. Social
4. Esteem
5. Realization of Oneself

Five Needs According to Sheth

Here are some instances for each of the five categories of requirements that Sheth identified:

1. *Functional needs* –Soap is an example of a functional requirement since it serves a specific physical function in the home.
2. *Social needs* –Social requirements - Needs that facilitate group identification (through symbols like group logos, for example)
3. *Emotional needs* –Feelings of happiness upon receiving a present are an example of an emotional need.
4. *Epistemic needs* –the need for knowledge or information, like a newspaper; and

5. *Situational needs* –situational, or the demands that vary depending on time and location, like urgent car repairs.

The Three-Needs Hypothesis of McClELLAND

McClelland, who had previously examined this topic, had recognized three sorts of wants, and we now know what they are: the need for accomplishment, the need for power, and the need for connection.

- Need for success; ambition; the desire to succeed in connection to a standard or goals; drive to excel.
- Need for influence, or the desire to influence others to act in a manner they otherwise would not have.
- Third, a desire for deep friendships and social connections.

Motives and Motivation

Now that we have a firm grasp on what people want and desire, we can turn our attention to what drives them. But before we get into it, we need to define the three linked concepts motivations, motivating, and motivation.

Motives: Individuals' actions are guided by their motivations. One definition of a motivation is an emotional condition that motivates an individual to do action.

By definition, anything that motivates someone is something they choose to do in order to focus their powerful emotions and impulses in a positive way.

To motivate someone is to tap into whatever it is that fires them up and gets them moving. At the most fundamental level, for example, our body has a need (let's say hunger), which translates into a drive (here, the urge is to seek food), and the objective is to meet the need (in this example to fee full in the stomach).

Positive or negative motivation

A person's drive might be good or bad. When a person feels a compelling pull toward a certain thing, person, or event, they are positively motivated. Personal motivation is another term for this. Negative motivation, on the other hand, is defined as any factor that prompts an individual to disengage from a certain situation or individual.

The Drive Behind It

The primary question that Consumer Motivation seeks to answer is, "Why do people shop?" The truth is that shoppers' motivations vary widely, making broad generalizations about what drives them to go shopping very challenging. Food shopping may be considered as meeting a fundamental human need. The issue is that most of us buy considerably more food than we need for basic sustenance, and a lot of the things we buy at the store are essentially just "luxuries" (relatively speaking).

Motivations on a personal level

Some types of shopping are more often linked with certain social roles than others (housewife, mother, student, etc).

Shopping as a diversion from the monotony of everyday life.

Shopping as "retail therapy" to lift one's spirits or relieve sadness is one kind of "self-gratification."

Educative value: Going shopping is a great method to get familiar with current styles and trends.

A trip across the mall may be all the exercise some folks get in a given week.

People visit businesses and shopping centers for a variety of reasons, but one of the most common is sensory stimulation, which includes the tactile experience of browsing items, listening to music, smelling perfumes, etc.

Considerations of the Common Good

Folks like chances to chat with others, whether it friends or random people at stores.

Some stores facilitate consumer interaction with essential reference groups, such as those who have similar interests or who are part of a social category to which the customer aspires.

For some, going shopping is a means to assert their authority and demand the attention of others, such as when interacting with store employees.

Some consumers take great pride in their bargaining skills, and "haggling" is seen as a fun method to exercise such skills while also saving money or getting a better deal on things. These groups are not exclusive of one another. At any one moment, almost 70% of the population frequents a shopping mall at least once a week, and their motivations for doing so might vary widely. Shopping is about so much more than acquiring a specific item; in fact, many individuals visit shopping centers with no intention of making a purchase at all.

Consumer Attitudes

Moods are temporary and less strong emotional states.

There is a spectrum of emotional responses that consumers might have to marketing stimuli:

Content of message from salesperson or ad; store or service environment; salesperson's demeanor; product's sensory attributes; tone and style of advertising;

Joyful spending

Consumption of goods and services for their own sake rather than to address an external issue is known as hedonic consumption. All of your senses will be stimulated by this:

A bubble bath provides tactile satisfaction, an original piece of art provides aesthetic satisfaction, a terrifying movie provides an emotional experience, and playing sports provides fun and enjoyment.

How invested do you think most of your target market's consumers would be in trying out the product before making a purchase? The term "involvement" has a more nuanced meaning in this context, referring to the extent to which users identify with the brand and see the product as vital to their lives. According to the course, students who are emotionally invested in a product are more likely to go through the whole PDP and make a well-informed decision. On the other side, if individuals are less invested, they are also less inclined to do extensive research or weigh all available options. Possible serious consequences follow from this. People may only do minimal searches, giving you an edge if you supply them with relevant information and make it accessible to them in a suitable manner. If a customer is making a decision between two brands based only on the information provided by the salesperson, it might be quite advantageous to incentivize the salespeople to disclose information about your brand. Alternately, one may attempt to sway consumers' level of investment in a product. It is hoped that by associating the use of toothpaste with "cavity prevention" in ads and on the advice of dentists, the priority that people give to brushing their teeth would grow.

Personality

The Latin term "persona" literally means "mask," and this is where our modern English word "personality" comes from. Examining the "masks" individuals put on in different situations is a key part of studying personality. People's projected and displayed personas, as well as the interior components of their psychological experience that make up what we term our "self," fall under this category.

Exactly what makes us who we are

We focus on three characteristics in our analysis of personality:
a) Personality, on the one hand, is a reflection of uniqueness on a person's part.
b) A person's identity does not change throughout time.
c) A person's character may develop through time

The uniqueness of each person is reflected in their personality.

One's personality is the result of a complex interplay of variables, and no two people are similar.

Second, the idea of "personality" is helpful since it allows us to divide customers into subsets defined by a single or set of characteristics.

1. Marketers study consumer behaviour in an effort to better understand their target audience and tailor their messages to the preferences of that group.

While a person's character may remain constant over time, their shopping habits likely will change often.

Influences on behaviour from psychological, social, and cultural contexts.

2. A Person's Character May Evolve

Major life changes, including having a child, losing a loved one, getting divorced, or switching careers, may have a profound effect on a person's character.

Second, as a person grows older, their personality develops and changes.
a) Generalizations about people's personalities may evolve as time goes on.
b) Personality experts believe that men and women are becoming more similar.

Analysis of Characteristics

Biological, Psychoanalytic, Dispositional, Learning, Humanistic, and Cognitive are the many viewpoints on personality.

Characteristics of Personality Theories

We will examine the three most prominent theories of personality. To name a few:

a) Freudian thought, to be specific.
b) The New Freudian Approach to Psychoanalysis.

c) Characteristic

Freud's Hypothesis

The foundation of contemporary psychology is Sigmund Freud's psychoanalytic theory of the individual's psyche. The foundation of this theory is the idea that fundamental human motivation and personality traits stem from deep-seated, unconscious wants or impulses, such as those of a biological or sexual nature.

The Three Faces of the Self: Id, Superego, and Ego

An individual's Id serves as a "storage" for their most basic, instinctual impulses, such as thirst, hunger, and sex, for which they have little to no care other than getting what they want as soon as possible. The superego is an individual's internalization of societal norms of right and wrong behavior.

a) The superego's job is to ensure that requirements are met in a socially acceptable way.

b) The superego acts as a "brake," slowing down the iimpulsive d's tendencies.

The ego is a person's conscious control; it acts as a monitor, attempting to strike a happy medium between the impulsive needs of the id and the social and cultural norms imposed by the superego. According to Freud, a person's personality develops over the course of many discrete phases throughout infancy and early childhood. The oral, anal, phallic, latent, and genital phases are all identifiable in infants and young children. How a person handles the challenges they face as they go through these developmental phases has a profound impact on who they become as an adult.

Freud's Id, Ego, and Superego as a Model for Mental Organization

As was said above, Freud concluded that the id, the ego, and the superego are the three components of personality that interact to generate all of our complicated activities. The Ego and Superego, as you can see, function in the conscious, the unconscious, and the subliminal levels of thought. If you want to have a healthy mind and plenty of psychic energy, you need to keep all three in check.

Analysis of Brand Identity in Light of Freudian Theory

People that place an emphasis on Freud's ideas recognize that customers' motivations for making purchases are often subconscious. Studies conducted by this group see consumers' purchasing habits and the contexts in which they engage in these behaviors as revealing aspects of their individuality.

According to the tenets of the Neo-Freudian theory of personality,

The idea that one's personality is essentially based on one's sexual and instinctive drives was contested by some of Freud's peers. They contended that interpersonal connections are crucial for maturation. Putting a focus on the individual's attempts to overcome emotions of inadequacy, Alfred Adler saw people as rationally attempting to reach diverse objectives, which he termed style of life. As Harry Stack Sullivan pointed out, individuals are always trying to make connections with others, whether it's platonic or romantic.

Primarily her research, Karen Horney zeroed in on the effects of parental figures, particularly the motivation to overcome fear. She suggested categorizing people as either cooperative, hostile, or distant. People who are compliant tend to approach people because they are motivated by a need to feel loved, valued, and appreciated. People that are aggressive are competitive and strive for success at anyone's expense. Detached people withdraw from social interactions because they want autonomy. The CAD is a validated personality assessment that draws on the above. It demonstrates many possible associations between ratings and consumer behavior with respect to certain brands and products. Many marketers have probably employed some of these neo-Freudian beliefs without even realizing it.

The Study of Personality Traits

When compared to the previous qualitative metrics characteristic of Freudian and neo-Freudian thought, trait theory represents a radical shift. Its primary emphasis is on the quantitative or empirical assessment of personality in terms of discrete psychological qualities known as traits. A person's traits are what set them apart from others and are something that tends to stick around throughout time. Research on consumer behavior is seeing a rise in the creation of single-trait personality assessments. The following categories of characteristics are often measured:

- Innovativeness in the marketplace, or the willingness of consumers to try new things.
- Consumer devotion to "worldly things," or consumer materialism.
- Consumers' propensity to accept or reject goods created in other countries is an example of ethnocentrism.

Researchers have come to assume that customers' personalities influence their decision-making across product categories, rather than with a single brand.

Differences in Characteristics and Buyers

To better understand customers and segment and target those consumers who are likely to react favourably to their product or service offerings, marketers are interested in learning how personality drives consumption behaviour.

Individual Differences in Consumer Creativity and Related Characteristics

Marketers need to know all they can about "consumer innovators," or those who are open to trying new things. Those risk-takers are often essential to the commercialization of innovative items. Differentiating consumer innovators from non-innovators has been aided by looking at their personalities. Some of the characteristics of people to be considered are as follows:

- Creativity on the part of the general public.
- Dogmatism.
- One's sociability.
- This pressing need to stand out from the crowd.
- Optimal dose of stimulation.
- Wanting a change of pace or novelty.
- Originality in the Marketplace

Consumers' receptivity to novel goods, services, and procedures.

Recent consumer studies show a correlation between creative Internet use and online shopping.

Dogmatism

A person's degree of dogmatism may be defined by how resistant they are to new ideas and information that runs counter to their preconceived notions. People who lack dogmatism are more inclined to choose novel goods over tried-and-true options. Customers who score higher on the dogmatism scale are more likely to trust advertisements that present the product's benefits as having been endorsed by an authoritative source.

Ethics in Social Interaction

A person's social character may be described as falling anywhere along a spectrum from inwardly focused to outwardly focused. Inner-directed customers are often the first to market with novel ideas since they evaluate things based on their own "inner" ideals or standards. And they especially like commercials that highlight useful features and individual advantages. Consumers who are "other-directed" are those who often seek to others for guidance and seldom try new things on their own. They are more likely to respond positively to advertisements that emphasize a positive social scene.

The need for individuality

Those who resist following the crowd are the ones who value individuality.

Maximum Effective Dose of Stimulation

It seems that although some individuals would rather live in a serene, uncomplicated setting, others would rather be immersed in a world full of interesting, complex, and out-of-the-ordinary events. People who are operating at their OSL are more likely to try new things, come up with creative solutions to problems, research goods and services before making a purchase, and be open to the introduction of modern retail spaces. The degree to which a person yearns for stimulation is proportional to the degree to which his or her OSL and reality match up. When one requirement meets another, both parties are usually content. If they're bored, it means they're not getting enough stimulation.

Looking for Something Different

In many ways, this is analogous to OSL. Variety and novelty seekers are the most common primary categories. A wide array of novelty-seeking behaviors seem to exist: exploratory

Vicarious exploration (where the consumer acquires information about a new or different alternative and then contemplates or even daydreams about the option), purchase behavior (e.g., switching brands to experience new and possibly better alternatives), and use inventiveness are all examples of how consumers engage with innovation (e.g., where the consumer uses an already adopted product in a new or novel way).

The third kind of novelty seeker is "use innovativeness," which is especially pertinent to technology advancements. Customers who have a strong need for novelty may also be drawn to products that boast versatility. To a certain extent, expanding their product offerings to meet the needs of customers who value choice is beneficial for marketers. The goal for every marketer is to strike a balance between giving customers too few options and overwhelming them with too many. According to this review, the consumer innovator is fundamentally different from the non-innovator in terms of their outlook on life.

Characteristics of a Thinking Mind

Researchers in the field of marketing are interested in the ways in which customers' cognitive personalities influence their purchasing decisions. There are two cognitive personality qualities that have proven effective in deciphering some aspects of shoppers' actions. To name a few:

A) the need for mental processing, and

B) the preference for either visual or verbal representations of information.

The Importance of Thinking

This indexes how much one needs or relishes engaging in intellectual activity. Customers with a high NC (need for cognition) are more likely to pay attention to the portion of an ad that provides a detailed explanation of the product being advertised. As a species, they have a greater affinity towards chilly tones. Low NC consumers are more likely to be drawn to an ad's secondary or tertiary features. Print attracts and retains their attention for longer, and their brand recognition is enhanced by their exposure to print. One's cognitive requirements may influence how much time they spend online.

Those who think visually vs. those who think verbally

Customers that are "visualizers" are those who learn best via images and videos and value items that highlight visuals. Consumers that place a premium on the written or spoken word are known as "verbalizers." This difference aids advertisers in deciding whether to highlight pictures or words. Overindulgence in consumer goods may lead to hedonic adaptation.

Commercialism and Materialism

People who place a high value on material belongings are said to be materialistic. They are materialistic and vain, they want to live lavishly yet aren't satisfied by their wealth, and they are self-absorbed.

Behaviour that is Overly Dedicated to Consumption

Consuming and possessing to the point of obsession lies between materialism and addiction. Consumption fixation is considered normal and acceptable in society, much like materialism. Certain traits are shared by customers who are fixated: 1. a strong (maybe even "passionate") desire for something. 2. A readiness to make significant sacrifices to get more instances of the item or class of products of interest. Third, spending a lot of free time and money trying to track it down. Many collectors and enthusiasts fit the description of the obsessed customer (e.g., coin, stamp, antique collectors, vintage wristwatch, or fountain pen collectors).

Problematic Consumption Habits

Consumption addiction is considered aberrant conduct. Compulsive consumers are addicted; they are essentially powerless over their behavior, which may have negative effects on both themselves and people around them.

The Characteristics of a Brand

It seems that customers have a tendency to attribute distinct brands across a broad range of product categories with varying descriptive "personality-like" features or attributes, which are the building blocks of brand personalities. Both practical (as in "provides safety") and symbolic (as in "the athlete in all of us") aspects may contribute to a brand's identity.

Personification of Brands

Personifying a brand is giving the product or service some kind of "humanlike character" that represents its qualities in the eyes of the customer. Consumers, it would seem, are able to reveal their true sentiments about businesses and goods via their associations with well-known figures. Finding or making the connection between a product's brand and a customer's identity is a crucial marketing objective. Sincerity, enthusiasm, competence, sophistication, and ruggedness are the five defining qualities of a brand's personality. The other fifteen components of personality (such as "down-to-earth," "daring," "reliable," "upper class," and "outdoors") all stem from these five core characteristics.

Colour and Character

In addition, consumers have a propensity to ascribe psychological significance to colour. Many companies and products use colour to convey a sense of character or identity. It would indicate that male buyers are more likely to purchase items that are blue. Colours like yellow signify "novelty" and black, "sophistication." The outside signage and interior decor of many fast food chains include eye-catching colour palettes that often include red, yellow, and blue. These hues have become shorthand for fast food and cheap eats. As a counterpoint, fine dining establishments often decorate with understated hues like grey, white, and tans to convey a sense of calm and relaxation. People's preferences for and aversions to certain hues might vary greatly from one country to the next.

You, Yourself, and Your Representation of Yourself

Individuals' product and service purchases, as well as their overall lifestyle choices, are strongly correlated with their self-images, or "perceptions of self."

Shop at stores whose "personalities" (images) align with their own (self-images). Elaborating on ideas like "me" and "we," "self" and "image," and "the extended self," consumer behaviorists investigate a wide range of psychological phenomena.

Self-Consciousness and Its Constituent Parts

When someone thinks about themselves, they see themselves as a specific kind of person.

One's sense of oneself is unique, a product of one's upbringing and life experiences. Products and brands are evaluated by consumers based on how well they mesh with their own mental conceptions of what those products and brands represent. There are goods that appear to fit with at least one person's sense of who they are, and there are others that seem completely foreign. There are four components to one's sense of self.

1. Customers' true perceptions of themselves in the marketplace.

1. 2. The desired image of oneself, as held by customers.
2. A consumer's social self-image, or how they see themselves in the eyes of others.
3. A consumer's ideal social self-image is how they would want to be seen by others.
4. In the eyes of some marketers, there is a fifth and sixth kind of identity.
5. Fifth, customers' projected future selves, or how they see themselves in the future. "Ought-to" attributes are those that a person thinks they "ought to" have because they are morally obligated to. There are a variety of consumer self-images that might be used in a variety of settings. Marketers would do well to give serious thought to the ramifications of the idea of self-image.

Marketers may target certain demographics by identifying consumers' defining characteristics and values, and then positioning goods and services as symbols for those identities.

Beyond One's Limited Boundaries:

Some argue that the things people buy "confirm" or "expand" their identities. According to the preceding, many different types of human emotion may be linked to different types of material things. An individual's sense of identity may be in a variety of methods: In fact, it does so by facilitating the individual's ability to achieve goals that would be very challenging, if not impossible, without it (e.g., problem-solving by using a computer). As a metaphor, it may make individuals feel stronger and more confident (e.g., receiving an employee award for excellence). through promoting one's standing (e.g., status among collectors of rare works of art because of the ownership of a particular masterpiece). If you leave your children or other loved ones a large sum of money or other valuables, you may give them a sense of immortality. conferring supernatural effects onto (a cameo pin inherited from an aunt, for instance, can be seen as a mystical amulet thought to bring good fortune to the wearer).

Psychographics, Values and Lifestyles

Markets may be segmented by socioeconomic status, way of life, and personality traits with the help of psychographics. The theory proposes that people may be understood by the brands and items they regularly buy and the ways in which they live their lives. These are some instances of how psychographics are used to market segmentation:

For researchers, nothing is more useful than social class, which categorizes people according to their economic standing.

Individuals may be categorized in terms of their lifestyle choices, including their values, beliefs, views, and hobbies. Market researchers and advertising agencies are continually developing new lifestyle segmentation models to better target potential customers for their companies' goods.

Personality, or an individual's distinguishing traits, are what set them apart from everyone else. It depicts how other people see the individual in question.

Segmentation Based on Psychological Traits

- Information on: personality, motivations, lifestyles, geographical distribution
- Consumers are categorized by
- Work, play, rest, and retail therapy are all examples of activities.
- Things that pique one's interest include:
- Perspectives on life, the universe, and everything

- *A consumer lifestyle is defined as,*
- *Participation in clubs, activities, interests, and volunteer work are all manifestations of this constellation of personal traits.*
- Analysis of Consumer Behavior and How Lifestyle Choices Affect It
- In terms of consumer habits, what do people generally want to see?
- Baseline for how and why people value their time.
- Lifestyle influences consumption habits.
- People categorize themselves into subcultures depending on their interests: athletes, bookworms, fishermen, and music nerds.

Classifying People According to Their Values and Priorities in Life (Vals)

- Realizers: those who are already prosperous and have enough resources
- Individuals who are "Fulfillers" are those who are "career focused," "practical," and "principled."
- People who are "Achievers" are career-focused, reliable, and consistent.
- Type X: The Young, the Bold, the Doers
- True believers: established companies with unwavering values
- People who struggle have, in comparison to high achievers, less opportunities.
- Do-it-yourselfers and action-oriented Makers: a tough existence

Social Class

When discussing a society's stratification, we refer to social classes.

Which means:

Promotions to higher levels of responsibility can bring with them greater social standing. Each member of society may be located anywhere along a spectrum, or range, of social positions, which we might refer to as "social class." Social scientists, however, have categorize this range into a few of distinct groups.

The Effect of Socioeconomic Status

- Gives one a feeling of one's own uniqueness
- imposes a standard of conduct as "acceptable"
- Classes exchange norms, goods, rituals, and activities

- The Commercial Sector's Reaction to Consumers of Varying Financial Means
- To reach the low-income market, it is necessary to:
- However, some businesses are conflicted since their clients aren't seen as loyal.
- Makes comprises a significant portion
- Focus on what matters most by using value-driven tactics

ILLUSTRATIVE CASE

A new smoke detector from a recognized electronics manufacturer has been designed with an indicator that causes the alarm to sound once per minute when the batteries are low and need to be changed. To illustrate, let's say the corporation finds that many detectors' batteries are too weak to adequately function the alarm for some time before the "beep" feature is enabled. Should the maker (a) issue a recall and modify the smoke detector, (b) discontinue producing the alarm and send notices to affected owners, or (c) keep selling the device while warning customers that they must routinely replace the batteries?

Question

If the corporation has a firm grasp of how consumers behave, they will be more equipped to choose the best course of action.

Consumer motives: personal, social motives

Personal motives refer to the individual needs and wants of a consumer that drive their purchasing decisions. Examples of personal motives include the desire for convenience, comfort, or status.

Social motives, on the other hand, refer to the influence of other people and societal norms on a consumer's purchasing decisions. Examples of social motives include the desire to conform to a certain group or to be perceived as fashionable.

The contemporary marketer's foundation is the adage "The customer is always right." Every purchase a customer makes is said to be motivated by some underlying need. Therefore, the reasons for a consumer's purchase are directly related to his goals in making the purchase. Consumers' motivations come from a wide range of sources. Buying decisions are influenced by a number of different elements. When a product or service meets a customer's expected value, the consumer is more likely to make a purchase. To repeat, if a marketer knows why a consumer wants to buy a product, he has a better chance of making the sale. For instance, a consumer may be encouraged to purchase an umbrella during the rainy season. The need to clean one's soiled laundry is similar to the need to purchase detergent. 'Buying motivation' refers to the reasons why a consumer decides to make a purchase.

A consumer will make a purchase for what are known as "buying reasons," which include but are not limited to the satisfaction of wants and needs. Again, "purchasing impulses" refer to the "internal to the best extent possible the "feelings" of a consumer or purchase. People's desires to make a purchase are driven by a variety of emotional and psychological factors. A buying motivation is any factor that influences a consumer's decision to purchase a product or service. What you'll study in this section is:

The intent of buying inspirations

Numerous writers have made substantial contributions to the body of work on the topic of personal selling buyers' motivations. The following are some definitions of what motivates consumers to make purchases that have been proposed by a select few of these individuals:

A motive is a "drive or desire for which a person wants gratification," as described by W. J. Stanton. When a person wants something so badly that they're willing to spend money to get it, it's called a "purchasing motivation."

"Buying motivations are those influences or factors that generate the drive to buy, motivate action, or decide decision in the acquisition of goods and services," writes D. J. Duncan.

An internal drive that compels or inspires a person to do action; this is how Prof. S. Davar described motives.

Motive, as defined by Berelson and Steiner, is "the inner condition that energizes, activates, or moves, and that leads or channels behavior towards objectives."

Prof. William G. Carter has provided a comprehensive list of consumer motivations, including "money, vanity, acquisitiveness, rivalry, adornment, cleanliness, collecting, amusement, construction, companionship, mental culture, appropriateness, ambition, inhibition, reverence, affection, tastes, sex, limitation, curiosity, self-preservation, sympathy, gratitude, patriotism, and so on."

After reviewing these definitions, it becomes clear that a "purchasing motivation" is a psychological human need that inspires customers to purchase things or services in order to meet their requirements. A buyer's motivation may be defined as the "why" behind their purchase, and can take the form of any number of factors including desire, stimulation, cognition, drive, instinct, or sentiment.

The Role of Buying Motives in Individual Sales

It's important to grasp the idea of "Buying motivations" for the following reasons:

1. First, a salesperson may hone their craft by learning to identify and appreciate his or her customers' underlying motivations for making purchases. He will be better able to meet the customer's expectations about the product's quality, price, size, color, etc. once he learns the reasoning behind the purchase. Furthermore, the salesperson will be in a better position to lead and influence the customer's purchasing behavior if he has a firm grasp of the customer's purchase motivation. If a salesman can grasp this idea, it will help him excel in his current position and open doors to more promising ones in the future.
2. It helps with product planning since marketers and businesses can better anticipate their clients' wants and needs thanks to the information provided by buyers' motivations for making purchases. Under this, numerous industry specialists do in-depth market research in an effort to learn what motivates their target customers to make a purchase. They make an effort to learn the preferences of the target market with regards to things like color, size, features, occasions, design, and so on. As a result, these professionals or businesses make choices about the product's development.
3. Supports price choices, which are crucial to a company's ability to stay afloat or expand in the marketplace. Therefore, before settling on a pricing for a product, a company should do a thorough examination of the relevant facts. Insight into consumers' underlying reasons for making a purchase, whether logical or emotional, is invaluable to businesses. The price sensitivity of consumers may be broken down into several segments according to the reasons they make purchases. Customers who make purchases out of pure logic tend to be more price conscious than their emotional counterparts.
4. Person-to-person selling, advertising, direct marketing, sales promotion, publicity, etc. are all part of a company's arsenal of promotional tools for getting the word out about its wares. Marketers may get insight into the factors that influence their target audience's purchasing decisions by learning about the consumers' motivations for making a purchase. If you know how logical or emotional your intended audience is, you may tailor your message accordingly. Effective communication with the intended audience requires a promotion mix that takes into

account factors such as the sort of advertising appeal utilized in the message, the message's body content, etc.

5. Determining Distribution Channels Some customers may rather purchase directly from the wholesaler. They would rather not purchase goods through a wholesaler or merchant. Customers who shop for "self-protective" reasons are driven to buy. Therefore, a marketer must evaluate clients' "purchasing reasons" before making any logistics-related decisions.
6. It helps a company's reputation by making sure its consumers are happy; businesses succeed in this endeavor by identifying and responding to their clients' wants and requirements. Goodwill in the market is established when a company has a solid reputation in the eyes of its customers, which in turn generates repeat business and referrals.

Customers are more likely to be devoted to a business once they have had a positive experience with it; this is the seventh benefit gained through customer motivation analysis. Building trust with your customers is a certain way to keep them as loyal customers.

TYPES OF CONSUMER MOTIVES

Buying motives can be classified as follows (Figure1):

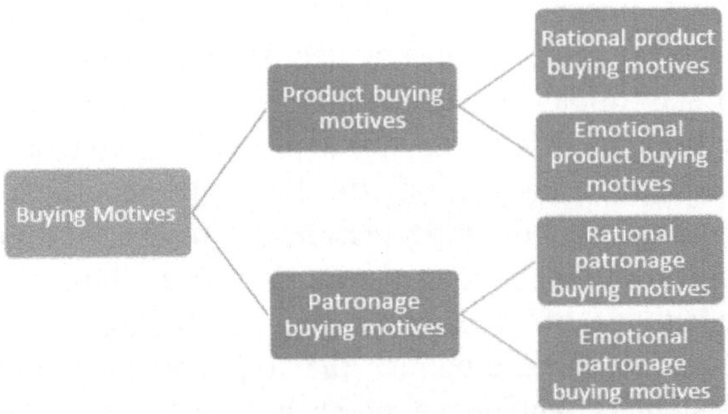

One category of factors that influence a consumer's purchasing decisions is what is known as "product purchase motivations." Several characteristics of the product itself, such as its size, color, packaging, quality, number, design, etc., all play a role in generating this enthusiasm.

The reasons people purchase a thing may be broken down into two distinct categories: logical and irrational.

Justifiable factors in making a purchase

After giving serious thought to all of the factors involved, a buyer makes an informed decision to acquire a product. Buyers' rationales are considered to be at play in such a transaction.

Listed below are some of the most logical product purchase justifications:

Customers' concerns about their personal safety are a major factor in determining which items they ultimately decide to purchase. For instance, before purchasing an iron safe or a locker to store one's jewelry or other valuables, one should carefully inspect the safe or locker for any potential weaknesses in terms of strength, size, security, etc.

Financial considerations: the product's operating or maintenance costs weigh heavily on consumers' minds before making a purchase. People typically choose to purchase those

products or commodities whose operation or maintenance expenses are cheap in comparison to the market average. Customers in the medium income range, for instance, are more likely to choose diesel or CNG-powered vehicles because of their cheaper pricing compared to gasoline. They also have greater gas economy than gasoline-powered vehicles.

The product's price is one of the most important considerations for consumers before making a purchase. Customers often look at the pricing of many alternative products before settling on one to purchase.

One of the factors that contributes to a consumer's final choice to buy a product is whether or not they find it to be a good fit for their needs. A savvy shopper knows what he needs and only buys what he wants. If a buyer has a tiny home and needs a dining table, he or she is more likely to choose a smaller, more compact one.

A product is considered versatile if it can be used for more than one purpose. The product's adaptability plays a role in the consumer's final choice to buy.

The product's durability, defined as its higher quality and extended lifespan relative to competitors. One such aspect that affects a customer's propensity to buy is the item's durability. Consumers are willing to pay a premium for something they know will last a long time. For furniture, for instance, consumers would often pay more for a more expensive but more desirable wood like teak or rosewood.

People are more likely to purchase goods if they are easy to use. Take, for instance, a common household gas range. Here, the customer wants the easiest-to-use model available.

Influencing a purchase using one's feelings

When a consumer makes a purchasing decision based on feelings rather than facts, it is said to be irrational. Emotional purchasing impulses are posited to be at play in such a transaction.

Examples of emotional product purchasing reasons are as follows:

One of the biggest intangible motivators for purchasing is a desire to display one's status or pride. Consumers who want to maintain or improve their social standing often buy things that they take pride in owning. Such is, among other things, a penchant for diamond jewelry, the acquisition of the most recent iPhone model, the purchase of a brand-spanking-new luxury car, etc.

Aspirational: Some consumers purchase items only because they see other individuals have them. In other words, some shoppers strive to set themselves apart by purchasing items that are similar to those of their peers. If a young man sees that his buddy has just purchased the most up-to-date model of a certain product, he may feel pressured to do the same. In a similar vein, a housewife wants to purchase a diamond ring since her sister and mother also have them.

The most prevalent kind of emotional purchasing is based on feelings of love or affection. People often make purchases motivated by feelings of love or devotion. For example, a son may purchase a pricey watch as a token of his appreciation for his father, whereas a mother would give her daughter a pricey ring as a symbol of her value to her.

One of the emotional purchasing factors is the need for uniqueness or individuality. Some individuals, for instance, choose to dress a certain way in order to distinguish themselves and emphasize their uniqueness.

A consumer may also be motivated to make a purchase because he or she has an interest in doing so that is just based on the desire to indulge in some kind of entertainment. People purchase things like stereos and guitars because they want to relax and have fun.

The power of habit as an involuntary purchasing motivator cannot be overstated. Some products become indispensable to consumers after they've developed a dependence on them. Many people develop dependencies on substances like alcohol, nicotine, some types of soap, sleeping drugs, etc.

Motivations for purchasing favors

The term "patronage purchasing motivations" refers to the reasons why customers consistently make purchases from the same store. Retailer- or store-specific incentives including accessibility, selection, credibility, and a favorable credit policy all contribute to this compulsion.

The two main types of customer loyalty are based on logic and emotion while making purchases. Yes, let's study them.

i) Logic behind the purchase of patronage

When a customer makes up their mind to buy something after giving it a lot of thought and deliberating over all of the options available to them, they have made an informed choice. Patronage purchases are thought to be motivated by a mix of both emotion and logic.

- Here are some examples of reasonable reasons to make a patronage purchase:
- The most prevalent rational patronage purchasing incentive is convenience, such as a store's convenient location or convenient business hours. A customer is more likely to shop at a store if it is at a handy location. Retailers like supermarkets, drugstores, dairies, and so on.
- Customers are more likely to frequent a store that has both convenient location and convenient business hours. A pharmacy open 24 hours a day, a grocery store with extended hours, and other 24*7 type convenience stores are all examples.
- Lower prices: Price is, and always has been, the single most important element affecting a customer's choice to make a purchase. The more competitive a store's prices are with those of its competitors, the more likely a customer is to shop there.
- Customers are always enticed to purchase more often when they are offered some kind of refund or discount.
- Incentives for patronage include extended credit policies and special discounts. The ability to get credit is one example of such a benefit. Many store owners offer their customers the option to buy goods on credit and keep track of these transactions in a register or other record. Payment is made to the seller at a later date, at the buyer's convenience.
- Customers are more likely to spend money at establishments that have a broad selection of goods. In this way, a customer's ability to make a variety of choices provides a rationale for shopping at a certain establishment.
- A store's reputation rises or falls on the shoulders of its proprietors, therefore it pays to be trustworthy and reasonable. If

a store or merchant has a solid reputation, customers will begin frequenting them on their own.

ii) Buying for emotional reasons rather than practical ones

When a customer makes a purchase from a business they are emotionally attached to rather than rationally examining all of the options available to them. Patronage purchases are thought to be affected by sentimental values.

The following are examples of emotional patronage purchasing motives:

- Customers may begin frequenting a store more often than usual due of its visually appealing interior design, product displays, or overall theme.
- Recommendations: Consumers' purchasing habits are often influenced by the recommendations of their friends and family. Customers are often influenced by the opinions of others close to them, such as members of their family, friends, and coworkers.
- Some consumers choose businesses or merchants based on the choices of others. That is to say, some consumers strive to mimic the behavior of other consumers by shopping at the same stores as the majority of consumers.
- One of the most powerful intangible benefits of patronage is the enhancement of one's emotional well-being. Dinner at a five-star restaurant is a popular choice, as are some high-end clothing labels.
- One of the underlying emotional patronage incentives is habit. It's not uncommon to observe customers repeatedly purchasing the same items from the same store, presumably out of sheer familiarity with the proprietor.

Reasons Why Customers Buy

The term "buyer motivation" describes the assortment of mental considerations that go into a consumer's final buying choice. These are the elements that influence a consumer's decision to make a purchase. A person's hunger might push them to buy food, while holidays can inspire the purchase of new garments. The "Buyer's Journey" is where the idea of "buyer motivation" first emerged.

A buyer's journey typically consists of three phases:

1. First in the buyer's journey is the step of just becoming aware of the options available to them. The buyer now realizes there is a problem, a need, or a desire. To rephrase, the shopper looks for clues as to what the issue is, such as whether or not he or she is hungry, thirsty, etc. Here, the purchaser has realized the issue at hand. When a buyer has a problem, a need, or a want, it serves as a catalyst to prompt them to start looking for solutions. The stimulus, however, may come from anywhere, not only the outside world. A buyer who starts looking for a restaurant because they're hungry is responding to an internal stimulus, whereas a buyer who starts looking for a restaurant because a buddy recommended it is responding to an external stimulus.
2. The shopper has a good grasp of the situation and is actively searching for solutions. The consumer has realized what it is he wants or needs. Presently, the shopper is looking into his available choices in an effort to choose one that best meets his requirements. The purchaser does their homework and learns about all of their choices. The buyer, for instance, may have been feeling peckish and therefore been investigating local dining options.
3. Third, decide: At this point, the buyer evaluates all of their alternatives and choose the one that best meets their needs.

The purchaser is certain that the selected solution will adequately address his concern or meet his need or desire.

Each and every one of a consumer's purchases is believed to be motivated by some kind of need. To rephrase, a buyer's decision to acquire anything is influenced by his or her goals in doing so. Physiological, social, and economic aspects of the individual consumer all play a role in fostering these motivations.

'Buying motivation' refers to the reasons why a consumer decides to make a purchase. The term "buying motivations" refers to the internal or external influences that motivate a consumer to make a purchase. To restate, a customer's "internal sentiments" are his "purchasing reasons," and he seeks to fulfill them entirely while making a purchase.

It's important to grasp the idea of "Buying motivations" because:

It helps with:

1. impromptu sales techniques
2. product development
3. price choices
4. The part it plays in the overall advertising strategy
5. Identifying potential outlets for product dissemination
6. Benefits the reputation of the company, number 6. Seventh, it helps to gain the confidence and loyalty of your customers.

An individual's reasons for making a purchase can be broken down into several subcategories: product buying motives, which can be further broken down into emotional and rational product buying motives, as well as patronage buying motives, which can be further broken down into emotional and rational patronage buying motives.

Prestige, emulation, love, uniqueness, enjoyment, and routine are all examples of intangible values that influence consumer decisions. Reasonable product purchasing criteria include security, cost-effectiveness, appropriateness, compatibility, adaptability, durability, and convenience.

Aesthetics, word-of-mouth, routine, imitation, and status are all examples of social influences that might influence a customer's purchasing decisions. Convenience, reduced pricing, credit facilities, a larger selection, and a good reputation are all important factors that contribute to a store's success in attracting and retaining customers.

The term "buyer motivation" describes the emotional state of the consumer at the time of purchase. In other words, they are the elements that influence a consumer's decision to make a purchase. Awareness, information search, and choice are the three primary phases of the buyer's journey.

Involvement-types of involvement

Why do we choose one brand or product over another? What makes us choose one store over another? To what end do we shop?

Some of us may find the questions to be as meaningless as the clichés, while others may find them to be axiomatic. The primary motivation, though, is to stress a quite basic principle of human nature. Human behavior is characterized as driven or goal-oriented in the first unit of this course. Even if some of us didn't see it that way before, it's still valid. Each and every one of our activities has a purpose, whether we are aware of it or not. Successful marketers "sculpt" their customers' motivations by fully comprehending those motivations.

However, the motivation may not be powerful enough to make the marketer feel either at ease or uneasy. Because there was no need or opportunity for the marketer to address the consumers on the significance of the choice that the consumers make for themselves, or because consumers just aren't aware of the significance of the purchase decision. At some point, the marketer must add their own weight to these motives in order to encourage customer action and achieve the intended outcome. The term "involvement" describes this step.

The NIIT case study at the beginning of the unit is only one example of many in which marketers have had to get consumers actively engaged in the process of being inspired and invested in making a purchase choice about a computer training program. The number of businesses like NIIT that recognize the importance of understanding the consumer's perspective is expanding.

WHAT NEEDS ARE AND HOW TO CLASSIFY THEM

The concepts of customer requirements and desires are essential to consumer motivation and engagement. This section is an attempt to elaborate on the idea of need.

Concept

The origins of the classification of needs and their interpretation remain murky. Need, desire, and demand are all synonyms that mean the same thing. So, a desire is a specific kind of consumption that serves to meet a need. How one person's needs are met by another is certain to be different from another's because of differences in background, education, and cultural upbringing. A French and an Indian student in the same training program can both become hungry during the noon lecture. If both of you haven't eaten since last night, your hunger levels are probably roughly the same.

However, the means by which various people achieve this goal may vary greatly. While the first may become excited about the possibility of a fried Parantha and pakauris, the second may be content with some cottage cheese, bread, and milk. The question of whether or not marketers can invent new desires hinges on a clear understanding of the difference between needs and wants.

Different Needs

Humans have an innate need for the basics of existence, such food, drink, air, and shelter. The term "biogenic needs" describes these requirements. However, people also have a great deal of non-primal requirements. The process of assimilating into a culture results in the development of certain psychogenic demands. The desire for prominence, authority, and acceptance are all examples. An Indian customer, for instance, may feel compelled to spend a large portion of his money on things that allow him to demonstrate his love and care for his family. Consumers might be inspired to make a purchase for purely hedonic or purely pragmatic reasons. Utilitarian demands are satisfied when items' objective, concrete qualities, like a household appliance's longevity, are prioritized by buyers. Automobiles with low fuel consumption, etc. Hedonic requirements are personal and contextual. A product's ability to satisfy a customer's need for adventure, assurance, or escape into a fantastical world is a key factor in the product's success. Naturally, a product's ability to provide both functional and emotional advantages may help sway customers' purchasing decisions. A Maruti automobile, for instance, may be purchased because of its stylish and elegant interior as well as its cheap operating costs.

Needs theories for customers

The categorization of human desires has been the subject of much study. Some psychologists have sought to identify a core set of requirements that would account for practically all observed behaviors. For example, Henry Murray devised a system that identifies 20 different demands that, when addressed, lead to predictable patterns of behavior. Aspects of autonomy (the ability to make decisions for oneself), dependance (the capacity to rely on others), and play (the pursuit of enjoyable activities) all fall under this category of needs. While generic models such as Murray's tend to account for a wide range of requirements and their consequences, others have honed in on a narrower set of needs and their implications. Those who have a high "desire for achievement," for instance, place a premium on success in their own lives. As a result, they are willing to pay a premium for commodities that serve as visible indicators of progress toward their objectives. Products that boast the purchaser's success would likely appeal to these individuals. Those women who were highly motivated by the prospect of achieving a goal were found to be the most likely to dress in a businesslike manner and the least interested in attire that drew attention to their femininity in a study of working women. The following are some other demands that are significant in understanding customer behavior.

- This desire is applicable to items and services that are consumed in groups and help combat feelings of isolation, such as team sports, bars, and shopping and social clubs. a) Need for affiliation (to be in the company of other people).

- Many goods and services provide customers a sense of control over their lives, satisfying a deep psychological need. Use cases for mobile devices and related accessories like pagers and mobile internet access provide an illustration of this kind of need.
- Products that claim to highlight a customer's unique features satisfy this urge for uniqueness (to proclaim one's particular identity).
- One popular theory on what motivates people is Abraham Maslow's Hierarchy of Needs (d). Maslow's theory is an overarching one that was created to investigate maturation and the achievement of "peak experiences." Maslow developed the theory of a "hierarchy of needs," which classifies people according to how strongly they feel about a certain issue. If you choose a hierarchical approach, you have to complete one set of requirements before moving on to the next. Marketers have adopted this universal theory of motivation since it (indirectly) describes the sorts of product advantages consumers could be searching for at various life stages and in different contexts.
- A person's "ultimate" ideals, such as justice and beauty, should become their primary driving force as they go up the hierarchy. Unfortunately, it's not easy to go to that place (at least consistently), so most of us have to settle with rare glimpses or peak experiences instead.
- According to Maslow's hierarchy, one's more advanced needs must be met before one can focus on the lower ones (i.e., a starving man is not interested in status symbols, friendship, or self-fulfillment). Yet, this order shouldn't be seen as unyielding. Given that a single item or service may fulfill many distinct types of wants, its use in marketing has been oversimplified. For example, sex is considered a primitive instinct for humans. This is a universal truth throughout the animal world, but it's clear that the situation is more nuanced for humans. It's possible that this kind of exercise might be beneficial at any stage of Maslow's hierarchy. Taking Maslow's hierarchy at its value also has the issue of being culturally specific. It's possible that the hierarchical assumptions only hold true in the West. The sequence of the stages may be called into question by those with a different cultural background (or even by those with an eastern cultural background). A religious person who has accepted a

vow of celibacy could disagree that meeting one's physical demands is necessary for happiness. Many eastern cultures also function on the idea that the needs of the group (belongingness requirements) are more important than the needs of the individual (esteem needs). While this hierarchy is commonly used in marketing, it's more important that it serve as a reminder that consumers' priorities for satisfying their needs may shift over time (i.e., "you have to walk before you can run") than that it provide a precise specification of how a consumer moves up the ladder.

What drives us: motives

An individual's motivation is the driving force behind their actions, yet it is not always obvious or quantifiable. In addition, there may be many sources for the same action. The consumer may be oblivious to or unwilling to acknowledge the existence of the need that he or she is striving to fulfill, adding more difficulty to the task of identifying motivations. These obstacles mean that analysts often have to deduce motivations on their own. Certain studies believe that a large number of purchasing choices are not the product of conscious, rational judgments, even when some consumer requirements are definitely utilitarian and pretty simple. On the contrary, there are times when individuals act for reasons they aren't even conscious they have.

Motivation as a concept

To be motivated is to be influenced by or subject to the processes that lead to one's particular pattern of behavior. It takes place whenever a desire to fulfill a need is felt. When a desire is aroused, it creates a condition of tension that compels the consumer to look for ways to alleviate it. To alleviate this stress, consumers might purchase goods and services that aim to meet their needs. This is the goal of many businesses.

Goal

The buyer is the one to realize a need exists. A person may have a hedonic need (the want to experience pleasure) or a utilitarian need (the need to obtain some functional or practical advantage, as when buying a sturdy pair of shoes is necessary) (i.e., an experiential need, involving emotional responses or fantasies). Ultimately, the customer wants to feel a certain way.

Drive

It's always the case that the consumer's actual experience falls short of their ideal one. Tension is raised as a result of this chasm. The degree to which this tension must be alleviated is what drives the sense of urgency the customer experiences. We refer to this level of excitement as a "drive."

Want

One's particular collection of experiences, cultural background, etc., all have a role in shaping the exact route one takes in satisfying a fundamental need, as indicated before. Want is one kind of need, and it is the result of the interaction of the aforementioned variables.

Theories of What Drives People

The theory of motivation rests on a number of key assumptions. In the following, we'll examine a few of them in further detail:

a) The Instinct Theory of Motivation

Earlier theories of motivation attributed actions to instinct, or preprogrammed behavioral tendencies that cross species boundaries. This viewpoint has recently been extensively debunked. One reason is because it's hard to demonstrate either way that an instinct exists. The claim that consumers are driven to purchase status symbols by the need to seem successful is seldom convincing.

b) The Theory of What Drives Us

For proponents of the notion of "drives," the emphasis is on the physiological requirements that lead to unpleasant levels of arousal (e.g., your stomach grumbles during a morning class). The stress that this state of alertness causes motivates us to take action to alleviate. It has been suggested that relieving stress is a fundamental process that controls human behavior. Tension, in the context of marketing, is the uncomfortable situation in which a person finds themselves if their consuming requirements are unmet. A person's mood may be affected by a number of factors, including hunger, financial constraints, and the inability to buy a new automobile. The word "homeostasis" is used to describe the condition that triggers goal-directed activity aimed at alleviating the discomfort and restoring equilibrium.

c) Expectancy Theory

However, problems arise when trying to use drive theory to explain some aspects of human behavior that go against its predictions.

It's more common for people to do actions that heighten rather than lower their drive state. One example is the common practice of postponing enjoyment. You may choose to skip lunch while being hungry if you have plans for an expensive supper out. The second situation is when individuals watch sexy movies on purpose, despite the fact that such stimuli tend to enhance rather than decrease sexual excitement.

Most modern theories on what motivates people to behave look more to mental than biological causes. The idea of expectancy proposes that rather than being driven only by intrinsic motivation, most human behavior is tugged by the anticipation of gratifying results, or positive incentives. To put it another way, when we choose one product over another, it's because we believe we'll benefit more in the long run. Hence, the word "drive" is employed here in a more general sense to include both physiological and mental activities.

Powerful Inspiration

Attaining success relieves pressure and diminishes drive (for the time being). Both the intensity of the customer's drive and the path taken by that consumer in an effort to alleviate that motivation may be defined. Determining how much effort an individual is willing to put out in pursuit of a certain goal as compared to another is one definition of MOTIVATIONAL STRENGTH. It is a direct reflection of the individual's true drive to succeed. There are several hypotheses put out to describe the factors that influence people's actions. People generally agree that they can only focus so much of their energy on any one task.

Mood-Inducing Guidance

The power and focus of an individual's motivations is undeniable. They have a goal-directed mindset in that they want to achieve something in particular in order to fulfill an urge. Marketers try to persuade customers that their product or service is the best option since there are usually several ways to achieve a given goal. If a shopper desires to fit in socially or present a specific image, he or she may pick among denim brands like Levi's, Wranglers, Flying Machine, and others like them, all of which make similar claims about the advantages they will provide.

The direction, or valence, of a goal or purpose may be either positive or negative, and as a result, consumers can have both positive and negative aims. When customers place a high value on a certain outcome, they orient their behavior toward that outcome, move toward it, and seek out products that will help them get there. In order to accomplish the good aim of enhancing his physical and social image, a customer may employ Allegro workout equipment.

However, not all actions are driven by a want to advance toward a target. On the other hand, customers may be on the lookout for ways to prevent a bad experience. They'll organize their spending and consuming habits in a way that lessens the likelihood of this happening. As an example of a negative objective, for many customers, it is to avoid being rejected. As a result, individuals will avoid purchasing items that carry a stigma in their minds.

Advertisements for antiperspirants and mouthwash, for example, often play on customers' negative motivation by showing them the embarrassing results of sweaty pits and foul breath.

Incentive crisis

Multiple factors may influence a consumer's final choice. Since marketers aim to meet the demands of customers, they may also be of assistance by suggesting ways out of sticky situations when competing goals (both good and negative) threaten to derail a consumer's decision-making process.

Confrontation between Different Methods of Approach

In this case, a person has the good fortune of being presented with a choice between two excellent possibilities. A student may feel split between spending the holidays at home with family and traveling on a group vacation. To provide another example, maybe he or she has to decide between two CDs that are equally appealing but only one can be purchased with the money at hand.

Challenges of Approach and Avoidance

As desirable as some goods and services may seem, they often come with unwelcome side effects. When we indulge in things like ice cream or costly perfume, we could have mixed emotions. The popularity of diet food programs like Weight Watchers, which offer wonderful food without the calories, and the widespread use of synthetic furs, which erase guilt about killing animals to make a fashion statement, are two examples of solutions that have helped to alleviate these tensions. Marketers often work to alleviate shoppers' feelings of guilt by persuading them that they deserve finer things.

Cognitive dissonance is a notion in consumer behavior that arises from this sort of incongruity. The idea behind cognitive dissonance is that when people's views or actions are at odds with one another, it creates an uncomfortable mental condition known as "cognitive dissonance." When two or more of your convictions or habits are at odds with one another, you may be experiencing cognitive dissonance. It happens often when a customer must decide between two options, each of which has its own set of pros and downsides. A consumer who opts for one product over another will experience the drawbacks of that product while missing out on the advantages of the other. As a result of this loss, the individual has a sense of discord and discomfort, which drives them to seek relief.

A strategy called cognitive dissonance reduction may help individuals deal with the internal struggle they experience when deciding between two options by encouraging them to minimize the internal contradictions that cause them stress. After making a decision, people often try to reassure themselves that they made the right call by "discovering" problems with the other choice or by finding new evidence in favor of the one they ultimately went with. Bundling many advantages together may help marketers overcome an approach-avoidance dilemma. Miller Lite, which claims to be "less filling" and "tastes wonderful," essentially lets the consumer "have his beer and drink it too."

Confrontation Between Two Avoiders

Consumers might literally be "stuck between a rock and a hard place" at times. They may have to decide between two bad options. Sometimes, a person has to decide between investing more money into an old automobile or purchasing a brand-new vehicle. Marketers often try to resolve this tension by highlighting hidden advantages of one choice over another (e.g., by emphasizing lease finance or easy payment plans to ease the pain of new-car payments). And there's also the issue of having to choose between starvation and working in deplorable conditions. One such instance of this sort of argument is the purchase of medication.

Participation of Individual Consumers

Involvement, along with motivation, is a key idea in stimulating customer motivations. The term "involvement" is used to describe "the amount of perceived personal relevance and/or interest triggered by a stimulus (or stimuli) within a given circumstance."

According to this interpretation, the consumer's incentive to digest information about a product at any particular moment depends on a number of factors, including the characteristics of the individual, the product, and the circumstances. Consumers are more likely to pay attention to and understand information they perceive as being relevant to their objectives when they are really invested in taking action to meet a need. However, the same information may go unnoticed if it is not deemed useful in meeting a need. When it comes to workout gear, one individual may read all he can get his hands on, spend his free time at sports shops, and so on, while another (lazier) person may just ignore it.

A person's level of involvement may be thought of as their level of motivation to analyze given data. A customer will be more interested in learning about a product if they believe it will help them achieve their objectives or fulfill their beliefs. To put it another way, when the right memories are triggered in the brain, it leads to a highly motivated mood that in turn motivates action (like going shopping, for example). The word "felt engagement" describes this intangible but real experience of being involved in something that matters to oneself. When consumers have a stronger emotional investment in a product, they pay closer attention to and make more of an effort to comprehend product-related advertisements.

One may think of the range of interest in a marketing stimulus as a continuum, with complete disinterest on one end and complete devotion on the other. Low-involvement consumers are characterized by inertia, making the same choices over and over again because they lack the drive to explore new options. Intense, passionate attachment is often saved for the few people and things in one's life that really matter.

Participation also modifies both the processing and activation of data. Therefore, the kind of information processing is determined by the degree of engagement of the customer. There is a spectrum from elementary processing, in which just the most fundamental aspects of a message are evaluated, to complex processing, in which the incoming information is elaborated upon by making connections to one's existing bodies of knowledge.

Involvement and all their components

Involvement, as previously described, may take several shapes. If a consumer's running shoes play a significant role in shaping his sense of identity, then he may be considered to have a personal investment in them. That investment tends to grow when he has something to prove, like a competition. Alternatively, for those who are really committed to shopping, the act of purchasing the shoes themselves may be a significant experience. Commercials for Nike and Adidas, for example, could be engaging since they feature athletes (e.g.; because they make us laugh, cry, or inspire us to work harder).

Involvement Types

Involvement appears to be a vague idea since it blends into other concepts and has varied connotations to different individuals. In fact, almost everyone agrees that there are a number of different, broad categories of participation.

a) Participation in a Purchase: How invested a buyer becomes in making a purchase depends on how urgently they feel the need to fulfill that purchase. In order to get more people invested in making a purchase, many retailers run promotions. For a perfume company's contest, ladies sent letters or called talk programs to share the gory details of their sexiest encounters. The manufacturer compiled the best of the winning tales into a romantic book. These booklets were then handed out free with the purchase of the fragrance. According to reports, sales increased dramatically.

b) A two-way exchange of messages and responses: Participation in the processing of marketing communication is referred to as message-response participation. Since viewers are expected to sit back and take in the show without actively participating (apart from "zipping" the remote), television is categorized as a low engagement medium. On the other hand, print is a very interactive medium. The reader plays a vital role in absorbing the content and may take a breather between passages to consider what they've just read.

c) This brings us to Self-Centeredness: Ego engagement, also known as lasting participation, describes how integral a product is to a person's sense of identity. There's a considerable potential for social fallout if the product doesn't work as advertised; the buyer's sense of identity might be harmed. The runner's shoes, for instance, constitute a key component of his sense of identity (i.e., they are said to have high sign value). This kind of participation is not contingent on the specifics of any one transaction.

Measuring involvement values

Several marketing strategies depend on accurate participation metrics. For instance, it has been shown via studies that viewers who are more invested in a program are more receptive to the ads that air during that show, and that these commercials have a larger possibility of persuading the viewer to make a purchase after seeing them. With so many different ways of thinking about engagement, it may be hard to agree on a single metric to use to evaluate the notion.

Creation of an Involvement Profile

Two French scholars have contended that there is no one, decisive factor in engagement. They argue for the creation of an involvement profile with four components to account for the fact that customers might be engaged with a product because it is a hazardous purchase and/or its usage reflects upon or affects the self.

a) The likelihood of making a poor purchase is affected by two factors: a) the significance and risk of the product (how much it means to the buyer and the potential repercussions of a poor purchase).
b) The delight factor of the product class
c) The Category's Symbolic Value

Classifying People According to Their Degree of Engagement

This method of assessment provides consumer researchers with a means of capturing the richness of the participation construct, and it also offers the possibility of using involvement as a foundation for market segmentation. Even though a product has low sign value for one group of customers, it may have high relatedness to the self-concept of another group, such as health fanatics or enthusiastic socializers, as one example. The business might adjust its approach to better suit the needs of various customer subsets based on their interest in learning more about the product. Keep in mind that cultural differences in product class engagement should be taken into account. Champagne may not have the same potential to bring enjoyment or be fundamental to self-definition in other nations, despite its high ratings in both symbol and personal worth among a sample of French consumers (e.g. Islamic cultures).

Methods to Boost Involvement

Although customers may have varying degrees of engagement with a product's message, marketers aren't helpless in the face of this diversity. Consumers may improve the chances that their product information will be received by being aware of certain fundamental variables that enhance or reduce attention and taking appropriate action. An easy win for any marketer is to increase a consumer's incentive to absorb important information by using one or more of the methods discussed in this section when crafting compelling communications.

Values and attitudes: Means and end chain model

Identifying the factors that influence customer choice is a challenging but crucial part of any marketing strategy. If a soccer mom needs a minivan, why does she choose an SUV? Is there a particular reason why a young person would choose Coke over Pepsi? Product characteristics are not the primary determinants of purchase in these situations. Consumers' reasoning extends much farther than that when making decisions. In order to generate an effective message, marketers need to understand what makes their target audience feel.

How, however, can you zero in on the specific causes of your distress? There is a strong method available to market researchers for deconstructing customer preference, but few of them are familiar enough with it to utilize it successfully. The method, known as "laddering," has been around for decades, but it remains a well guarded secret. With the use of laddering, businesses may learn more about their target audiences in order to better communicate with them and ultimately convince them to make a purchase.

The Time-Tested Model of Scientific Investigation. Researchers often undertake qualitative research to study customers' decision processes prior to quantifying the findings in a lengthy attribute-laden survey with a large statistically precise sample in order to better understand why consumers make product selections. Sometimes this strategy works, but other times managers are left wondering what they can do to make customers purchase their goods despite their initial hesitance.

The conventional method often looks at the product's features and advantages, but doesn't go into the customers' psychology to find the emotional triggers that really drive their purchases. The study's findings lead to marketing and communication initiatives that fall short of winning over consumers' hearts and minds. The question then becomes how to encourage customers to feel comfortable enough to reveal their true motivations.

Laddering as a means to a goal for this approach. Means-end analysis is a rigorous research strategy that makes use of the laddering interview. It helps us understand what motivates consumers by getting to the bottom of their decisions by delving into their feelings, the outcomes they fear, and the values they hold most dear. In this study, qualitative and quantitative methods were combined to create a new methodology. Expert interviewers use the laddering approach to collect qualitative data via in-depth interviews, with the data then being organized and processed for quantitative analysis. Researchers in the field of marketing employ this method to gain insight into consumers' decision-making processes so that they may more effectively influence those decisions via the mediums of advertising and public relations. Consumers' actions may be influenced by more convincing communications, which is the outcome of means-end research. Thomas J. Reynolds and Jerry C. Olsen compiled an outstanding resource on the topic in their book, Understanding Consumer Decision Making: The Means-end Approach to Marketing and Advertising Strategy.

The means-end strategy is predicated on the idea that customers would make more informed purchasing decisions if they are aware of the potential repercussions of their purchases. The end result is a value chain connecting the product feature with its functional consequence, its psychosocial (or emotional) consequence, and the underlying human worth.

In other words, the value chain from beginning to finish..

The earlier example of a consumer option being a soccer mom's choosing to drive an SUV rather than a mini-van serves to demonstrate this point. Starting with a product characteristic like "SUV does not have sliding doors" establishes the foundation for the subsequent stages of the value chain. Due to its lack of sliding doors, an SUV "has a more attractive look," which is a positive practical trade-off. "I feel trendy driving it" is a psychological or emotional result of a fashionable design. In conclusion, "approval of me personally by my peers" may be the underlying personal value that is appealing to those who value feeling current.

Minivan chain SUV

Laddering Interviews for Value Chain Construction. Facilitators in charge of constructing such value chains with end users need extensive training and experience, as you would expect. Laddering is the name of the interview method used to discover the value chains. In this qualitative technique, facilitators ask participants to fill in each "rung" of a ladder to explain, in their own words, why each component of the value chain is significant to them.

Using the above example as a starting point, the facilitator may inquire broadly about the respondent's preferences by asking, "Why do you drive an SUV instead of a mini-van?" The interviewer asks more in-depth questions to move the response steadily upward. It's important to obtain details at each rung of the ladder, but some replies like to test you by skipping around. If you don't answer each question in the ladder with a unique answer, it won't help with the analysis. Having respondents verify the ladder helps guarantee that their thinking process was represented properly. An interviewer and responder have the following conversation to establish a value chain in which SUV ownership correlates to social acceptability.

Interview

Ads for an SUV aimed towards soccer mothers, if this value chain holds true, would do well to emphasize the vehicle's appealing style as a means to project an image of being modern and hip. Commercials should encourage a certain frame of mind, and that frame of mind is one in which the personal importance of social approval is implied rather than shown.

Interviewer:	What is the primary reason you drive an SUV instead of a mini-van?
Respondent:	An SUV just looks better than a boring mini-van.
Interviewer:	What do you mean "it looks better"?
Respondent:	A mini-van looks like a sedan, and it has those ugly sliding doors.
Interviewer:	Why is it important to you not to have sliding doors?
Respondent:	Because I want to drive a vehicle with a more stylish design, like an SUV.
Interviewer:	Why is it important to you that your vehicle have a stylish design?
Respondent:	Because it makes me feel trendy and more cutting-edge to drive it.
Interviewer:	Ok, so the stylish design of your SUV makes you feel trendy. In the end, why does feeling trendy matter to you?
Respondent:	It makes me feel good! My friends like what I bought and think I'm trendy because I drive it instead of a mini-van.
Interviewer:	Just to make sure I understand you... you drive an SUV because it doesn't have sliding doors, making you feel like you are driving a stylish vehicle. Since it has a stylish design, you feel like you are trendy for driving it. Feeling trendy makes you feel good, because your friends like what you bought. Is that correct?
Respondent:	Yes.

Due of the extensive questioning necessary to elicit each rung on the ladder, the laddering interviewing approach has typically been used in a face-to-face, one-on-one interview. It may, however, be performed effectively over the phone or online with the help of cutting-edge software that enhances the ladder-building process and sums it up for responders in real time.

Adoption of an Online Channel as a Case Study

One of the world's largest banks has an initiative to promote its online self-service channel. The firm was able to win over early adopters, but it was struggling to win over the following generation. This is a typical problem in the technology industry, and it is difficult to solve by merely adding new product features, since the next generation need more than just more bells and whistles. Customers are being expected to drastically alter the way they are used to communicating and doing business. Why won't these consumers just stick with in-person or telephone support forever?

A means-end strategy with 75 laddering interviews was utilized to investigate the problem. Fifty people who don't use the internet channel were interviewed, and twenty-five people who do use the online channel were interviewed for comparison. For each group, you'll want to perform at least 25 laddering interviews, since that's the minimum number required for a reliable analysis. The average length of an interview was 30 minutes. Voice over Internet Protocol (VoIP) was used in these interviews; the facilitator spoke with the responder via their computer as they wrote their replies.

Each responder was questioned about their use of, or lack thereof, for the internet medium in the performance of personal financial management. Starting with a positive question like "what do you believe is the major benefit to utilizing the internet channel?" the interviewer constructed a positive ladder. Utilizing questions like "what do you believe is the biggest drawback to using the internet channel?" the interviewer constructed a negative ladder to get insight into the obstacles to adoption. While the inclusion of negative ladders isn't required in all laddering studies, it was especially pertinent here because of the study's aims.

Analyzing the Findings. Methods and Ends analysts perform coding on the study's ladders to provide numerical data for the analysis. The analysis's major deliverable is a Consumer Decision Map (CDM), which lays bare the most frequent decision routes (or value chains) that account for consumers' actions.

On the next page, you'll see an illustration of a CDM depicting the two most common decision-making channels followed by consumers who access a service through an online medium. Here we see how the interviews might go in two different directions: one focused on relieving anxiety and stress and the other on improving one's quality of life via the internet medium. The capacity to instantly obtain information and handle private business is the key factor in the left-hand choice route that leads to online channel adoption. Users may rest easy knowing they're always up-to-date on their money situation thanks to this feature. As a result, they may rest easy knowing that their future is safe financially.

3

REFERENCE GROUP AND CONSUMER BEHAVIOUR

Perception and consumer behaviour- Introduction of groups

Consumer wants and needs are sparked by a wide range of causes. You learned in the last lesson how much of an impact families have on consumer habits. In this lesson, we'll talk about how things like social status and the opinions of those in authority within our social circles may play a role in shaping our final decisions.

To begin, let's define the term "Reference Group."

Considered here are some facets of the complex interplay between individuals and the groups to which they belong as reference points. You know from firsthand experience that individuals you look up to have had an impact on the way you make purchases. This is especially true for things like apparel that need to be accepted by your social group. One of the main draws of studying social dynamics is the way in which interpersonal interactions shape individual behavior.

There are two ways in which consumer behavior might be affected by reference groups:

1) They provide guidance on what kind of life one should aspire to lead by setting benchmarks against which one may measure progress.

Two, they specify what one has to have in order to participate in that culture and maintain one's identity. You remembered from before that a person's reference group is any social group to which they refer and to which they feel a strong sense of identification. In other words, a person will use another group as a standard against which to evaluate how they fare. Similarly, consumers often consult social networks for information and insight.

2)Typically, people's social circles of reference are somewhat intimate and limited in scope compared to a whole social class. Actually, the notion of a reference group has its roots in work with relatively small groups. Family, friends, neighbors, congregations, workplaces, and sports teams are all examples. The family is seen as a primary social unit. As an added complication, different members of the same household may have varying responsibilities when it comes to making and consuming purchases. There are a number of other social groupings that have just as great an impact on our lives as the family does. They control our daily lives by dictating how we should look, act, and do duties in person.

3)When it comes to marketing, questions like "what impact do reference groups exercise on individuals?" and "how does reference group influence differ between goods and brands?" are of paramount relevance. The next sections will elaborate on these two concerns.

An Examination of the Role of Peer Groups in Consumption

Consumers are affected by reference groups in a number of ways, including conformity to group norms, exposure to new ideas, and changes in the desire to express one's values. By normalizing the public display of agreed-upon values and attitudes, they are able to influence customer opinion and behavior. Anyone who wants to fit in with the rest of the group will pick up on its norms and standards. Additionally, groups where members share similar social characteristics are more open to altering their perspectives than those where members have varying social traits. This means that group buying is a common occurrence, since individuals tend to purchase goods that their peers purchase. Keep in mind that people experience a strong feeling of belonging to a group because they get significant emotional or material support from their membership in that organization.

Norms and conformity demands from social circles can impact individual spending patterns. Every single member of a group is obligated to follow the rules that have been set. Members of a group may be subjected to direct or indirect forms of pressure to conform in order to ensure the upkeep of the group's normative framework. Among adolescents, for instance, social pressure might be felt when it comes to what they wear. Everyone has felt the weight of peer pressure to conform at some point in their lives. Of course, there's always a chance that the social pressure to comply has the opposite impact.

Grades of Participation in a Group: There are also three phases, or different degrees, of participation in a group. Terms like "compliance," "identification," and "internalization" have been coined to describe them.

An individual's thoughts and outlook are irrelevant to the need of compliance, which is limited to overt behavior.

The connection represented by identification is more tighter and more reliant than the one implied by compliance. A person identifies in order to keep a social interaction going. Similarly, the act of identifying oneself strengthens one's own sense of self-worth.

The final phase entails really believing the group's ideals. Internalization occurs when individuals make the group's values obligatory even when the group is not present.

With the exception of those extremely few persons who may be categorized as hermits, humans tend to be associated with others on a pretty frequent basis. Expectations that one's social interactions would facilitate the attainment of certain goals are a common driver of human activity. One way to meet this need is to take on a community service role; for instance, volunteering as an ambulance driver. For social reasons, someone else could look to a computer club for a group of like-minded people to hang out with. To take advantage of the savings that come with bulk purchasing, a third individual could decide to join a health food cooperative. Just a handful of the almost unlimited possibilities that motivate us to interact with others are listed above.

What is a Group?

Two or more individuals working together toward a common objective might be considered a group. That definition is sufficiently wide to include both a small, intimate "group," such as two neighbors who casually visit a fashion show together, and a big, formal group, such as a neighborhood.

Organizational Structures

We'll keep things simple by comparing and contrasting four ways of categorizing groups: principal vs secondary, formal versus informal, big versus tiny, and membership versus symbolic.

1. Primary and Secondary Societies

A person's main group is comprised of the people with whom they have the most frequent and meaningful interactions. This might include close friends and family, neighbors, and trusted coworkers. A person's interaction with others, however,

A person's secondary group might consist of those they interact with less often or whose views they place less value on.

That description makes it clear that the major and secondary groups differ most in how often and how significantly a person interacts with them.

Two Types of Organizations:

1) One helpful approach to categorize organizations is by the degree to which their structure, members' duties, and purpose are all laid out in detail for everyone to see. A formal organization is one that has clearly defined positions and responsibilities (such as a

president, treasurer, and secretary) and objectives (such as backing a certain political candidate, helping members' kids get better grades in school, or educating members on a particular topic).

One example of a formal organization is the local chapter of the American Red Cross, which has its own set of elected leaders and has regular meetings at which members debate issues of public importance.

On the other hand, an informal group might be something like four ladies who were in the same college sorority and get together for dinner once a month, or three coworkers who see each other often with their husbands.

2) Differentiating between large and small or simple and complicated groupings is frequently useful. One definition of a big group is one in which an individual is unlikely to know more than a small fraction of the members personally or to have a detailed understanding of the roles or activities of more than a small fraction of the other members of the group. Complex organizations like General Motors and the American Bar Association are good examples of massive groupings due to their many subordinate divisions and local chapters.

A small group's members, on the other hand, are more likely to know one another well and to be familiar with each person's contributions and responsibilities. Members of the staff of a campus newspaper, for instance, are typically all familiar with one another and understand one another's roles and responsibilities.

The study of tiny groups is of primary interest in the field of consumer behavior because the members of such groups are more likely to have an impact on the purchasing decisions of their individual peers.

3) Comparing Symbolic and Membership Groups

The distinction between real-life and fictitious groupings provides another another helpful categorization scheme. One's membership status in a certain group is determined by the criteria set out by that organization. A young housewife's membership group can consist of the other ladies she plays weekly golf with or wants to play golf with when an opportunity arises.

In contrast, a symbolic group is one in which a person's chances of being accepted as a member are low, even while the individual adopts the group's ideals, attitudes, and behaviors. Actual membership organizations provide a more direct and, thus, more persuasive effect on customer behavior.

To sum up, it can be said that tiny, informal, primary membership organizations are of considerable interest to marketers since they have the greatest potential impact over consumer purchase choices.

4) Audience-Relevant Societies

We will look at six fundamental consumer-relevant groups—family, friends, formal social groups, shopping groups, consumer action groups, and the workplace—to better understand the sort of influence that different groups have on people.

5) As a Unit, the Family

The people closest to a person, such as immediate family members, have the most impact on his or her purchasing habits. It is the family's ability to exert a strong degree of influence on the development of a person's values, attitudes, and behavior, as well as the individual's high frequency of contact with other members of the family, that makes them so significant.

Social Networks

In contrast to conventional organizations, which often have clear hierarchies and protocols in place, friendship groups are loosely organized and governed. In terms of absolute impact, friends are second only to family members in terms of their potential to affect a person's propensity to make a given purchase.

It's human nature to want to make and keep friends. Friends give company, a sense of safety, and a forum for discussing issues that one would feel uncomfortable discussing with immediate relatives. Forging social links with people outside of one's immediate family is an indicator of maturity and autonomy. Those looking for recommendations are more inclined to approach people they know who they perceive to have similar beliefs and perspectives.

Groups that meet formally

Formal social groupings are more impersonal and serve a different purpose for the individual than are friendship groups, which are closer in nature. Formal social groups attract members for a variety of reasons, including the desire to further one's social and professional networks, enhance one's career, or advocate a particular cause. Marketers are interested in formal social groupings since its members tend to buy the same things together. It's hardly surprising that local insurance agents, car salesmen, and accountants would be interested in the names of males who are members of a local men's club.

A consumer's decisions may be influenced by their membership in a formal social organization. Members of such organizations, for instance, often have the chance to talk casually about places to buy goods or services. It's possible that some members may adopt the shopping habits of more popular members.

Clubs for Retail Therapy

The term "shopping group" is used to describe two or more individuals who go out shopping together, whether for practical reasons (such as buying groceries) or for recreational purposes (such as buying clothes to pass the time). The origins of such communities may be traced back to the bonds of family and friendship. Commonly, individuals like

people tend to group buy with others they perceive to have greater expertise in or familiarity with a certain product or service. Going shopping with friends adds a social component of enjoyment to an otherwise mundane but essential activity. It also lessens the possibility that a consumer may make a choice that is unpopular with their peers.

Few studies in marketing or consumer behavior have looked at shopping groups in depth. While there are similarities between group and individual purchases, one study of buyers' actions in stores uncovered notable distinctions. Three-person shopping parties varied more from their initial purchase intentions (they purchased either more or less than originally anticipated) than did either solitary shoppers or two-party groups, according to the study. The research also indicated that those who shopped in groups were more likely to make impulse buys since they had more time to browse the store's selection.

In-home shopping groups are a subset of shopping groups in which a number of ladies join together at one person's house to "party" and promote a certain brand of goods. Marketing professionals may show off their wares to a large audience all at once with the help of the house party method. Undecided visitors are more likely to make a purchase after seeing the selections of their companions. And since they are visitors in the house of the sponsored hostess, some of the guests may feel obligated to purchase.

Groups That Fight for Consumers

In reaction to the consumerist movement, a new kind of consumer organization called a consumer action group has formed. Since the 1960s, this demographic of shoppers has grown in prominence, giving them more of a say in how products are made and sold.

There are two main types of consumer action groups: those that form to fix a particular consumer mistreatment and then dissolve, and those that form to fix systemic issues that have been going on for a long time. Tenants who organize to publicly display their displeasure, cause-specific consumer action organizations include tenants who are unhappy with the level of service offered by their landlord and neighbors who band together to protest the opening of a fast food restaurant in their middle-class area.

Group Projects

Employees spend a significant portion of their waking lives at work, sometimes more than 35 hours a week, giving coworker groups sufficient time to have a significant impact on the purchasing decisions of its members.

Customers may be swayed either by a company's official work group or by an informal friendship/work group. Those that formally collaborate on projects constitute a group. One or more team members have a great deal of leverage on the beliefs and actions of the others in regards to customers because of their close and long-term working relationship. Coffee breaks, lunches, and after-hours discussions are all opportunities for members of informal work groups to influence the consumption habits of one another.

Place in Society

Every person of society may be placed anywhere along a spectrum of social classes. The social sciences, however, have segmented this spectrum into a handful of distinct categories. Therefore, we use this theory, wherein social class is employed to categorize people and households.

As defined by sociologists, social class is "the separation of members of a society into a hierarchy of separate status classes, so that members of one class have approximately the same status and the members of all other classes have either more or less status than the members of each other class."

Social stratification and its defining features

The defining features of a certain socioeconomic class

1) People in the same socioeconomic group tend to have similar attitudes and behaviors.
2) Class structure is hierarchical
3) Social class is not determined by a single factor but rather is a multi-factor weighing system that includes one's profession, income, money, education, position, prestige, etc.

S. No	Status, Value & Prestige enjoyed	Social Class	Factors affecting Social class
1	Low	**Lower Class**	Lower level occupation with no authority, less income, and no education or minimum education, For example, labour class or clerks etc.
2	Medium	**Middle Class**	Graduates, or postgraduates, executives' managers of companies with authority, drawing handsome salary of which certain amount can be saved and invested. For example, executives or middle level managers of companies.
3	High	Higher Class	Authoritative person, drawing handsome salary, very often professionally qualified, working in a very senior position or a person born into a rich family, with a good background of education.

Individuals may rise or fall in social status on a continuous scale rather than in discrete steps.

Advantages and Disadvantages of group

Advantages of groups include:

1. Shared knowledge and resources: Group members can pool their knowledge and resources to achieve a common goal.
2. Increased creativity and diversity of ideas: A group can provide a diverse range of perspectives and ideas, leading to more creative solutions.
3. Greater efficiency: Tasks can often be completed more quickly and efficiently when divided among multiple people.
4. Improved motivation and morale: Group members may feel more motivated and engaged when working together towards a common goal.
5. Social support: Being part of a group can provide emotional and social support for its members.

Disadvantages of groups include:

1. Groupthink: The pressure to conform to the opinions of the group can lead to poor decision-making.

2. Social loafing: Group members may feel less responsible for the outcome of a task, leading to less effort and reduced productivity.
3. Communication problems: Miscommunication and conflicting ideas can slow down progress and lead to frustration.
4. Conflict and power struggles: Groups can experience conflict and power struggles between members, which can harm the group's cohesion and productivity.
5. Difficult to manage: Groups can be difficult to manage and coordinate, especially when group members have different goals and motivations.

Reference Group

The influence of social status

- "Imposes a set of 'normative' conduct while also imparting a feeling of identity"
- Values, belongings, traditions, and extracurriculars are all shared throughout classes.
- A Marketer's Reaction to Customers With Varying Incomes
- Low-income consumers make up a sizable segment of the market, but some businesses are hesitant to target them because they aren't certain that they would be loyal clients.
- Aim for the value you can provide.
- Collectives Used as a Benchmark

Consumers often look to peers or family when making major purchases. This simple idea sheds light on how the opinions and actions of others shape one's own consumption-related worldview. It also sheds light on the means through which collectives might influence consumers to alter their habits in desirable ways.

Define the term "Reference Group."

The term "reference group" refers to any individual or set of people that an individual uses as a standard against which to measure his or her own values, beliefs, and actions. This idea is more applicable since it does not need customers to identify with a concrete group, regardless of its size or composition (i.e., the group can be symbolic: prosperous business people, rock stars, and sports heroes).

Normative reference groups are those that have a significant impact on societal values and norms. The family is an example of a child's normative reference group, and it is likely to play a significant role in shaping the child's general consumer values and behavior (such as what foods to choose for good nutrition, how to dress for specific occasions, where and how to shop, and what constitutes "good" value).

The term "comparative reference group" is used to describe groups that are used as norms for very particular or precisely defined types of attitudes or behaviors. A family in the neighborhood whose practices you like might serve as a benchmark for your own (the way they maintain their home, their choice of home furnishings and cars, the number and types of vacations they take).

Social class and market segmentation. social factors, social class and consumer behaviour.

The use of both normative and comparative reference groups is crucial. Both normative and comparative reference groups have a role in shaping individuals' views and actions as consumers. It is probable that the fundamental values and behavioral patterns formed early in a person's development by normative reference groups are reliant to some extent on the unique effects of comparative reference groups.

Expanding the Scope of Reference Groups

Reference group is a term that, like many others derived from the behavioral sciences, has evolved through time. In their original form, reference groups were used to refer solely to those people with whom a person had personal contact (e.g., family and close friends). The scope of this idea has expanded throughout time to include not just oblique but also direct impacts exerted by individuals or groups. Movie stars, sports heroes, political leaders, and TV personalities all fall under the category of "indirect reference groups," since they are not people with whom the average person has regular face-to-face interaction. An individual, a few close relatives, a larger family, a voluntary organization, a social class, a profession, an ethnic group, a community, or even a country might all serve as referents against which a person's general or particular attitudes or actions could be judged.

Classes of Peer Support Systems

A person's reference group may be categorized according to the extent to which he or she identifies with the group and the extent to which the group positively or negatively affects the person's values, attitudes, and behaviors. There are four distinct reference groups that arise when these elements are compared and contrasted:

1. A contractual group is one in which one participates or with whom one has frequent personal contact and whose beliefs, attitudes, and standards one endorses. As a result, being part of a

contact group may help to shape one's beliefs and actions for the better.

2. A person who does not currently belong to or interact with a group in person may consider joining an aspirational group in the future. Participate as a Full Member. It has a beneficial effect on the person's outlook or actions.
3. Third, a disclaimant group is one with which a person is affiliated or with which they have regular contact but with whom they strongly disagree on fundamental issues of belief and practice. As a result, they tend to embrace beliefs and practices that run counter to those of their peers.
4. A person who does not participate in or have in-person contact with a group because they disagree with its members' principles, attitudes, or behaviors is said to be part of a "avoidance group." This causes the individual to adopt views and practices that are at odds with those of the community.

Take Ron for example, he is a senior at the state university in the southern United States, and he is majoring in advertising. As the school's vice president of the Advertising Club, Ron is a part of a contractual organization. To further his work, Ron plans to get a Master of Business Administration degree. He clearly views MBA holders as a group to which he aspires to join. While he like working as a reporter for the school newspaper, he disagrees with the recent editorials (supported by the majority of the faculty) that encourage students to embrace a more conservative political outlook. As a result, today's newspaper workforce operates as a bunch of caveat-makers. Finally, Ron has firsthand experience with a large number of students who have dropped out of school during their final year.

Reference-group effects of contextual variables

Various person and product characteristics, as well as a number of social elements, determine the extent to which a reference group affects an individual's behavior. Some of these mechanisms by which consumer behavior is influenced are discussed below, along with their effects and explanations.

1, Knowledge and Practice

Anyone who has used the service or product in question personally, or who can quickly and readily get all relevant information, is less likely to be swayed by the opinions and actions of others around them. However, a person who has no or limited familiarity with the product or service in question, and seeks the guidance or example of others more often than someone who does anticipate to have access to objective facts about it (e.g., someone who thinks that relevant, advertising may be misleading or deceptive). Insightful conclusions may be drawn from studies on imitative behavior about the ways in which customers with little product knowledge are more influenced by the opinions of others around them, for better or for worse. If a medical student wants to impress his new girlfriend, he may take her to a restaurant that he has been to before and enjoyed or one that comes highly rated in the local newspaper's Dining-Out Guide. If he doesn't have any direct experience with this topic and can't find any reliable sources, he may ask around for some advise or try to act like the doctors he looks up to by bringing her to a restaurant they like.

2. The Authority, Charm, and Influence of the Peer Group in Question

A shift in customer attitude and behavior might be prompted by the presence of a reference group that is seen as credible, appealing, or powerful. For instance, customers are more likely to be convinced by someone they see as trustworthy and informed when they are seeking reliable information about the performance or quality of a product or service. In other words, individuals are more prone to be convinced by authoritative sources. Those are more inclined to embrace a product, brand, or set of behaviors when they believe doing so would get the approval of people with whom they identify, provide them with social status, or provide them with financial rewards.

Customers who are worried about the disapproval or punishment of a particular individual or group may choose for goods and services that conform to the standards of that person or organization. Power groups, on the other hand, are less likely to influence individuals' perspectives than are other reference groups that consumers follow due to the credibility or attractiveness of their members. A person's conduct may change because of the influence of another person or group, but that person or group's influence is unlikely to cause a change in the individual's own beliefs or values.

When a person is in a new environment or experiencing a new set of circumstances, their worldview may shift to reflect the values and norms of a new reference group. Examples of this may be seen in the way a young female attorney

may shift based on her location and function. She could wear staid business suits to the workplace throughout the day and then switch to far more outlandish attire once she gets home.

3. Product Visibility & Awareness

The potential impact of a reference group shifts depending on how obvious a product is to others, either visually or audibly. Products that stand out and are easily recognized as belonging to a certain category are said to be "visually noticeable" (e.g., a luxury item or novelty product). A product doesn't need to be flashy to be noticeable; it just has to be something that stands out when you talk about it. In particular, people will consider the opinions of those who matter while making purchases of highly visible and status-revealing goods (such a new car, fashionable apparel, or expensive furnishings). When shopping, consumers are less likely to use a peer group as a reference point when purchasing less flashy products (such canned fruits and laundry detergents).

Reebok is a popular brand of high-status running shoes because its wearers can be easily identified by the flag emblem on the medial side of each shoe.

4. The Role of Peer Influence on Purchasing Decisions

A person's social circle may have an impact on both their product category and brand (or type) preferences. Product-plus, brand-plus goods are exactly what they sound like. When it comes to making a purchase, reference groups often only have an impact on which product category is chosen. Product-plus, brand-minus goods are exactly what they sound like. Brand (or product category) preferences may also be influenced by peer pressure. The term "product-minus, brand-plus" describes these goods. Finally, there are certain goods for which reference groups have no bearing on either the category or brand choice; we refer to them as "product-minus, brand-minus" items. In the mid-1950s, it was proposed to categorize a limited number of product categories into four groups based on the applicability of a reference group appeal for the items and brands in question.

5. Peer Influence and the Pressure to Conform

In marketing, the power of reference groups to influence individual consumers is of great relevance (i.e., to encourage conformity). A reference group's ability to exert such sway depends on its meeting the following criteria:

1. Educate or raise awareness about a product or brand;
2. Allow the person to evaluate his or her own beliefs in light of the group's norms and practices;
3. persuade the person to adopt beliefs and actions that are in line with the expectations of the group;

4. justify an individual's purchase of the same goods as the majority.

A famous experiment meant to compare effects demonstrates the power of reference groups to influence consumer adherence.

Referencing a successful group may be beneficial in many ways.

There are two main advantages for the marketer when using reference group appeals: more brand recognition, and lower risk perception.

The Number One Benefit: Greater Public Recognition of Your Brand

Advertisers may capture and keep the interest of potential customers more easily and effectively with reference group appeals than with many other sorts of promotional efforts. This is especially true in celebrity-based reference group appeal, when the used celebrity is already well recognized by the target audience.

The very fame of the celebrity serves to boost the product's profile.

With so many quick and identical advertising announcements on television, this provides the marketer an edge in standing out to viewers.

Having a lower sense of danger

There is some evidence that making an appeal to a consumer's sense of community might reduce their sense of risk when making a purchase. The customer's doubts regarding the product's quality may be allayed by the endorser's or testimonial-positive giver's example: Some instances of how appealing to an established social norm might reduce shoppers' sense of danger are shown below.

a) Celebrity: These are some of the common responses of fans of a specific celebrity to a testimonial or endorsement from that star. Take the statement, "She wouldn't make a commercial for that product if she didn't feel it was truly fantastic."

b) Expert. Concerned buyers often seek the opinion of a real or perceived expert before making a purchase. That's why we can say things like, "If he claims it works, then it must work."

c) Consumers who have concerns about how a product will effect them individually are more likely to be swayed by an endorsement or testimonial from a regular person. Sayings such, "Others who are just like me have found this product to be helpful,"

Type	Definition	Example
Testimonial	Based on personal usage, a celebrity attests to the quality of the product or service	Sachin and Adidas
Endorsement	Celebrity lends his name and appears on behalf of a product or service with which he/she may not be an expert	Sachin and Boost
Actor	Celebrity presents a product or service as part of a character endorsement	Shahrukh Khan and Santro
Spokesperson	Celebrity represents the brand or company over an extended period of time	Shahrukh Khan and Tag Heur

Roles Played by Reference Groups and Methods of Persuasion Employed

There are four distinct categories of reference groups that may be identified based on the role they play and the level of impact they have.

It should now be obvious that in order to function, reference groups need members to agree upon and abide by a shared set of standards about behavior, contributions, and standing within the group. Norms, as previously mentioned, are the unspoken rules or standards of behavior that are ascribed to members of a community. In addition, different people play different roles in group buying as they try to choose the best product from among many similar options. These include the influencer's, the gatekeeper's, the decision maker's, the buyer's, and the end user's.

Within a group, there have been specified positions of authority. Individuals having a high social standing within a group are likely to have more authority and sway over its decisions. Some purchases, like a fancy outfit or a flashy automobile, are made to flaunt one's socioeconomic standing.

The group's impact will vary depending on the context in which it is being used as a reference. Normative, comparative, status, and dissociative groups are the four broad classifications of social groups.

Comparison Groups for Normative Purposes

An individual's sense of self in a social setting is shaped by the values, rules, and perspectives of the groups to which he or she belongs. A group's norms reflect its members' consensus on what is best for the group as a whole. As an illustration of the normative effect on attire, consider dress codes. Similarly, social standards impact how much food and drink are consumed during a gathering.

Influence applied by a group to encourage members to adopt its values and practices is called normative influence. Because of their prominence in the home, a group might exercise normative influence on the acquisition of clothing, furniture, and appliances. Even inconspicuous goods like mouthwash may be subject to normative influence due to the threat of social exclusion. However, informational impact may exist even while normative influence is unlikely for items like veggies. Influence exerted by a group in the context of normative influence is also known as utilitarian influence because it is grounded on the idea that people want to earn the approval of their peers.

Variables Used as Benchmarks

Consumers are continually gauging their opinions against those of individuals in their social circles. This is done so that they may feel good about the way they act and think. Therefore, comparing oneself to other members of the group and determining whether it will be helpful is the foundation for comparative influence. Newcomers to a community tend to settle among those who are most like them, bolstering their own preexisting worldviews and patterns of behavior. This is also true of advertisements that feature spokespersons who readers would recognize as being like themselves.

A reference group is a set of norms against which one's own views, values, and attitudes may be evaluated. Consumers may be impacted by a reference group even if they do not interact with its members directly, according to reference group theory.

Value-expressive impact arises when a comparison reference group is employed to express those values. One example of value expressive impact is smoking cigarettes in peer groups when this is socially acceptable. In fact, sharing the group's core principles is a certain method to earn everyone's approval and develop strong bonds with everyone else there.

Independent Groups of Reference

These examples make up the counter examples. A person tries not to act or dress like members of the dissociative group because they feel that doing so would be a kind of identification with the group, which they would want to avoid.

Separation from a community may happen when a person prioritizes success at work above belonging to a social group. The consumer may try to distance themselves from the dissociative group by not purchasing goods and services often utilized by members of that group.

Group Dynamics and the Effects of Peer Pressure

Referencing Organizations for Current Situations

The aim of joining such communities is to feel accepted by other members. A person's ability to be affected by such a group is not contingent on their membership in the organization. The term "aspiration group" is used to describe the group when an individual is not a part of it.

Group Dynamics, Peer Pressure, and Personal Authority

Consumer behavior is affected by social power, which in turn is affected by factors such as socioeconomic class and the impact of reference groups. Understanding the social power of these organizations on consumer behavior requires looking at the many ways in which they exert influence. The five pillars upon which social authority rests are as follows. Included in this group are:

1. The Strength of Incentives

Power to bestow benefits onto others. Monetary incentives, swag, and intangibles like kudos and a pat on the back are just a few examples of The more the amount of authority, the larger the payoff. Products, like clothes, may be used in certain contexts to get the benefits of social approval.

2. Power to Compel

The power to withhold rewards or issue threats. As a result, individuals might be pressured into conforming to social norms, such as dressing in approved attire. It is common practice to use pressure to sell other products, such as deodorant, mouthwash, and life insurance.

3. Legal Authority

Because the group has the authority to affect others simply because they are members of it, legitimate power is inextricably tied to cultural or group values and entails the approval of what ought or should be done.

4. Indirect Referent Power

One's sense of belonging to and identification with a group provides the foundation for referent power. The desire to join or be a part of the group has given birth to this. People who have a lot of referent power tend to spend it on things that add to their position in society. Customers are asked to follow the example set by buying the suggested product.

5. Expertise

Consumers trust the opinions of those they consider to be experts within the group.

It seems that a person may be drawn to and adhere to group standards from these different sources of power, either in pursuit of praise or recognition or in reaction to coercive force.

Influence of Reference Groups and Its Determinants

People are open to and actively seek out the guidance of their reference groups because of the perceived advantages it offers. Friendship, knowledge, and contentment are all possible outcomes of the conversation. However, there are a number of variables that determine how much of an impact a person's 10 closest friends have on their actions.

1) The person's level of knowledge and experience: someone who doesn't know much about a product or service will likely ask their friends and family for opinions. When a customer lacks knowledge or expertise, they are more prone to the suggestions of salespeople and others.

2) Secondly, the credibility of the reference group has a significant impact on the extent to which it is able to influence customers' perceptions, opinions, and actions. More and more people will look to it as a source of data on product quality.

Reference the impact of groups on products and brand names

The decision to purchase a certain brand is frequently influenced by the purchase decisions of others around them, rather than any desire to conform to social norms. People talk at great lengths about objects they enjoy and detest during social events, sharing anecdotes about their own experiences with these items. Therefore, the potential impact of reference groups on a product or service's success should be carefully considered. Products or services with significant group use or connotation should be positioned in a social setting when advertised.

Some research suggests that the visibility of a reference group has a direct correlation to the impact it has on consumers' product and brand preferences. There are several degrees of conspicuousness, each of which may have an impact on how items and brands are marketed. It is possible to evaluate conspicuousness along two dimensions. They are a product's uniqueness and its exposure. The ownership stakes are what we mean when we talk about "exclusivity." This suggests that the presence of a product becomes less noticeable when it is owned by a larger percentage of the population. If a designer claims that only 11 men in the world would wear his shirt, for instance, he achieves this level of exclusivity by limiting the number of shirts made from each pattern. Figure 3 shows this clearly. Products that are necessities on the left and luxury items on the right stand for the exclusiveness aspect of conspicuousness. Most people will have and use the things that are considered necessary, but they won't draw much attention to themselves. Luxury goods, since they are possessed by a smaller number of people, tend to stand out more prominently when they are seen.

Second, there's the issue of how obvious something is. This is the process through which other people become aware of and recognize the product and brand. This has an impact on consumers' preferences for certain brands.

Types of reference group

Different kinds of reference groups may be just as beneficial as one another, and they don't even have to meet in person. People who are part of a reference group are often referred to as referent others. Figure 1 demonstrates the four distinct reference group types you should be acquainted with. A breakdown of the groupings might look like this:

1) Organizational Membership vs. Non-Membership: A person's affiliations are the communities to which they belong. On the other hand, aspirational organizations are ones that don't need membership.
2) Referencing groups may be either formal or informal
3) A group's status as "main" or "secondary" depends on how often its members interact with one another. Both formal and informal settings may function as primary groups. One's key informal groups are the people with whom one has the most frequent touch, such as one's family, friends, peers, and business partners. The secondary formal groups are highly organized and not as well knit as the primary ones. Accordingly, groups that primarily interact via infrequent activities, such as going shopping or joining a club, are considered secondary groups.

4) There are two sorts of aspiration groups: anticipatory aspiration groups, which a person plans to join in the future, and actual aspiration groups, which they have already joined. Part of the group's allure is based on the expectation that it will one day be at the very top. Symbolic ambition groups are ones that a person may admire from a distance but is unlikely to join in reality, such as elite sports teams. Businesses use famous people to appeal to consumers' symbolic ambitions for certain items.

Depending on the nature of the influence being exerted, different types of reference groups have different levels of relevance in marketing. All of these diverse reference groups have one thing in common: they are all utilized by consumers as a standard against which their own behaviour, opinions, and values may be measured.

There is a more direct impact on a consumer's belief formation, taste development, and preference formation from primary groups. Many advertisements include groups of people enjoying a product together, whether it's a group of friends out for drinks or a family enjoying breakfast.

Group Dynamics and the Effects of Peer Pressure

It incorporates the public-private distinction to highlight the visible component of conspicuousness. Products used in public settings get greater attention than those used in private settings. Incorporating each of these dimensions yields four distinct classes of goods. The power of peer pressure might be especially strong when it comes to publicly accessible luxury. This is because so few individuals really possess these items. In addition, people will take note of the manufacturer and model of the goods because of how widely available it is.

Since fewer individuals tend to indulge in private luxuries, just owning one might make one feel more special than others. Because such items are not readily available to the general public, there will be less external impact on the product's branding or aesthetic.

In the case of products that serve as public needs, the impact of reference groups is minimal. However, due to the product's prominence, reference group effect on the brand will be substantial.

Take timepieces on the wrist, which are often classified as needs. Due to their widespread availability, the decision of whether or not to wear a watch is less likely to be influenced by peer pressure. In spite of this fact, the brand may be vulnerable to reference group influence since wristwatches are so conspicuous.

Because of the low visibility of private requirements, the effect of the reference group is minimal on the product and the brand.

Therefore, the impact of reference groups varies according on whether the goods and brands in question are considered public needs, private necessities, public luxuries, or private luxuries. Luxury items purchased in public tend to have a greater collective impact than essentials purchased behind closed doors, as predicted by reference group theory. The following inferences may be made regarding the impact of reference groups using the typology shown in the matrix:

1) Impact on Product/Brand (Public Luxuries)

However, smoking is permitted more often in certain communities than others. If smoking is commonplace, members of the group may have a clear favorite brand of cigarettes. As a result, it's probable that both the product and the brand will be heavily influenced by the reference group.

2) Product-Only Influence (Private Luxuries)

Some product categories, like air conditioners and home computers, are so unique that just owning one is adequate representation of group norms. For example, if a family buys a computer for their house, their neighbors and friends would inevitably use it, leading to a proliferation of home computers in the community.

3) Brand Effect (Public Necessities)

You can count on everyone having tried a certain product at some point. Clothing, home furnishings, periodicals, and bathroom soaps are all examples of goods that fall under this category.

This eliminates the possibility of groupthink affecting the final output. Group dynamics start to have a role in how the brand is perceived. Thus, a subculture may use a focus on high fashion to set itself apart. Casual clothes may be emphasized by yet another. For another demographic, reading sophisticated periodicals may be the norm.

4) There Is No Peer Pressure (Private Necessities)

For certain items, there is a correlation between poor product and brand presence on social media. When the power of the reference group is little or nonexistent, this is the situation. When consumers find a product with desirable characteristics, they purchase it. A loaf of bread is not likely to be influenced by a salesperson since it is a low-risk, low-visibility product.

Attempt the next task and see how you fare.

Fill out the list below with the names of the organizations to which you belong, such as your family. Which demographics have the most impact on how you shop for certain products? Identify the group's likely classification as a separate entry.

Using Focus Groups for Marketing

Advertisers utilize the reference group notion to encourage customers to buy goods and brands by showing such items being eaten in positive social contexts, endorsing the products with famous and beautiful individuals, and even enlisting members of stereotypical groups as spokespeople.

For reference group influence to work, ads need to focus on the demographics of the product's buyers and the particular reference groups that play a role in the product selection. The first step for every advertising campaign is to define the demographic and lifestyle parameters of a control group. Once this happens, advertisers will be able to create campaigns that really work.

It has been shown that advertising may be used in three different ways to influence consumer behavior based on the opinions of others in similar social situations:

Group Dynamics and the Effects of Peer Pressure

1) Endorsing goods and services with the help of famous people

Marketers invest heavily on famous people in the hope that their target demographics would have a favorable emotional response to the celebrity's endorsement of their product. The lives of celebrities are a reflection of the consumer's idealized version of their lives.

2) Using well-known people as spokesman for your goods.

Advertisers often employ professionals in the sector as a reference group to bolster their campaigns. Professionals aid potential buyers in assessing an advertised goods.

3) The third strategy is to have well-known people promote the product.

The spokesperson appeal is the third kind of reference group appeal. This speaks to the average person. It shows the customer that someone with similar tastes and needs has purchased and enjoyed the product. Most people appear to relate with individuals like themselves when it comes to messaging about public health, which is why the common man appeal is so powerful in public health announcements.

There are two advantages to using reference groups in advertising. That's because they provide people standards by which to judge products. Even more, because of their own fame, their usage raises awareness of the goods among consumers.

Informative transmission and the importance of opinion leadership

Once the reference groups have been established, the next step for marketers is to zero in on the opinion leaders and early adopters within those groups so they can effectively communicate with them.

Every organization has its head, or more accurately its most influential member: One person's ability to informally influence the opinions of others is referred to as "opinion leadership."

Societal Factors That Affect Buying Habits

Individuals who are influential because of their behaviour or outlook and who convey this information to those who are interested in it. They have sway over others because they are better informed about the product or service than others around them, whether from exposure to marketing, word-of-mouth from those who have used the product, or direct experience. Assuming there are opinion leaders or influential who operate as providers of communication and, other customers who behave as receivers, the phenomena of opinion leadership is intriguing to marketers.

Leadership in shaping public opinion is not uncommon. About half to three quarters of the population acts as both an opinion leader and an opinion follower. Opinion leaders are often friends, neighbours, or co-workers since these relationships for casual chats about the product.

It is thought that persuasion campaigns directed towards opinion leaders will be more successful because of the influence they have on the actions of their followers.

The mechanics of thought leadership

What is the process of interaction between individuals? How does this news make its way from the media to the public at large? Do influential people act as intermediaries in this sharing of knowledge?

It has been said that the two-way flow of communication best exemplifies the process of opinion leadership. This theory proposes that information travels from the media through influential individuals and finally to the broader population. Due to their central role in the chain of transmission, opinion leaders are portrayed in this two-way communication process as direct recipients of information from impersonal marketing sources.

After further refinement, the two-step flow theory became the multi-step flow model. This accounts for the fact that interpersonal communication is the dominant mode of dissemination of knowledge among humans. That is to say, blame cannot be placed squarely on the shoulders of the media.

The pinion leaders, the gate keepers, and the opinion receivers or followers are the three groups who receive information from the mass media in a step-by-step process, as described by the multi-step flow model. These three parties may exchange messages with one another.

According to the multi-stage flow model, leaders of public opinion do not have any influence over a passive set of followers.

Additionally, this is an informal and interpersonal kind of persuasion. In this exchange, one person, the opinion leader, typically imparts knowledge and counsel to the other. Opinion leaders are likely to spread the following types of data about products:

1) Product usage instructions
2) Which brand is the best among these options?
3) If you're looking for the best shopping options?

Influential Opinions and Targeted Products

However, market authority varies from product to product. As a result, a person who is a follower of opinion in one product category may become a trendsetter in a different category. The market leader in one area of products isn't always going to stay there. On the other hand, there is some evidence of a correlation between the opinion leaders in closely linked product categories. Those who hold influential positions in the consumer electronics industry, for instance, may also hold such positions in the home appliance industry.

However, it does not seem that opinion leaders are influential across a wide variety of unrelated product types. Since opinion leadership is a two-way street, it is not uncommon for an opinion leader to switch roles and become an opinion receiver for a different product.

The research shows that those who have a lot of experience or interest in a certain field tend to be seen as opinion leaders in that field. Most influential people in a field focus only on one kind of service or good to which they provide information and recommendations. As a result, you could discover, for instance, that thought leadership in the realm of apparel is not always correlated with thought leadership in the realm of, say, kitchen appliances. Once again, those who are considered to be leaders in the dentistry industry are not always considered to be thought leaders in other industries.

Opinion leaders' individuality and drives

Analyzing the Characteristics of Influential People

Is it possible to create a profile of an opinion leader based on any distinguishing features? This is significant for marketers because identifying these key individuals will allow them to better shape the purchasing decisions of their target demographic.

Opinion leaders are more likely to use products in the category, research shows. They're more invested in the category as a whole, read more publications catering to their interests, and are therefore more versed in it. In addition, they are more likely to try new things while shopping than their following are. They have local networks of acquaintances and social contacts, making them more likely to spread the word. In addition, people place more trust in leaders of thought because they see them as objective. Their guidance is often based on personal experience. Influential people tend to be more unconventional in their outlooks and behaviours, more secure in their own skin, more open to new experiences, more worldly, and more socially at ease with taking risks.

What Drives Prominent People in Their Fields?

There are three hypothesized factors that drive influential people to express their views. One reason may be that they use talk about the items they've purchased to help them feel better about those purchases. It's also possible they're trying to persuade a nearby acquaintance. Self-involvement, in which people seek validation of their own opinion, is another possible explanation.

Influential People: Their Sociodemographic Profiles

Opinion leaders, according to certain research, are often younger people who have achieved more success in life (through things like education, wealth, and social standing). Many influential film critics are young and unmarried. Married people are more likely to spend money on groceries. Medical service information providers, on the other hand, tend to be single.

Exposure in the Media

Do any particular channels exist for communicating with those who hold influential opinions? Yes. There is evidence from a number of studies that suggest that opinion leaders have a heightened interest in a certain product.

Group Dynamics and the Effects of Peer Pressure

They are opinion receivers in general, those who take in information from just certain types of media. Leaders in the public's estimation tend to get greater media coverage. This is especially true with content catering to their specific interests. Leaders in a field tend to spend more time at the movies and in front of the TV than the average person. And they consume more periodicals than everyone else. More content is shown that is directly related to their interests. There is a bigger audience for specialized and technical publications that cover the category of products they fall under. They may better advise their friends, family, and neighbours by reading publications tailored to their specific interests. However, it is not required that influential people get greater coverage in the mainstream media.

Social class and consumer behaviour- Introduction social class categorization

People generally have a sense of the existence of social classes and their own place within them. This is due to the fact that certain individuals have access to better jobs and greater social standing thanks to their educational background and/or profession. Practitioners of the medical, legal, and civil service arts all fall within this category.

However, some individuals, at least, experience discomfort when discussing socioeconomic class because of the harsh reality it portrays. Consideration of social class is valuable in the marketing environment because of the information it may provide regarding consumer market behaviour and the presence of market segmentation. Many of the characteristics of the things we want are influenced by our socioeconomic status, including the colors and styles we find appealing, the sizes we tend to like, the kind of places we frequent, and the strategies we use when we go shopping.

A definition of social class.

When discussing a person's place in society, we talk about their "social class." As shown in Figure 5, your socioeconomic status is contingent on factors including your level of education, profession, property ownership, and income. As a result, people in a society end up categorizing themselves into a hierarchy of social classes, from the very wealthy to the very poor, with those within the same class being on relatively equal footing.

Consumers in a given social class have preferences and consumption habits that are unique to them, making the hierarchical nature of social classes relevant to marketing. This leads them to choose brands that are popular among people of similar or higher socioeconomic status. Some goods may be avoided if they are associated with being of a lower social status. Consistent with this behavior, social class has been defined as the relatively permanent and homogenous divisions or strata in society, which are distinguished by differences in occupation, income, level of education, material wealth, political and religious affiliation, circle of friends, and even accent.

Different social classes also have varying degrees of status, power, and privilege. In reality, social class is used to characterize distinctions in social rank and norms within a community. One uses the word "status" to communicate the concept that various social roles are valued to varying degrees. In other words, status is a socially designated position and a socially attributed function that leads to certain behaviors in persons.

Instead of focusing on people as individuals, social class looks at their families. Many aspects of a family's interactions with the world outside its walls are shaped by the fact that its members all live in the same home and adhere to the same set of values. Thus, we speak of a social class to describe a large group of families that are roughly comparable to one another and wholly distinct from other families. Therefore, social class may be seen as the end consequence of significant groups within a population that have roughly the same lifestyles and are stratified according to their social position and prestige.

Members of the same social class are more likely to interact officially and informally with those of the same class, rather than with those of other classes. There is a correlation between social status and pattern. Class affiliation and the kind of coworkers one mixes with affect the dynamics between friends and family. People's feeling of community is strengthened via such interactions.

CLASS AND SOCIAL STRATIFICATION

Strata, or social groupings, are what the word "social stratification" describes. It's common for members of any social class to think of members of other classes as socially superior or inferior to themselves. It's common knowledge that some groups in any society enjoy privileged treatment, while others are subjected to prejudice and discrimination. In terms of social stratification, those who are placed in the same tier have a greater propensity to socialize, work, and play together. By mutual consent, stratification exists in every human community and culture. Cultural norms are what give it legitimacy. The specifics of the various stratification systems reflect these variations between civilizations.

As a consequence, two types of stratification systems have emerged. One is based on bloodline, while the other is merited. Earned status is based on a person's actions and performance, whereas inherited status is based on a person's history and is present in every stratification system. The class system and the caste system are the two most common ways of organizing people in society. Our own nation, and rural India in particular, is a prime example of a caste system that has persisted for thousands of years. With the caste system, there are clear borders between social classes and little opportunity for advancement. Cultures that place a high value on the caste system and, by extension, hereditary status, tend to be more closed than those that place a higher value on earned status and, therefore, more social mobility. Open systems lack the clear boundaries and historical significance of closed ones.

Maintaining an appropriate level of separation between social groups is seen as desirable.

Class membership is less rigid and static under the more fluid class structure. This indicates that a person's social class is not fixed by their parents' status but rather may rise or fall over time. The upper classes become the normative group for the lower classes to aspire to because of the possibility of moving up the social hierarchy via hard work, education, and opportunity.

The importance of social stratification lies in the fact that different strata have different norms and beliefs. Lifestyle, spending habits, and consumption traits all reflect these distinctions and offer a foundation for market segmentation.

Class and social impact

The term "social influence" refers to the awareness of, and the impact of, other individuals and groups on our decision-making processes. People of a certain socioeconomic status are more likely to buy a certain brand of goods, and such purchases serve as a cultural touchstone for others.

Category of Influence on Society

It's important to distinguish between the two forms of societal impact. The first kind of social influence is normative. This pertains to the way in which customers' social circles affect their purchasing choices. Consumers may behave like sheep and try to fit in by purchasing only socially acceptable items and brands when faced with the intense pressure of normative social influence. In the marketing system, consumers are subtly pushed towards conformity through the availability of similar products at drastically reduced prices as a result of mass production; this, combined with the persuasive power of social pressure, is highly suggestive of a deliberate effort to shape consumer behavior in a uniform direction.

Informational influence is another sort of social pressure. Customers often consult with their peers for advice before making a purchase or deciding where to dine or see a movie. Though they could be swayed by the data, they won't feel compelled to change their behavior in response to it.

Direct information transfer may take the shape of a variety of spoken or written forms of communication, whereas indirect information transfer might take the form of observation. Suppose a buddy of yours tells you that he just bought a cross pen, that he's really enjoying using it, and that you should consider doing the same. Explicit interaction, to put it another way. Or, you may deduce that it is a nice pen since a buddy is happily using it and decide to buy one for yourself. To put it another way, this is a kind of indirect communication.

Furthermore, there are three distinct contexts in which informational impact might take place. You can learn something either by actively seeking it out, by having a member of your reference group offer it, or by seeing how someone else learns it. Although commercial sources are significant (for specific categories of items), personal sources of information are often more influential. This is because people are less likely to trust advertisements and salespeople than they are to trust their friends, neighbors, and family members for product recommendations. This is because individuals are more likely to place their trust in individual accounts as opposed to those provided by corporations.

Both of these methods of exerting influence on customers rely on the latter's participation in a shared social identity construction process. Consumers have a strong need to be included in and identified as part of a positive social group, and this phenomenon, known as consumer identification, is a reflection of this. Consumer goods are typically used as outward symbols in this kind of identification.

Now try your hand at the following challenge:

There is a common perception that people from different socioeconomic backgrounds have different worldviews and values. Think about what separates the top classes from the lower classes and write down at least three distinct psychological distinctions. In each scenario, please specify the kinds of goods you see these socioeconomic groups purchasing in large quantities.

Social class and consumer behaviour- Introduction social class categorization

As you pointed out, education and employment, including salary as a measure of job performance, play a significant role in determining one's place within each social class. However, it is also influenced by the hobbies and activities that a family enjoys together and by the level of social acceptability within a certain socioeconomic class. Thus, social class is not determined by a single factor, such as wealth or education, but rather by a composite of several such factors.

Historically, one's economic standing has been used as a proxy for social standing. This includes elements such as one's employment, educational attainment, the value of one's home, and the quality of one's immediate neighborhood. Marketers are interested in socioeconomic aspects since they can readily obtain the data as part of any inquiry. Market profiles may then be created for the prospective clientele.

Different systems of classification for social status exist. They're arranged in a hierarchy that starts with an upper echelon and ends with a lower one. To order the many strata of society, several systems of categorization have been devised. Commonly, people will utilize a system like Warner's Index of Social Status Indices (ISC).

Four indices of socioeconomic status are used in Warner's Index. They are one's line of work; one's financial situation; and one's living quarters. According to Warner, there are six distinct social strata in every given civilization.

1. Upper-upper class
2. Lower-upper class
3. Upper-middle class
4. Lower-middle class
5. Upper-lower class
6. Lower-lower class

The proportion of people in each socioeconomic group seems to change throughout time, with the majority living in the middle and lower classes. Among the highest classes, mass marketing doesn't really apply, but it works well for the middle class. Yet, companies would do well to aim their marketing of specialized products towards the well-to-do. There is a tiny but dedicated audience for these products among the wealthy with well-developed palates.

Down addition, marketers have zeroed in on four distinct demographics they believe will benefit most from them. Figure 6 depicts these many socioeconomic groups, which include the well-off upper class, the middle class represented by white collar workers, the prosperous working class, and the less fortunate lower class.

For advertising reasons, we characterize the socioeconomic classes in terms of the demographics from which they are derived. Therefore, using demographic data, we find:

Upper-upper-class society: This group represents the country's elite in terms of money and social status. The lower socioeconomic groups might use this as a benchmark. Due to its insignificance, it is not a sizable market niche.

Those in the upper middle class are the new elite. Money is a recent invention. It's a group of high-achievers, such as CEOs of multibillion-dollar corporations, prominent attorneys, and the visionaries behind the world's most influential companies. It is a significant market for high-end niche products.

Those with modest success make up the upper-middle class. Managers with advanced degrees, members of the academic elite (such as doctors, lawyers, and professors), entrepreneurs with mid- to large-sized enterprises, and high-ranking business executives and managers, as well as the younger men and women who are on track to join them in the future are all included. Products in this category are primarily concerned with their housing and overall aesthetic quality.

In the lower-middle class, you have the average person and the highly compensated worker. The self-employed and those without management responsibilities fall under this category. People in this group often have some college experience in addition to their high school diplomas, but they do not rise to senior leadership positions in their respective organizations.

The Working Class consists of unskilled and low-skilled laborers and is the biggest socioeconomic class.

Workers in the blue (Khaki) collar sector who earn a living wage and have discretionary income make up a significant portion of the mass consumer goods industry, together with the middle classes.

Members of each of these strata may be considered either disadvantaged or privileged based on whether their household income is above or below the norm for the stratum. The middle and working classes, the market's biggest demographic, are of particular interest to many businesses since they buy a disproportionate share of the things they promote.

The relationship between social class and ways of life

It is not only one's present socioeconomic standing that shapes one's outlook on life, but also one's parents'. People have a propensity to follow a specific pattern of behavior because of the way they were socialized. Therefore, it is commonly accepted that some aspects of one's way of life are indicators of, and correlate strongly with, one's socioeconomic status. This allows us to see the various socioeconomic strata as distinct subcultures, each with its own norms of conduct, beliefs, and practices.

Studying how people from diverse socioeconomic backgrounds form distinct sets of beliefs and habits might be aided by a careful examination of social classes. Those in the upper-upper class, for instance, may not feel the need to splash out on the priciest brands in an effort to gain social favor since they already enjoy a high level of status. Whereas the upper class may be less likely to indulge in conspicuous consumerism, those in the middle and lower classes may be more likely to do so.

Accordingly, while selecting effective marketing appeals to interact with members of these various social class groups, it is important to take into account the disparities in lifestyles among them. This doesn't prove that people from the same socioeconomic background act similarly. Actually, it is seen that within each socioeconomic class, there is a wide range of ways in which individuals achieve their aims and show their beliefs via their purchasing pattern, Differences in lifestyle as a function of socioeconomic status are seen in Figure 7.

Social stratification and consumer habits

Consumers' spending habits are shaped less by financial means than by their social standing and aspirations. Using the idea that individuals of comparable social classes tend to congregate in their same or nearby neighbourhoods, social class indicators have also been connected to demographic and geographic data.

This causes the emergence of ethnically, racially, and socioeconomically homogenous neighbourhoods.

Food, housing, clothes, and furnishings, and even religious ceremonies, may all serve as symbols of social rank. Especially in civilizations where financial success is equated with social standing, material goods may stand in for one's own value. House, automobile, clothes, food, furniture, and appliances are all purchased in accordance with the norms of one's social class and one's relative position within that class.

Customer behaviour and why they buy

Different socioeconomic groups have distinct shopping habits and sets of priorities. Reread Figure 7 if you need to. It's been shown that people from different socioeconomic backgrounds have distinct preferences when it comes to what they purchase.

Upper class

The upper class enjoys the benefits of wealth, social standing, and political influence. Because of their money, they are able to enjoy social status. To maintain their status, the affluent can afford to purchase the appropriate things, join the right organizations, and hang out with the proper crowd. The wealthy upper class also has more disposable money than the rest of the population. Because of this, they make for a very desirable target market for services and products including leisure activities, high-end fashion, and local and international travel.

Group Dynamics and the Effects of Peer Pressure

Upper-middle-class people

That's the group that just became wealthy. They want to adopt the refined manners of the well-to-do. Therefore, this demographic may represent a sizable market for high-end products because of their emphasis on ostentatious spending. It's not uncommon for middle- and lower-class consumers to adopt a product first popularized by the affluent.

The term "trickle down" describes the result of this phenomenon. Therefore, the middle and working classes are employed as proxies for the higher classes in marketing. In addition, there are those at every rung of the socioeconomic ladder who are always trying to improve their lot in life by material means.

This is what you'll discover in ads featuring attractive ladies in high-class settings. Commercials like this prey on the aspirations of the working poor.

The Middle to Upper Class

The middle class consists of those who have achieved some measure of accomplishment. They tend to be clubgoers with a wide variety of interests in the arts. They are driven by a desire to advance professionally and financially. Typically, the upper-middle class serves as an aspirational benchmark for them.

Lower-middle-class people

The pursuit of social standing drives this community. They look for houses that are properly cared for and nicely furnished, and are located in safe and pleasant areas. Consumers shop with their peers' approval in mind.

Middle-upper class

Members of this group don't plan beyond the immediate future. Instead of looking up to the next socioeconomic class for inspiration, it looks horizontally inside its own.

Because of the differences in spending habits across socioeconomic groups, marketers have taken notice. In the eyes of the marketer, the various socioeconomic groups should be seen as separate subcultures with their own norms of behaviour, consumption habits, and goals. The underlying assumption is that customers' desires and needs do not originate from an indefinable, amorphous sense of wanting. They have been shaped by their upbringing and social surroundings. Individuals' requirements within social classes are thus shaped by the kinds of social interactions they often engage in. The culture at large provides an enabling environment for such pursuits.

Therefore, different socioeconomic groups use and buy different kinds of products. The wealthy tend to be the primary consumers of luxury goods and services like holidays. Once again, the affluent want items that help them stand out from the crowd, are in style, and are a reflection of their refined tastes. As a result, every day, individuals of different social groups communicate the rules and values of their social culture to one another.

Consumer Search Behaviour and Purchasing Habits

It has also been shown that different socioeconomic groups purchase for different reasons. People from higher socioeconomic status brackets are more likely to purchase for fun. As a result, they choose businesses that exude an air of refinement and culture. For their clothing requirements, for instance, members in this socioeconomic group tend to shop at upscale specialty stores. One's socioeconomic status seems to influence one's choice of retail establishments.

There is a notable difference in the amount of research done before, and even during, buying across socioeconomic groups. In general, those in the middle and higher classes do more research into products online before making a purchase. They will do extra research, such as reading newspapers, brochures, and reviews, before making a major purchase like an appliance. Poorer shoppers, on the other hand, are more likely to depend on in-store displays and salespeople. Consumers in the lower socioeconomic classes have less resources at their disposal.

Propaganda and Economic Status

Those in the higher classes react to more nuanced appeals that use material goods as markers of status and individuality. Therefore, advertising targeting the affluent works best when it emphasizes intangible rewards. People of lower socioeconomic position are more receptive to advertisements that illustrate racial relationships and give answers to real difficulties. They're receptive to ads with striking visuals and no-nonsense copy. When communicating with people from varied socioeconomic backgrounds, it's crucial to consider how to best frame your message.

Class division and market segmentation

Marketers can easily divide the population into several subgroups based on their socioeconomic status. In fact, some researchers have argued that social class is a more accurate indicator of consumer preferences than income level alone.

Therefore, social class has been proven to be more indicative of expressive consumer behaviour than money in regards to things like private club membership, farm home ownership, car type, shopping habits, and brand loyalty. Therefore, it is essential that marketing materials, methods of distribution, and points of sale all properly tie into customers' socioeconomic status. Although income has shown more reliable than social class in dividing markets, the debate over whether is the more useful variable for doing so has raged on for quite some time. It seems that the product and the circumstance determine which one is preferred. It has been discovered that the social class variable is more important than the income variable when it comes to the acquisition of status symbols and costly items like sofas. What's crucial for market segmentation is that there be commonalities among the values, beliefs, and actions of people in the same socioeconomic group.

It has been shown that when it comes to large, non-status-signifying purchases like kitchen and laundry equipment, income is a stronger predictor than age or marital status. Finally, for product categories like televisions, vehicles, and apparel that are highly visible, serve as markers of social status, and require modest spending, the combination of social class and income has been proven to be better.

Social class lifestyle and buying behaviour

Various groups of people in a culture are given different statuses. Different factors are used to categorize people into distinct social strata. The transition across socioeconomic strata is reflected in distinct consumption habits. Understanding how different socioeconomic groups make purchasing decisions is critical for any business.

Cultural context for research on social stratification

You should realize that the human propensity to both distinguish oneself from one another and to associate together based on similarities or consistencies is the most basic and interesting of all human occurrences. One of the most important marketing ideas, market segmentation, is built on this idea. You may be aware that the whole market may be broken down further into smaller, more manageable segments based on their shared qualities. All the people in one subgroup have a lot in common, yet they're quite distinct from everyone else. Different groupings and subgroups exhibit distinct behavioral traits. This is what we in the social sciences call "social structure." It indicates that a population or market may be segmented into smaller groups according on the ways in which its members behave. There are several ways that consumer groups might be organized. There may be discrepancies in customer demographics. One way in which people might be different is by the amount of information, skills, and resources they have at their disposal. We characterize these variations in consumers by reference to the idea of social class. Again, cultural norms and preferences may distinguish one set of customers from another.

Consumption patterns, lifestyles, and behaviors varies among socioeconomic groupings because of the wide range of underlying social structures. So, it's important to learn about different social systems. An advertiser might benefit from this kind of research on customer habits. As a result of this discovery, businesses are very interested in learning about many facets of social stratification.

Demographic information that might improve their ability to predict customer behavior and *tailor their efforts to meet their needs.*

An Overview of the Idea of Social Classification

Each community has its own system of social stratification, which serves to distinguish its people from one another. Inequality in social status and status exists everywhere in the globe. Despite their claims of being "classless," class inequality is nevertheless present in many modern nations. It's important to keep in mind that every human culture has some kind of layered social structure in which people are classified into different social classes. Some people in society use these to oppress others. In their work, Kingsley Davis, David Berkman, and John Gilson make reference to this. It was said in "Consumer Behaviour" that all of humankind's social evolution is rooted in violent class conflicts. There are the oppressors and the downtrodden, the wealthy and the impoverished, the lord and the serf. It indicates that individuals are not given the same opportunities or burdens. Families, schools, and religions are all important socialization mechanisms that play a role in passing this system down from one generation to the next. According to the definition provided by Loudon and Bitta, social stratification occurs when "members of a society rank one another into higher and lower social positions, which establishes a hierarchy of respect or status." (1) People in lower social strata have less access to resources like money, power, and reputation and fewer privileges. We have a culture where secretaries are highly valued and compensated but ministerial employees are not, despite the fact that both contribute to the common good in different ways.

Economic status and other factors can contribute to the stratification of society. The distinction between secretaries and staffs is not only one of salary, for example, and this has to be firmly established. Economic theory can shed light on the effect of income bracket on consumer behavior, but sociology is needed to decipher the role of non-monetary factors like social standing. A marketer's ability to identify and assess target markets might benefit from an examination of the causes and consequences of social stratification within a culture or subculture.

Institutional and Cultural Factors That Shape Social Hierarchies

Every member of a society may be classified into one or more predetermined roles. Statuses are used to identify these different roles. We hold several positions in the community at once. A guy may, for instance, be a student, an instructor, and a parent all at the same time. At any one moment, one status is more prominent than the others. The preponderant master position refers to a person's level of authority. One person may have several masters during his lifetime.

Each of these statuses has a different purpose. Roles are culturally established patterns of appropriate conduct. A status is something like being a member of the House of Representatives or the

Senate. A member of parliament (MP) has specific responsibilities that come with the job. A member of parliament (MP) may be called upon to perform legislative duties, political duties, and ceremonial duties. It's worth noting that taking bribes, for example, is not acceptable conduct for a member of parliament.

It is possible to classify systems of social stratification, in which differences in rank and position are enforced, as either open or closed to social mobility. The term "social mobility" refers to a person's or group's capacity to rise from one social strata to another. The Hindu caste system, which is prevalent in India, is an example of a closed social hierarchy. Those who are born into a certain caste are supposed to remain there permanently. The United States, on the other hand, is a more accepting place than many other nations. There, a person automatically joins the social class to which his parents belong at birth. In any case, he has the ability to rise or fall in social status either on his own efforts or on the whims of chance. Three primary types of social stratification were discovered by Engel, Blackwell, and Miniard. They are "castes," "estates," and "social class."

The caste system is a more established and time-tested method of social division. The caste system gives great weight to familial relationships. When comparing the highest and lowest castes, there is a significant gap in terms of authority and social standing. The bulk of India's caste structure is founded on religious beliefs. People of various castes seldom mingle and are restricted in their ability to move freely among them.

Medieval Europe also had an even more established system of social stratification called the estate system. Each party's responsibilities and rights were spelled out in detail under this structure. Power and ties to others were fundamental to this style.

Nowadays, people are divided into several social classes using the modern class system. Almost all modern, urbanized cultures have it. Since disparities in social interaction and consumption are often attributed to differences in socioeconomic status, it is crucial for marketers to get an understanding of these class distinctions.

Stratification as outlined by Max Weber

From what has been said, it is clear that people in a society are placed in a variety of social strata, each with its own set of responsibilities. It's intriguing to speculate about the mechanisms that civilizations use to allocate individuals to various economic and social classes. Mr. Max Weber devised a framework that may be utilized to examine the social divisions that exist within a community. This system proposes a six-factor grading scale for classifying social groups. They are as follows:

(1) social status;
(2) profession;
(3) material assets;
(4) social engagement;
(5) awareness of one's social class; and
(6) value system.

In the sections that follow, we'll go further into each of the aforementioned six factors:

- Social standing: hardly everyone in a given society has equal esteem. People with varying degrees of prominence elicit varying responses from us. The degree of prestige one has in a given society determines which social strata one belongs to.
- One's prestige correlates inversely with their level of education, but not with their employment. A person's job status is a strong indicator of the many social classes that exist in a society. Your occupation is the single most significant determinant of the degree to which you are honored, admired, and respected. In the United States, professionals in the medical field, such as doctors, are held in higher esteem and often get more compensation.
- People's possessions may be a factor in classifying them into different social groups. A society may be stratified into tiers based on the quality and quantity of its members' material possessions.
- Another characteristic that may be used to divide a society into classes is the people its members come into contact with on a daily basis. It is difficult to quantify an individual's social contact, despite the fact that it is one of the most essential elements in classifying cultures.
- "Class awareness" is "the extent to which individuals are aware of themselves as members of a particular social group."
- Not all members of a society are aware of the existence of social stratification. Those who are somewhat aware of social stratification have a better chance of integrating into the top classes.
- Values are the standards by which we judge our actions and the actions of others. These are commonly held convictions about appropriate social conduct." It is feasible to classify a person inside a group according to the extent to which they possess a set of shared values when that group has a shared set of abstract

beliefs that organizes and relates a large number of concrete attitudes."

The following six factors may be used to categorize or stratify people in any given civilization. Remember that these factors are interconnected and have mutual effects when utilizing them to draw conclusions about social stratification. Among the six factors, he should keep in mind that status is the most important.

To Define and Expound Upon the Concept of Social Class

For decades, the indicators of social class (such as level of education, employment, and income) have been helpful in determining what kinds of data and interpretations are most important to various socioeconomic groups. In every culture, there exists a hierarchy of people who are seen more or less deserving of respect. This classification system yields distinct socioeconomic strata. Members of the same socioeconomic class tend to have similar beliefs and lifestyles. This group consists of individuals who are similar to one another in terms of their economic prospects, social standing, way of life, outlook, and patterns of conduct. Every society that relies on an industrialized economy also uses a class system to divide its population. In this way, persons are categorized based on how society at large perceives them.

People of the same socioeconomic strata tend to be held in high respect and regard. What this means is that their thoughts and actions will be informed by a common set of shared ideas, attitudes, and values. A person's social class may be defined as the demographic he has the most in common with. Warner defined social class as a hierarchy in which certain members of society are seen as better than others and are treated differently because of this perception. This definition includes the concepts that the person must take part in the social interaction of the class and be considered as a peer by its members. As described by Loudon and Bitta, it consists of a set of persons who occupy roughly equivalent social roles. Schiffman and Kanuk offer an additional comprehensive definition of social class by arguing that it is the division of members of a society into a hierarchy of distinct status classes, such that members of each class have relatively the same status and members of all other classes have either more or less status.

Kuhl said that big families with shared characteristics and distinctive distinctions from outsiders may be considered a social class because of their place in society. His reasoning disproves the hypothesis that socioeconomic status can be inferred from individual income. People in the same salary bracket but have different jobs (say, a CEO at a private company and a professor at a public institution) may not really be all that similar. This means that a person's financial level is not a reliable predictor of his class membership. It's possible that one's line of work is a more accurate indicator of socioeconomic status than education level. However, those with the same job title but different worldviews are sometimes classified as members of distinct socioeconomic strata. Consumers act according to their attitudes and ideals. Therefore, looking at people's daily routines might provide some useful insight on their socioeconomic status. Members of the same socioeconomic group tend to exhibit a shared lifestyle by purchasing and using the same brands and services. This analysis leads us to the following conclusion: a social class consists of a significant number of families that share the same social standing and prestige and who behave in the similar ways.Therefore, a person's purchasing habits and consuming preferences are shaped by their socioeconomic status.

Traits that define a certain social strata

Various traits distinguish between social classes. The distinguishing features of each social stratum will be discussed below. One of the most prominent features of a social class is that it is limited in some way. 2) they have a hierarchy, 3) they don't overlap, 4) they're comprehensive, 5) they have power, 6) they're visible, 7) they're varied, 8) they don't allow for free-form activity, 9, they're consistent, and 10) they're always changing. Now, let's take a quick look at these features:

- There are clear boundaries between socioeconomic strata: It is implied by "bounded" that there are distinct boundaries between the various social strata. Because of this divide, two distinct social groups are created. A sharp dividing line like that makes it easy to see who belongs in a certain category and who doesn't.

The social orders exist in a hierarchical structure. This indicates that they are standing upright. The order of social classes is hierarchical, with higher-status members of society occupying higher echelons and lower-status members occupying lower echelons.

In accordance with the tenets of the social class system, one may only identify with one social class at any one point in time. That doesn't imply any kind of freedom of movement between socioeconomic groups. Over time, a person might advance from one group to another. However, generally speaking, a person only ever belongs in one social class.

Every member of society belongs to one or more social classes; there is no such thing as a "classless" person in a society with social classes. One's social status is inherently assigned to him regardless of his actual wealth. There is evidence that different socioeconomic classes have different levels of influence because of differences in consumption patterns. To what extent one is influenced, however, is a function of one's level of class consciousness.

- They give off an air of prestige. "status" refers to one's perceived standing in society. Someone's social class determines whether or not he will carry himself as a person of high or low status. There is an unspoken assumption of superiority among those of one socioeconomic class over those of another. Again, one's unique qualities will determine his place in the group. Professors at the same institution, for instance, do not all have the same social standing because of differences in background and personality.
- There is more than one criterion used to divide people into different social classes. They have numerous constituent parts and are thus called multidimensional. Our society does not divide individuals into distinct classes based on a single factor, such as money, but rather uses a variety of factors. Influence, profession, education, inheritance, and household size are among factors that are taken into account when determining a person's social status.
- They limit actions; with rare exceptions, people in a given social class are only allowed to mingle with others of the same class. People also like to associate with others who share their socioeconomic status, worldview, and temperament. Conversations between people regarding goods, shops, and related subjects are limited by this one-dimensional kind of engagement. People in the upper class may discuss a product whose name is unknown to others in the working class.
- They share similar norms, values, beliefs, interests, hobbies, lifestyles, and purchasing patterns since members of the same socioeconomic class tend to congregate together. In what ways will they be distinct from those of other social classes? Marketers may more easily segment their target audiences by targeting just those people who share their socioeconomic status.
- That said, the idea of social class is not static; rather, it evolves with time. This means that people might rise or fall in social status over time. Again, as society reevaluates the value of different social strata, the prestige of any one social group may rise or fall through time. There has been a shift in the social standing of air hostesses in the United States as a result of shifting public opinion towards this occupation. As a result, they now find themselves in a different social strata.

Meaning, Quantification, and Classes in Society

A marketer's success in a nation depends on his or her ability to accurately gauge the many socioeconomic strata that exist there. Several methods exist for assessing socioeconomic stratification. The ability to identify and understand the characteristics of different socioeconomic classes throughout the world is also essential for every successful marketer. This will aid him in targeting the appropriate demographic with his offering.

How Can I Tell If Someone Is Part of a Particular Class?

The characteristics of persons from different socioeconomic backgrounds are of interest to marketers. They might consult with sociologists, who have established straightforward methods for identifying people's socioeconomic classes. Knowing customer demographics is essential for marketers when developing targeted campaigns. People's socioeconomic status is based on a variety of things. One's employment, one's performance, one's belongings, one's affiliations, one's level of education, and one's level of influence are the primary determinants of one's social class.

What occurs when you meet someone for the first time in your line of work? Typically, you start by inquiring about the person's occupation once you've learned his name. You may learn a lot about a person by how they respond to the second inquiry. According to consumer behavior analysts, a person's profession is the most reliable predictor of social status. Prestige rankings for jobs are often in line with common perceptions about associated factors including pay, educational requirements, and access to influential positions. It is often accepted that university professors belong to the middle class, whereas secretaries, generals, and wealthy businesspeople are placed in the upper class.

Individuals' social standings may also be inferred from their own performances and accomplishments. The majority of our nation's attorneys are middle-class people. However, Dr. Kamal Hossain's skills and accomplishments as a lawyer place him squarely in the elite class.

- Artifacts and possessions: a person's social group may be inferred from the kinds of things he has. It seems to reason that middle- and upper-class individuals will have noticeable differences in the clothes they wear, the furniture they use, the kind of home they live in, and the equipment they possess and use. The home a person lives in, the clothes he wears, the car he drives, and the equipment he uses may all be indicators of his socioeconomic status.

• We feel at ease when we mingle with and spend time with others who share our interests, beliefs, and habits. The people with whom one interacts or associates may have a significant impact on their perceived social status. Friendship, dating, and marriage tend to occur among those of the same socioeconomic status.

• One of the most reliable indicators of socioeconomic status is a person's level of education. No doubt, you won't find many Ph.D. holders among the lowest social strata. However, today's middle class nearly exclusively consists of those who have bachelor's degrees.

• Power: not everyone in a society has and uses the same amount of power. Those who have and use greater authority are seen as belonging to a higher social class in a complex society. Ministers, generals, and secretaries often get the treatment accorded to those in the upper classes because of the prestige associated with their positions.

Methods for Assessing Societal Standing

We've already established that people's socioeconomic status is often evaluated along four dimensions: their employment, their level of education, their income, and, to a lesser degree, their living quarters. Here we have the elements of prestige that are tied to actual accomplishments. Age, gender, and socioeconomic background of one's parents are examples of non-academic elements of status. However, the issue arises as to the most efficient means of measuring such factors. There is a variety of tools at our disposal for assessing socioeconomic status. There are three main methods that marketers use to categorize people by socioeconomic status: (1) the reputational approach, (2) the subjective approach, and (3) the objective approach. Now, in a nutshell, let's talk about them:

Method Based on Reputation

Lloyd Warner, an early researcher in the field of social class, created the reputational method for doing so. Just the word itself implies that a person's social standing is based on his or her standing in the community or among their peers. In this approach, participants are asked to rate the social standing of their acquaintances. The strategy relies on an interview format to collect data. The interviewer will question a random sample of respondents about their friends, coworkers, and neighbors in terms of those individuals' perceived social status. Rather of coercing respondents into giving their thoughts, we take into account their honest, unprompted comments.

Objective Criteria

The term "subjective method" denotes that it is open to the influence of the person using it. People are asked to assign themselves a class ranking using this approach. Self-evaluation is based on an individual's own knowledge and perspective, not on the opinions of society at large. The issue is that people tend to overestimate their own social position. Also, they tend to avoid avoiding the underlying meaning of social stratification. Thus, the marketer may get an erroneous impression of the true size of each socioeconomic group using this approach.

An Impartial Methodology

The objective technique assesses socioeconomic stratification by using objective indicators, such as census data. There is no favoritism or prejudice of any kind. Neither of the aforementioned methods is immune to the influence of prejudice. In cases when a person's peers may not give him an accurate social ranking—for example, if they dislike him or want to maintain a positive picture of themselves—the reputational approach might be useful. The subjective approach has a bias since people tend to overstate their own importance in comparison to that of others. The objective technique uses demographic characteristics such income, employment, education, type or region of dwelling, organizational activity, and material possessions to determine a person's place in society. Single factor/item indices and multiple factor/item indices are two examples of objective methods.

- SFII, or Single Factor/Item Index: It uses only one factor—age—to determine one's social standing. This technique is often less accurate than well-developed multiple item indices in predicting an individual's social position or standing in a society due to the fact that an individual's total status is impacted by a number of characteristics. However, the influence of certain status aspects on the purchasing process may be estimated using the single item index. Income, profession, and level of education are three popular single item indices used by marketers to categorize their target audiences into different socioeconomic brackets.
- One's financial standing and ability to make purchases are both reflected in one's income. Income and social standing are linked. On the other hand, there are several issues with utilizing money to categorize people into social classes. It's not always clear to researchers whether they should focus on household or individual earnings, pre- or post-tax earnings, or even wage vs total earnings, among other scenarios. The collection of reliable income statistics is also

challenging. Although there is a link between the two, lifestyle can't be guaranteed just because one has a higher income. It's possible that the salary of a university professor and a car mechanic are comparable. However, these two people's social standings and ways of living will be quite different from one another.

- A person's level of education is seen as a valuable indicator in gauging their overall happiness because of the impact it has on their own interests, preferences, values, and attitudes, societal stratifications of people. Further, educational attainment can be quantified with relative ease, making it a viable indicator of socioeconomic standing.
- The occupation field is the most popular single-item index. The working class of a person might be inferred from his or her economic status. However, there is a strong association between education and income and the profession one has. The use of one's employment as a proxy for one's social standing is problematic due to the fact that it is notoriously hard to establish clear norms for the vast array of occupations that exist in any given community. To address this issue, a classification system based on factors such as level of education and salary may be created.
- MFI Index (Multiple Factor/Item Index): Predicting people's social classes using a multi-item index might be more reliable. More than one demographic factor is used in this approach, allowing for a more nuanced assessment of social stratification. In recent years, academics have created a plethora of multi-item indexes. Common techniques include Warner's Index of Status Characteristics (ISC), Hollingshead's Index of Social Position (ISP), and Coleman's Computerized Status Index (CSI). Warner's approach (ISC) is the most popular choice among the three. As two of them are among the most common, let's take a quick look at them now.

Warner's Index of Typical Social Positions (ISC)

Most people agree that this particular multi-item index is the best way to differentiate across various socioeconomic strata. Factors such as employment, income, housing type, and square footage of living space were used as indicators of socioeconomic status. Warner assigned varying weights to each of seven distinct criteria while defining each of these four dimensions. According to this system, people may be placed into one of six different social groups. These types of groups will be the focus of further discussion in this tutorial.

Hollingshead's Index of Social Standing (ISP)

The Hollingshedad Index of Social Position is another established and extensively used technique of categorizing people into social groups (ISP). This strategy uses both occupational and financial status as proxies for social stratification. The goal of this strategy was to provide an accurate depiction of a family's standing in the community as a whole.

Comparing Different Societal Groups and Their Distinct Features

All societies have their own distinct social strata. As you may be aware, society divides its members up into several "social classes," or groups of people who have similar worldviews and habits. There are many methods to classify people in society, but W.L. Warner's system is commonly recognized. There are six different types of society that he found people to be divided into. Upper-upper, lower-upper, upper-middle, lower-middle, upper-lower, and lower-lower are the six frequently recognized social strata. Marketers care about socioeconomic strata because it informs their choices about how and where to distribute their products and how they talk to customers.

People from long-established affluent families, frequently with money passed down through many generations, make up the upper-upper class. In general, members of this category are regarded as model citizens. People who belong to this category tend to want more affluent areas and larger houses. They are characterized by a concern for the welfare of others. They like to shop in high-end boutiques that cater to the elite. People in the higher classes may like splurging on luxury goods, but they don't want to flaunt their success. It's safe to say that this demographic represents a sizable opportunity for businesses dealing in high-end goods and services such as fine art, rare jewels, exotic vacations, and one-of-a-kind creations. Customers have unique service needs while purchasing a variety of products. Most of their money comes from inheritances. Because of their rarity and affluence, the general populace views them as superior. They send their kids to elite private schools and expect them to eventually attend and excel at the nation's top colleges. They spend money as if it doesn't matter to them, but they don't brag about it either. Those from the higher classes often give direction and financial backing for community events. There is evidence that they have held positions as trustees for various organizations, including healthcare facilities, schools, non-profits, and churches.

Lower-Upper Class: These people have expensive houses in the finest neighbourhoods and enjoy luxurious lives, but they lack illustrious heritage. They lack the social graces of the well-to-do. There are occasions when their average income exceeds that of upper-middle class households. However, their financial success has occurred more recently and was not passed down through the family. " They are the newly affluent, the class of people who have lately become wealthy but who are still not fully recognized by the higher classes. There are four types of people that belong here: successful business pioneers, prominent attorneys, and very successful medical professionals. They have been seen trying to model their lifestyles after those of the wealthy. Society at large refers to them as the "new rich" and the "new successful elite" of this generation. In many cases, this demographic has a more noticeable consumption trend. The way they spend their money communicates a lot about who they are in society. They are the main consumers of luxury goods such as houses, vacations, clothes, cuisine, and furniture. They are not welcomed among the ultra-rich since their fortune was obtained during their lives rather than being passed down from previous generations.

Businessmen, professionals, and owners of medium-sized businesses with a decent amount of success make up the upper-middle class. People in the upper middle class tend to have advanced degrees and a strong will to succeed. They encourage their children to pursue their dreams and provide a supportive atmosphere for them to do so. They are not as financially secure as the upper middle classes. The upper middle class as a whole is either not concerned with their genealogy or does not care about it at all. They are seen as the "eyes and brains" of society due to their high levels of education. They are upstanding people with strong morals and honest character. Their main source of money is not their investments, but rather their salary. Those in the upper middle class often got there because of where they worked or where they went to school. They participate in a wide variety of extracurricular events and pursuits. Upper-middle-class spending is more publicized than wealthy spending. Typically, their purchases are tied to social rank or other indicators of social standing. They contribute to social causes, enjoy a comfortable lifestyle, and engage actively with other people in their social group. Members of this socioeconomic group care deeply about the standard of living they provide for their families and guests, and as a consequence, they design and decorate their houses accordingly.

White-collar employees who make a decent living and can afford relatively pleasant lives are the backbone of the lower-middle class. The members of this group are known to be very frugal. People in this category often own their own businesses, educate, work as technicians or salespeople, or are employed in an office setting. Any community will have a sizeable population of people who fall under this category. They are the most conformist to societal norms and values, prioritizing home life, morality, and religion above everything else. As a means of gaining social standing, they attempt to do the right thing and invest in trendy products. They forego luxuries in order to provide their kids a better education and lift them out of poverty. They lack trust in their own preferences and hence choose to acquire mass-produced goods. They put forth more effort than most people do while shopping since they find deciding what to buy to be difficult and time-consuming. It turns out that they are quite sensitive to price changes.

The middle class is the most numerous socioeconomic group in the majority of nations. This group consists of the hardworking majority. These people want to make sure that their current situation is safe and sound. They have low-skilled or unskilled occupations that don't pay as much and need less education. They put a significant chunk of their money toward basic needs like food and housing. They place a premium on social standing and rely heavily on their immediate families for both material and emotional assistance. Their homes are smaller, and their routines are more predictable. Due of insecurity, most of their purchases may be characterized as being made on the spur of the moment. A larger portion of their revenue comes from salespeople, and advertising. This social group is the least likely to participate in community events and has few contacts outside of their own group. They value now gratification more than future security.

Those in the Lower-Lower Class are unskilled workers, those with low-status jobs, the jobless, and those who rely on government assistance. Since their income is so low, they are effectively homeless. Daily survival is usually the focus of their existence. Members in this socioeconomic group have low levels of education and tend to reside in rundown areas. Neither desire nor chance has given them a reason to better their situation.

The Effects of Socioeconomic Status on Marketing

It's important in marketing to understand how consumers' socioeconomic status affects their purchasing decisions.

Here's why a marketer has to be aware of different socioeconomic groups:

Every culture has some kind of stratification based on economic and other factors. Class has significant disparities in consumer behavior. Consumers from diverse socioeconomic backgrounds shop and are served differently. Socioeconomic status is a significant predictor of brand loyalty and financial conservatism. In light of this, it's important to consider these while developing a marketing plan. As a result, marketing initiatives may need to be developed with various socioeconomic groups in mind. A thorough understanding of the socioeconomic classes and their behavior patterns may aid in making educated decisions about the advertising message, the media platform, the product's design, pricing, and distribution channels. Several puzzling facets of consumer behavior may be better understood via the lens of social class research.

Researching consumers' social classes is of interest to marketers because of the link between socioeconomic position and spending habits. What he buys, where he buys it, how often he buys it, how he pays for it, what drives him to buy, and how he makes that choice all constitute his shopping behavior. When making business choices, the idea of social class may be both analytically helpful and relevant. A marketer's ability to strategize across product creation, market segmentation, pricing, and distribution is hindered without an understanding of social classes, their traits, and their influence on customer behavior.

The Wealth Gap: The Real-Life Differences Between the Upper and Lower Classes

Because people from different socioeconomic classes have different priorities, beliefs, and habits, understanding these differences is crucial for marketers. Because of these differences, various socioeconomic groups have varied product preferences, necessitating specialized approaches to advertising. Differentiating markets and crafting targeted messaging may both benefit from a deeper understanding of these variations. Now, we'll create a profile that accurately reflects how people of various socioeconomic backgrounds really live.

Typical Example of a Person from Different Socioeconomic Groups' Way of Life

As such, the following parts will focus on how people from diverse socioeconomic backgrounds lead their daily lives.

Luxury goods and the lives of the rich and famous: Because of their travels, interactions, and friendships, they have a global perspective. They act like members of the upper class because they are members of the upper class: they are well-mannered, respectful of others, concerned about the welfare of the community, generous benefactors, and members of or leaders of influential social and cultural groups.

People in the middle-to-upper socioeconomic bracket combine elements of the upper-uppers' emphasis on virtue with those of the middle-to-uppers' ambition for material achievement. They are making ostentatious purchases with their newly acquired cash. Many of the emblems of their social standing are material in nature. They like giving the impression that they are cutting edge by purchasing and employing cutting-edge technology.

People in the upper middle class tend to be goal-oriented and focused on their careers. They show it by moving up the corporate ladder quickly. Participation in a wide range of civic and cultural activities is another indication of their will to succeed. They also have a high level of social activity. The members of this group strive relentlessly to improve their lot in life. They flaunt their wealth with flashy homes and expensive possessions.

Lower-middle-class people value clean, well-kept homes. They take pride in maintaining a tidy home environment. They like dwellings close to major thoroughfares. They're always thinking of ways to improve their work at home and in the office. As home life is crucial for this demographic, they invest a lot of time into domestic chores like dusting and vacuuming. They always stress the importance of good behavior to their kids. We find that they engage in vigorous religious activity. Their way of living is not seen as very original.

The Upper-Lower classes prioritize comfort and luxury in their daily lives. They take pleasure in each passing day. Daily life for this group is on establishing and maintaining healthy relationships with other people. In order to determine what constitutes acceptable conduct, they cast their gaze outside. Women in this social stratum devote a sufficient amount of attention to their children and domestic responsibilities. They have narrow perspectives on the world and have difficulty adapting to new situations. Rather than looking for new opportunities, they are more inclined to focus on safeguarding their current situation. They lead humdrum existences in unremarkable metropolitan neighborhoods, occupying modest homes.

Poor people's way of life: They see themselves as helpless puppets who are acted upon by the surroundings. They frequently choose to live contrary to the values held by the middle class. Credit card purchases are common within this group. They're terrible parents who barely get by day-to-day. All hope is lost in the end for them.

Consumer Behaviour across Socioeconomic Groups

You should now realize that people from the same socioeconomic class tend to have the same consumption habits. Like-minded individuals have common norms in terms of worldview, lexicon, and material belongings. As a result, one's socioeconomic status is strongly correlated to his opportunities and challenges. As an example, it might influence a person's fertility and their children's odds of making it through childhood. A person's vocation, religious beliefs, early upbringing, and level of schooling may all be affected by his socioeconomic status. A person's purchasing habits are influenced by his socioeconomic status, just as it is by many other elements of his life. As a result, it dictates the goods and services that people purchase and utilize. It also has an effect on the way a person shops and the places he frequents. The following table provides a snapshot of how people from different socioeconomic backgrounds shop.

Class	Patterns of Buying Behavior
Upper-upper	People of this class are not conspicuous buyers/consumers. They purchase or inherit large houses. They buy conservative clothes. They patronize exclusive shops. They avoid mass merchandisers. They travel extensively. They purchase expensive and unique products.
Lower-upper	They pursue a gracious living. They spend their wealth conspicuously in purchases. They purchase large houses and luxury cars. They buy more expensive clothing, food, and furniture. They spend substantially in foreign travel.
Upper-middle	They buy expensive houses to indicate their social positions. They purchase products such as insurance to achieve financial security. Though their consumption may be conspicuous, they are found to be cautious to ensure that their purchases are socially acceptable. They usually buy high-quality products in pursuit of gracious living.
Lower-middle	They usually rent houses. But, sometimes, they are found to buy houses to be respectable in the society.

	Their houses are usually well maintained through the purchases of decorative items. They usually buy standard design and moderately priced one piece offurniture at a time. They are usually price sensitive, andshop covering a wide variety of stores and shopping areas. Joint shopping by husband and wife is more common in this class.
Upper-lower	They live in small houses or flats. They favor national brands, are usually more brand loyal. They spend less on housing and more on household items. They spend smaller proportion of their incomes on travel. They usually prefer to shop at nonexclusive stores. They are attracted more by the promotional offers and inducements. They also prefer credit purchase facilities.
Lower-lower	Their purchases are impulsive in many cases rather than planned. They spend larger portion of their incomes on daily necessities. They spend very less on theirchildren's education. They prefer to shop at local storeswhere they know the owners and can get easy credit terms.

The Role of Socioeconomic Status in Buying Decisions and Its Implications for Marketing

• Social stratification is of great interest to marketers because of its correlation with customer behavior. Many businesspeople assume a connection exists between income level and customer spending habits. As a result, they resort to the idea of social class to shed light on consumer habits. Several studies have looked at how different socioeconomic groups' habits at the store compare. Some of the most important takeaways for marketers from these types of research are covered in more detail below.

• Economic Status and Retail Activity: People's retail preferences, in particular, may be accurately predicted based on their social status. The stores people frequent are strongly correlated with their socioeconomic status. It is possible for people from various socioeconomic backgrounds to buy the exact same product or brand from different retailers. It's a fact that most women across socioeconomic strata love to shop. However, different socioeconomic groups enjoy life for different reasons. Several sociological research have indicated that women of lower socioeconomic status take pleasure in shopping for and receiving new clothing and home goods. Those in the middle and higher classes, on the other hand, value a pleasant shopping experience complete with exciting store displays and a variety of unique products. The ladies of the middle and higher classes shop more often than those of the lower classes. Comparatively, upper-class individuals shop swiftly, whereas those in the middle and lower classes often take their time and enjoy window shopping. Shops that provide discounts, lines of credit, and a welcoming atmosphere are more popular among the lower classes than upscale establishments. Those in the high and upper middle classes tend to shop extremely methodically. The research shows that they have a deeper understanding of the many facets of shopping. People in the middle class put in more effort to get good deals since they care about their finances. The lower classes tend to make more habitual purchases and rely more heavily on in-store information sources.

- There is a connection between socioeconomic status and media consumption. Studies have shown that the middle and upper classes spend more time at the movies, libraries, and bookstores than the lower classes do. They cut down on their TV time. Middle and upper class individuals are more likely to read newspapers and periodicals that provide analysis and commentary on current events. On the other side, the working class tends to read more fiction, women's magazines, and tabloid newspapers. Compared to those in the middle and higher classes, those in the lower classes are less likely to subscribe to newspapers. People from lower socioeconomic backgrounds are more likely to be glued to the screen than those from higher socioeconomic backgrounds. Those in the upper and upper-middle classes are drawn to shows like game shows, comedies, magazine shows, and variety shows on television, while those in the lower classes prefer to watch shows like chat shows, documentaries, late-night movies, and dramas. Most low-income individuals read magazines that exaggerate the romance and celebrity lifestyles of actors and actresses on television and in movies.

- Engel, Blackwell, and Miniard showed that people from different socioeconomic backgrounds engage in different levels and types of search while making decisions. Lower-class people are at a disadvantage when it comes to sifting through information since they have less resources at their disposal. They are shown to do less research before to making a purchase. They are reported to rely on the advice of family and friends when making major purchases. The middle class, on the other hand, is more likely to depend on commercial resources like the media. It's also shown that they do more obvious searches.

• Those from various socioeconomic backgrounds have varying reactions to various forms of marketing communication. Lower class individuals do not understand advertising and promotional messages that use connotative connotations, and as a consequence, they are not interested in them. People of various socioeconomic backgrounds also have diverse interpretations of the symbols and language employed in advertising messaging. Even the tone of one's voice and one's speech pattern might be interpreted differently depending on one's social standing. There is some evidence that those who sound more affluent are seen as more believable by those in higher social strata than those who seem less well-off. Commercials that focus on regular living and provide answers to common issues are more likely to appeal to the working class. Incentives like "price-cuts," "buy two, get one free," and similar promotions may have a greater impact on the lower classes when used in advertising. People from the middle class want to make sure that the reward is worthwhile. People respond to these kinds of solicitations by doing their best to use common sense. However, those in the upper middle class have a negative outlook on such things, and research shows that they are less likely to believe advertising promises and more likely to dismiss emotional advertising appeals. Different, high-class, fashionable, humorous, and one-of-a-kind allures may entice the wealthy.

• Brands of expensive products (furniture, appliances, and vehicles) bought by consumers may also be influenced by their socioeconomic status. Rich people tend to purchase larger quantities of more costly, more rare, and more well-known brands. When it comes to purchasing physical products, they care more about appearances. The middle class aspires to seem successful by acquiring luxury items like those enjoyed by the wealthy. People in the middle class are more interested in purchasing the brands of consumer items that signal social approval. Brands of durable items are often chosen by lower-class consumers based on several criteria: price, durability, convenience of use, and function performance.

• Social Class and Recreational and Leisure Activities: A person's socioeconomic status affects both the way they use their free time and the kinds of recreational and leisure activities they choose to engage in. Many individuals from the middle class and below spend their free time playing indoor games, watching television, and hanging out with their friends and family. It's common to see men and couples in the middle and higher classes spending time apart. However, middle-class households are more likely to have husbands and spouses spend time together on leisure activities. Outdoor sports and activities, such as hosting social and cultural events and participating in a variety of civic groups, are popular among the upper class in their spare time.

Managers in the field of marketing must consider the impact of different socioeconomic groups on the aforementioned factors. They need to understand that customers' purchasing decisions are impacted by socioeconomic status. They should also be aware that individuals of various socioeconomic backgrounds respond differently to promotional and advertising messaging. Marketers should pay attention to socioeconomic class when developing strategies for marketing activities since it affects consumer spending, media consumption, information seeking, and leisure pursuits. To be successful in today's era of client wealth and awareness, a marketer has to develop distinct segmentation, product design, pricing, advertising, and distribution strategies for various socioeconomic groups.

A Perspective from the Family on Determination Making

Family members often make purchasing decisions together. A person's consuming habits are heavily influenced by their family in various ways. A youngster might learn the finer points of candy consumption by watching an older sibling; likewise, a youngster can learn the worth of hard currency by witnessing his or her parents. Buying a vehicle, planning a vacation, and deciding between a nearby university and one further out are all examples of the kinds of consumption choices that families often make together. Many businesses aim their marketing efforts towards families because they represent such a large potential market for their goods and services.

Group Discussion:

There are two main causes for the prominence of the home or family unit in consumer decisions:

The average household makes several purchases each year.

Family members may have a significant impact on an individual's purchasing behaviour.

Decisions on what to buy as a family or as a unit are heavily influenced by who makes those purchases and who uses the goods. An individual may buy food and soap for the whole family, but only use it themselves; a member of the same household might buy cosmetics or shaving cream for himself or herself. In contrast, it is common practice for couples to make large purchases like a house or automobile together, often enlisting the help of their children or other relatives.

Family outings to the mall often entail many people making purchases of apparel and accessories, an activity which carries a substantial measure of social impact by members of one's immediate family; for example, a parent may authorize and pay for a kid to buy an item of clothes, but that same child's adolescent sibling may have some say in what their parent buys.

It doesn't matter how many people are in the family at the time of a purchase, everyone in the family gets a say in what is bought. It is unfair to expect her to change her behavior as a person just because she is a mother of two small children. It doesn't rule out the possibility that the preferences and influence of other family members factor into her decision making. However, before choosing on a certain communication or advertising approach to attract their group, marketers should think about the consuming conditions and the family structure.

How do you define a family?

A family consists of two or more people who live together and are connected by blood, marriage, or adoption. The term "nuclear family" refers to a household consisting of a father, a mother, and their minor or minors children. The extended family consists of the immediate family (mother, father, and children) and any further blood relations (grandparents, aunts, uncles, cousins, and in-laws). Family of orientation refers to the one into which one is born, whereas family of procreation refers to the one created via marriage. Members of the most fundamental social group who share a dwelling and work together to meet their own and communal needs comprise a family.

The phrase "household" refers to a group of people living together in a single dwelling, regardless of whether they are connected to one another or not. Even though they're sometimes used interchangeably, "household" and "family" mean quite different things. When analyzing information, it's crucial to make a distinction between these two concepts.

Due to the increasing prevalence of unconventional families and non-family homes, marketers are increasingly privileging the household as a unit of analysis. One person resides in the vast majority of non-family homes. Non-family households that are still present include instances when seniors are staying with strangers. People of opposite sexes sharing housing, friends sharing an apartment, and couples of the same gender all fall into this category.

Family and household structural factors

Structural factors include things like the age of the family breadwinner, whether or not they are married, whether or not they have children, and whether or not they are gainfully employed. Analysts who study customer behavior, for instance, care much about questions like how many kids a family has and whether they do. Families with children have a larger need for many necessities, such as those listed above, but a lower need for many luxuries, such as vacations, fancier restaurants, and fashionable apparel for adults.

Alterations to the production system can have an impact on the goods available for purchase. In Japan, for instance, a group of IT firms has banded together to standardize home-monitoring and -management systems.

Influencing Societal Factors on Homes and Families

The social aspects of family consumer decision-making are often overlooked by marketers, although they are crucial to a full comprehension of the dynamics of the home. Cohesion, flexibility, and communication are three social factors that provide light on how families work.

Cohesion refers to the closeness and support shared by members of a family. It's a measure of how emotionally attached members of a family are to one another. A family's level of cohesion shows how closely its members feel knit together or isolated from one another.

Adaptability is the degree to which a family can adjust its dynamics in response to environmental and developmental pressures. How effectively a family adapts to new conditions is a good indicator of how well they will do in the long run.

- Movement on the other two dimensions is impossible without effective communication. As the requirements of family members change over time, it's important for everyone to be able to openly discuss those changes with one another and get positive feedback.
- Flexibility and unity. Restricting growth in the areas of cohesiveness and flexibility, negative communication skills (such as double messages, double binds, criticism) hinder the capacity to openly express emotions. Whether you want to know if your loved ones are pleased with a recent family purchase, you'll need to have a conversation between yourself.
- Understanding the functions offered and the responsibilities played by family members is helpful in determining how the

family makes purchasing choices and how the family impacts the future buy behavior of members.

Roles of family

There are four primary roles that families play that are especially essential when discussing consumption habits. The first is financial security, followed by emotional care, then a healthy way of life for everyone in the family, and last opportunities for everyone to interact with those beyond the family.

(1) Financial Security

Providing for one's dependants' material needs is undeniably a fundamental family role. There has been a dramatic shift in how the family handles the burden of providing for its financial well-being. Men should be the primary breadwinners and mothers and fathers in today's society, just as they always have been. As a result, children now play a different role in the economy. Even if some teenagers do find employment, they seldom contribute to the family budget. Their dependence on their parents for support remains unchanged. However, for some of them, pocket money is sufficient for them to make their own choices about the kind of discretionary purchases they make.

(2) Emotional Companionship

One of the primary roles of the modern family is to provide its members with emotional sustenance. In this role, the family helps its members through tough times by providing emotional and practical support. Greeting-card firms have marketed cards specifically for parents to present to their children so that working parents may more easily express their love, affection, and support.

The offspring. For example, there are several educational and psychological institutions in most towns that aim to aid parents who wish to aid their children in bettering their learning and communication abilities or, more generally, better adjusting to their circumstances.

(3) Suitable Family Lifestyles

Setting a reasonable standard of living for the household is another crucial role that families play in terms of consumer behaviour. Time obligations and other aspects of family living significantly affect purchasing habits. For instance, the growing number of married women who have jobs outside the home has increased demand for quick-and-easy meal options and fuelled the growth of the convenience goods industry. With both parents in the workforce, there is a shift away from prioritizing quantity over quality when it comes to family time. Hotels are catering to families by offering various weekend packages in an effort to make up for the lack of valuable family time.

(4) Family and Children's Social Development

One of the most important roles of families is in the socialization of its members, particularly its young children. Most of this process involves teaching kids norms and beliefs that are in line with the society they're growing up in. Some examples of these include following a set of moral or religious precepts, maintaining a certain level of personal hygiene and presentation, speaking and acting in a respectful way, and deciding on an acceptable course of study and professional trajectory. A youngster learns social skills (such as etiquette, ambitions, values, and other attributes) both explicitly and implicitly through their parents and older siblings. Parents who are searching for guidance on how to socialize their preteen children are a common target of marketers.

Generational Patterns in Families

Over time, families go through several phases that each bring forth unique changes. The term "family life cycle" has traditionally been used to describe this progression (FLC). Future developments in society may necessitate renaming the idea "home life cycle" (HLC) or "consumer life cycle" (CLC). To illustrate how the life cycle influences consumer behavior, however, we shall use the term FLC.

Characteristics of the Family Life Cycle

The conventional FLC analyzes consumer behavior over the lifecycle, from engagement to retirement, including marriage, parenthood, childrearing, the death of a spouse, and emigration. The table below details these phases and the typical actions of consumers at each level. However, buyers don't have to go through each step in order; some may skip many.

Stages in Family Life Cycle	Economic Circumstances	Likely Buying Behavior
Bachelorhood (Young, single staying alone)	Earning reasonable good salary, no financial burdens	Buy, basic kitchen equipment basic furniture, two wheeler, vacation with friends
Parenthood (young married just attained parenthood)	Better off financially, though home purchases at peak, less liquid assets, not able to save more.	Buys baby food, toys, diapers, chest & cough medicines
Post parenthood (growing children or grown up children)	Financial position improved with wife working, probability of home ownership on the higher side).	Concentrates on home improvements. Buy more tasteful furniture, car, home appliances, and magazines. Interested in vacation packages.
Dissolution (retired & lone surviving spouse)	Income though good, not interested in spending. At times drastic cut in income is likely.	Buy more medicinal products ant other products like the retired people. Seeks more of attention, affection and security conscious.

Young Singles

Single young adults may choose to live alone, with their nuclear families, with friends, or with a cohabitant. Despite having modest incomes, many buyers have few financial commitments and see no need to put money down for the future or retirement. It's not uncommon for them to blow all their income on luxuries such as a new automobile, a fully furnished apartment, the latest trends, a social life, a few drinks, exotic restaurants, and expensive holidays.

Newly Married Couples

In most cases, a newlywed couple without children will be better off financially than either of them was before they tied the knot. These households often squander a large portion of their earnings on luxuries such as new automobiles, expensive wardrobes, exotic holidays, and entertaining guests at their homes. They seem to be more receptive to advertising and have the greatest purchase rate and highest average purchases of durable goods (especially furniture and appliances).

Full Nest I

When a first kid is born, the parents must determine whether one will remain at home to care for the infant, or if both will go to work and pay for daycare. At this point, many families are settling into their first homes, acquiring all-new baby gear, and stocking up on staples like diapers, baby food, toys, sleds, and skates. These demands lessen a family's capacity to save, and they often leave both the husband and the wife feeling unhappy with their current financial situation.

Full Nest II

Now that the youngest kid is old enough for school, both parents are working, and financial stability has increased. In most cases, this leads to an improvement in the family's financial situation, but it also results in increased consumption. Children continue to have a significant impact on the family's spending habits; they have a hand in deciding whether or not to purchase big quantities of food and cleaning supplies, bicycles, music lessons, clothes, sports equipment, and a computer.

Full Nest III

When both parents are in their forties, the household's financial situation normally continues to improve due to the increased incomes of the main wage earner, the second wage earner, and the children's occasional and part-time work. In most cases, a family will invest in new furnishings, new high-end equipment, and new educational opportunities when they get a large sum of money. During this time, families often increase their computer spending by purchasing extra PCs for their older children. It's possible that a family's financial situation may be more precarious than usual if a significant number of its children decide to pursue higher education.

Married, No Kids

A married couple without children is more likely to have extra money for philanthropic endeavors, vacations, and fun than a single person of the same age. Couples in this situation are more likely to have two incomes and hence may retire early if they save enough.

Older Singles

People who are 40 or older and unmarried may have been married before and are now divorced or widowed, or they may have never been married and are now living alone or with a cohabitant. Even though this demographic has more disposable money than ever before, they are feeling the pinch of retirement savings requirements due to the lack of a second income as they age.

Empty Nest I

The current state of the family's finances is the one with which they are happiest. Now that they're grown and can provide for themselves, the family can devote more resources to savings. At this point in time, the couple's priorities shift from providing for the necessities of their children to satisfying the needs of the pair themselves. They do this by investing in their homes, buying luxury goods, going on exotic holidays, driving SUVs, eating out, taking road trips, and buying stuff for their grandchildren.

Empty Nest II

But now the breadwinners are no longer contributing, and that means less money in the bank. Medical care and related products, as well as pharmaceuticals, become the primary focus of consumer spending. However, many of these families are still energetic and healthy, which allows for activities like traveling, exercising, and volunteering. Many retirees choose to work part-time in order to maintain their social networks and financial stability.

Unaccompanied Survivor

Those who are alone must either work or stay at home. To continue making ends meet (rather than relying on savings) and keeping up social ties, a spouse who has previously worked outside the house may often keep or return to the workforce after their partner passes away. In this phase of life, people tend to spend less money on necessities like clothes and food and more on experiences like medical care, travel, entertainment, and services. Those who are unemployed often have lower disposable earnings, therefore they may opt to remarry or move in with friends to save costs and increase social support.

Retired Solitary Survivor

Although their income may be lower in retirement, lone survivors' spending habits are similar to those of the general population. They have the means to purchase a broad variety of goods, subject to their level of lifelong savings. Because of the decisions they have made in life, these people have unique need for love, care, and safety.

Marketers use the FLC stage descriptions to analyze marketing and communication strategies for products and services, but they also typically add information about consumer markets to do things like analyze consumer needs, find niches in the market, and develop marketing strategies that are more tailored to individual consumers.

Methods of Making Choices Within the Family

Products are used by families even though they are often purchased by individuals. Choosing which things to purchase and where to go shopping.

There are many people involved in the process of deciding what things to sell, when to sell them, and how to sell them.

Performing Your Part

Talcott Parsons, a sociologist, identified two types of role behaviors common in families and other groups: instrumental and expressive.

Individuals in a group take on instrumental roles when they execute tasks related to the economy, the group's performance, or both.

Supporting other family members in making decisions, expressing the family's aesthetic or emotional needs, and sustaining family standards are all examples of expressive responsibilities.

Members' Responsibilities in Buying for the Household

There are at least five roles that people in a family may play while making purchasing choices together. It is common for there to be more than one actor in a part. Marketers must engage with customers in all of these roles, keeping in mind that various members of the same household will take on varying roles based on the context and the nature of the offering. For instance, kids consume a wide variety of things, such as breakfast cereals, toys, and apparel, yet they may not be the ones making the purchases. Children may be influential decision-makers and end-users, but parents are often the primary purchasers in a family.

Responsibilities within the Family

Roles or chores, such as washing the laundry, making meals, setting the dinner table, bringing out the trash, and walking the dog, must be carried out by one or more family members in order for the family to operate as a cohesive unit. Family responsibilities are evolving along with the rest of our society.

1) Key Consumer Functions in the Home

Each member of the family will have a unique purpose in the final product. A stay-at-home mom discovers a novel kind of juice while at the grocery store and decides to bring it home to her family. The choice she ultimately made to

- There is no indirect familial impact on this purchase. She makes the final decision and makes the purchase, but she isn't necessarily the one doing the cooking and isn't the only one who will be eating the food. Products like televisions, automobiles, audio systems, furniture, and other household necessities are often decided upon as a group rather than individually.
- In a typical family, eight people take part in making decisions. Examining these functions sheds light on how members of a family behave in their different consumer roles:
- One kind of family member who may sway a consumer's decision is a "influencer." The housewife informs her family about a new restaurant in the area, and her husband and teenage children are impressed by what they hear.

2) Gatekeepers: Relatives who have sway over other relatives' purchasing choices because of their access to information about a product or service. The adolescent kid who desires a racing bicycle may steer his father toward the brand he favors by withholding knowledge about other manufacturers.
3) There are the family members who may make the final decision on whether or not to purchase a product or service. The husband and wife could make the decision to get a new fridge together.
4) Buyers are the members of the family who actually purchase a product or service. It's not uncommon for a housewife to be the one who shops for the groceries, pantry staples, and personal care items that the whole family uses.
5) The Preparers: the individuals of the household who are responsible for transforming the product into its consumable

form. The homemaker may make the family dinner using uncooked veggies, lentils, spices, oil, and other things.

6) Users, or consumers, are the people of a household who actually utilize or make use of the product or service in question. The automobile, the TV, and the stereo are open to all members of the household.
7) Family member or members that service or repair the product to ensure its continuing pleasure are called "maintainers."

Family members who decide to get rid of something or stop using it are called "disposers."

Influencing Spouses and Resolving Consumer Conflicts

Husbands and wives often try to sway one other toward their preferred conclusion while making purchases. There are six methods of persuasion that have been effective in mediating disputes between husbands and wives that stem from their divergent consuming habits:

The term "expert" refers to a situation in which one partner makes an effort to sway the other by presenting them with more advantageous knowledge about the available choice options. For Use in Cooking

Legitimacy refers to when one spouse tries to exert power over the other by virtue of seniority in the home.

(Housing purchase)

Bargaining is when one partner in a relationship tries to persuade the other to give up some of his or her power in return for something of greater value at a later time. (Jewelry)

A reward is anything offered by one partner to the other in an effort to change that person's conduct.

(FMCG)

An emotional response is an effort to influence your partner's actions by appealing to their emotions.

(Means of limiting reproduction)

The term "Impression" refers to any effort by one partner to persuade the other to change their actions.

Purchasers who are adamant about not negotiating prices

When a husband or wife has a dispute or conflict with the other over a particular purchase choice, they may resort to one of these influencing methods to sway the other person. We've all had those times when we wanted to try a new place to eat, see a new movie, or take a different approach to a family vacation. These examples are only a small sampling of the virtually infinite number of possible family consumption disputes that may arise and need to be handled.

Children

Any parent will tell you that as soon as their kid learns to talk, the youngster will try to exert control over family choices ("Buy me a cookie," "I want a Barbie doll," "Let's eat at McDonald's"). Young adults are more likely to take an active role in the household's consuming activities. More than half of the youngsters in a survey of kids aged 6 to 14 said they had input on major family purchases like vacation spots, audio systems, and personal computers. Children seem to play significant roles in both the sparking of interest in and the final choice to buy a new computer, according to other studies.

As it pertains to consumer behavior, the parent-child dynamic might be seen as one of influence and yield. To be more specific, kids try to persuade their parents to buy stuff (to yield). It's easy to observe how youngsters try to persuade their parents to buy certain products (like laundry detergents) after seeing commercials for them on television when they're out grocery shopping.

Young Adults and Teens

Discretionary spending is common among teens, and many of them really do it. Grades 7-12 pupils (high school kids) have the most passion for sports and physical activity. 16–19 year old boys are more likely to spend their money on things like movies, dates, entertainment, car costs, and clothes, while 16–19 year old ladies are more likely to spend it on things like clothes, makeup, and perfume.

The adolescent market may be broken down into subsets based on their preferred way of life. The adolescent market has been segmented into four distinct groups, as shown in the accompanying figure. Those in the marketing industry who want to target a certain subset of adolescents might benefit from this kind of segmentation approach.

Marketing to families

Specifically, family marketing examines the connections between the buyer and the family consumer, as well as the buyer and the purchase decision maker. Family marketing recognizes situations when there may be more than one decision maker for a purchase, and in certain cases, there may be more than one customer. As can be seen in Figure, the family marketing model consists of nine cells that each describe a unique buyer-consumer interaction. Advertising and product placement may be tailored to the buyer-user connection of each product, as seen in the matrix.

There are many moving parts in a family's decision to make a purchase, but answering the following questions may help shed light on the many buyer-consumer dynamics at play.

1) Whom are you shopping for?
2) I'm curious about the main players here.
3) What is the backstory behind the acquisition?
4) Whose desires are being met and when?

Insights into the Family Business Marketing Technique

These questions and their possible responses may not reveal every connection that marketers need to think about, but they do reveal a family marketing strategy that links customers and goods according to each member's influence or purchasing power. Marketing strategies in the restaurant business have recently shifted toward targeting whole families. The restaurant industry's need to increase revenue is undoubtedly behind the push to attract families.

External Factors Affecting Determination

When it comes to making big choices, how do husbands and spouses each think they weigh in? In addition, what does this imply for business owners and advertisers? Holidays, electronics, appliances, and household furnishings are typical examples of areas where couples work together to make a choice. Women's jewelry, men's leisure wear, interior paint and wallpaper, and baggage are all examples of product categories where consumers often engage in autonomous decision making. Marketers may target the most important person of a home by tailoring their message to them, based on where on this "map" that individual falls.

The Role of the Discernment Process

At each level of the decision-making process, spouses exercise varying degrees of influence. The time it takes to get from searching for relevant information to making a final selection may be quite short for many low-involvement products, but it may be longer for riskier or highly involved products that the whole family will be using. Most noticeable shifts may be seen in carpets, rugs, and living room upholstery, as well as refrigerators, family cars, and other household appliances. Travel plans are often decided upon by consensus in a family. Particularly for items with a lengthy planning cycle, several campaigns may be planned to meet with particular interests.

Occupational Factors' Impact

Once upon a time, marketers could look to pre-modern notions of role structure to ascertain which member of a given household was more likely to make a certain purchase. Traditional purchasing roles persist, although in dual-income households, men may be ready to pick up a few groceries and working wives may drop the family vehicle down for an oil change. Modern couples are less likely to have one person take on the role of sole shopper than in the past, but they are still eager to shop together for big-ticket products.

Considering the Role of Gender

As the gap between the sexes closes, more and more choices are being taken collectively by both partners in a marriage. Qualls looked at how families made choices in areas including travel, transportation, education, financial security, and home ownership. Previous research has found that either the woman or the husband often takes the lead in making purchases of these kind. According to a recent survey conducted by Qualls, making choices on important life factors like a child's schooling and living situation is now routinely done in tandem. Joint decision-making is increasing in high-risk product and service categories as women's economic power grows and attitudes become more equal.

The informal effect of friends, neighbors, and acquaintances on our-consumer related choices, and the structure and dynamics of the processes that shape consumers' behavior, is a matter of enormous relevance to consumers and marketers alike. This kind of sway is typically referred to as "word of mouth" or "opinion leadership." We also take into account the characteristics and motives of both thought leaders and followers.

Opinion leadership is defined as....

One's ability to informally influence the behavior or outlook of others, who may be opinion seekers or just opinion receivers, is known as "opinion leadership." Informal sway is emphasized in the notion of opinion leadership. Word of mouth describes the informal spread of information and influence amongst individuals.

This individual is a trendsetter in terms of thought and may also be a follower in the future. The term "opinion seekers" is often used to describe those who actively seek out information and recommendations on things.

These influential people often belong to a certain social group and use that group's communication infrastructure. The most significant benefit of word-of-mouth advertising is that it spreads quickly via a network of individuals who are not directly connected to the commercial selling source or the company itself. The power of formal word-of-mouth communication to influence consumer choice frequently exceeds that of widespread advertising.

Qualities of Influential People

Now, let's examine what makes opinion leaders tick. Characteristics of Opinion Leaders Describes some of the most prominent traits shared by all influential people.

- Influential people know more than the average person and care deeply about the subject at hand.
- To take a more active role in the product category
- Create and maintain friendships and social connections in your immediate area.
- Possesses the Capability to Broadcast Information
- Possess an excellent reputation
- Can take chances because they have increased confidence, sociability, and global awareness.

When people are eager to share their positive experiences with a product they have just purchased, they are often considered to be opinion leaders. Involvement allows them to verify their own assumptions and conclusions.

They're younger, better educated, wealthier, and more professionally successful than the general population.

They have plenty of media experiences. Watch more shows and movies. You should familiarize yourself with relevant information periodicals and technical publications as well. As a result of their increased product expertise, they will be better able to convey accurate and comprehensive product information to the general public.

Marketers consequently use opinion leaders as a case study, and their tactics are assessed and formulated with these individuals and their positions in mind.

1) Credible product information is often assumed to come from opinion leaders. People who are looked up to as authorities are termed opinion leaders. They aren't shy about sharing their thoughts since they've thought about it and researched it well.
2) People who are considered to be opinion leaders tend to be outgoing and knowledgeable. They have unique perspectives

because of their extensive background as customers and users. Their advise is highly trusted since it is usually based on direct experience. Furthermore, people like engaging with them because of their outgoing personalities.

3) As a rule, opinion leaders provide their followers both positive and negative data, which boosts their credibility and makes it more likely that the followers will act on the data.
4) Influential people may be relied upon for both guidance and information.
5) Media coverage of influential people, particularly in positions of leadership, has increased.
6) Influential people often serve as first movers in their respective industries.
7) Influencers' personalities, social standings, and demographics all have product-specific implications.

A Snapshot of Influential People's Thoughts

We need to research a leader profile to learn how to spot influential people.

Typical Characteristics

- Innovativeness Interest
- Knowledge and a desire to share it
- Self-Confidence
- Gregariousness Special-interest
- Exposure in the media
- Distinction in Thought Between People of the Same Age
- same standing in society
- Engagement with people beyond the core group

Leaders in Opinion: A Snapshot

Opinion Recurrence and Convergence

In most consumer research projects, we find that more than half of the persons surveyed fall into the "opinion leader" group in relation to a set of products that those respondents had chosen for themselves. The prevalence of consumer opinion leadership indicates that at least one product or category has captured the attention of consumers to the extent that they are willing to discuss it and provide suggestions to others.

According to studies done in the business, there seems to be a specialized group of leaders in the market. These shoppers have a wealth of knowledge about a broad variety of items, stores, and market trends.

To be a market maven, you need have some of the following qualities:

a) They are both proactive in starting conversations with other shoppers and responsive when asked for market data.

b) Their impact goes beyond the sphere of high-involvement goods, despite the fact that they superficially meet the profile of opinion leaders in that they have high levels of brand awareness and tend to test more brands.

c) Industry mavens stand out from other types of opinion leaders because their sway is based less on direct product experience and more on a breadth of market knowledge that allows them to see trends and opportunities before the masses.

Circulation of Data

Opinion leaders, as seen in the diagram, actively seek out and spread information to their followers gleaned from the media and other credible sources. The response from the group to the opinion leaders is shown by the dotted line.

Mutual Exchange of Thoughts and Information

As you may have seen, the public frequently receives its views from opinion leaders, who in turn get them via the radio and print media. This is the thinking underlying the so-called "two-step flow of communication" hypothesis, which depicts opinion leaders as direct recipients of information from impersonal mass-media sources, which then transfer (and interpret) this information to the public. According to this hypothesis, the opinion leader acts as a conduit between the detached news media and the general populace.

The dissemination of news via the media is shown as a multi-stage process in an all-encompassing model of interpersonal communication. The new model recognizes the reciprocal nature of informational and influential exchanges, in which opinion leaders may have an impact on, but are also impacted by, the opinions of those they are leading.

Thought-Leadership Positioning and the Company's Marketing Objectives

As long as there have been marketers, they have known the impact that opinion leaders may have on customers' tastes and purchases. Marketers are always on the lookout for ways to boost positive chatter about their products and services among friends and family. Product developers recognize the power of recommendations from satisfied customers, so they make an effort to create items that will spread easily by word of mouth. A successful new product will generate buzz among consumers.

When reviewers panned a film but audiences gave it high marks, it was proof of the effectiveness of word of mouth. Some marketers have made concerted efforts to artificially create, or mimic, opinion leadership in cases when it does not naturally arise as a result of the distinctiveness of the product or the marketing approach.

Each product category has its own set of influential voices. The marketer, armed with data, anecdotes, and common sense, must ascertain what part an opinion leader plays in the current state of affairs about the product or service. Customers provide feedback and opinions about the product's usefulness and functionality in the marketplace. If customers' experiences fall short of their expectations, the marketer should take appropriate action to address their concerns.

In order to lessen this, it is helpful to draw on the insights of influential people. Influential people like the company of others and often participate in organized activities. In certain markets, very prominent "professional opinion leaders" exist for particular types of products.

Professional hairdressers are influential voices in the hair care industry. Pharmacists play an essential role as key opinion leaders for healthcare goods. If you're looking to buy a personal computer, you may want to get the advice of a computer expert. The goal is to single out these influential people so that targeted marketing efforts may be made.

Opinion leaders provide insight into product categories and customer preferences via marketing research. For clients to positively react to the company's marketing mix, many tests should be conducted, such as the product usage test, pre-testing of the advertising material, and the chosen medium. The sample should come from the most influential people in the field. Several strategies, such as "fashion advisory boards" in clothes shops or offering free third meals with the purchase of two, have been used successfully in retail and staff sales.

Famous personalities and current customers may be leveraged as a source of credibility in ads by sharing their positive product experiences and impressions with the wider audience. Commercials featuring influential people may help spread positive word of mouth about the product to a wide audience.

Technology Spreading

As customers, we are constantly drawn to anything novel, whether it be an idea, a product, or a service. The issue of how quickly an idea will spread is always a concern for the company testing it. Thus, it may be concluded that there is always some degree of danger associated with doing anything new. After much study, the company will launch a groundbreaking new idea or product. As a result, it is clear that the act of spreading new ideas across an organization is vital.

Diffusion

The diffusion of a new product or invention from its creators to the general public is an example of a macroprocess. Adoption is a microprocess that focuses on the steps one customer takes before choosing whether or not to embrace a new offering.

The term "diffusion of innovations" refers to the gradual dissemination of a new product, service, or concept among members of the target market via various channels of communication (such as mass media, salespeople, and casual discussion).

Some innovative product developments that found widespread favor among buyers.

Dissemination of the New Product's Value

1. Eureka Forbes Vacuum Cleaner Convenient home delivery of a lightweight, user-friendly vacuum cleaner to help you maintain your house in tip-top shape demonstration.
2. Fire extinguisher
A fire safety portal (actual value)
extinguisher.
3. Holding tank made of plastic
(Sintex) A cheap and easy substitute for
water storage container made of metal or cement
4. Utensil cleaner
(Rin) cake A bar of pre-mixed scouring solution.
as an alternative to powder, which tends to go to waste.
5. Repellant for mosquitoes
A smoke-free, chemical-free mosquito repellant called matt (Good Knight).
the absence of smoke, ash, cream, and mosquitoes
6. Disposable diaper (Huggys) that is drier and more comfy than cloth diapers.
cloth diapers for infants.

Popular examples of novel goods and services quickly adopted by the general public

Diffusion Process

Stages in adoption process	*Steps in extended decision-making*
Awareness	**Problem recognition**
↓	↓
Interest	**Information search**
↓	↓
Evaluation	**Alternative evaluation**
↓	↓
Trial	**Purchase**
↓	↓
Adoption	**Post-purchase evaluation**

For any given social group or invention, the pattern of spread will look quite similar across time. Normal diffusion processes exhibit a sluggish rate of spread or acceptance. It first increases swiftly before experiencing a sluggish phase. The product is an instant success in the quick diffusion process. Quickly, new ideas are shared across many people. Instantaneous popularity leads to delayed dissemination later on. A product's diffusion or spread in a slow diffusion process is sluggish because consumers embrace the product gradually as they get more familiar with it.

Diffusion is the gradual spread of a new concept, practice, or product across a social system (a target market) via various channels of communication (mass media, salesmen, or casual talks). To break this procedure down into its four component parts:

1.A New Approach
2.How we get our messages across
3.Structure of Society
4.Time

Transmissive Diffusion

These analyses reveal that there is a period of time between the introduction of a product and the point at which the market becomes fully saturated. Therefore, it is important for the marketer to comprehend what factors influence the diffusion of innovations within a particular market group, and how the preferences of early adopters vary from those of late adopters.

1.New Approach

There are a number of ways that a new product or service has been defined.

Definitions from the standpoint of the corporation producing or selling the product are called "firm-oriented." The company considers a product to be "new" when it has not previously been used by the company.

Definitions that take a product-oriented view give attention to the characteristics of the product itself and the impact those characteristics are expected to have on customers' current habits. Of the three possible forms of product innovations, the one with the least disruptive effect on existing patterns is continuous innovation, which involves the introduction of a slightly different version of an existing product rather than an entirely new one. Discontinuous innovations necessitating consumers to adopt new behavior patterns include television, fax machines, and the Internet; dynamically continuous innovation, which may involve the creation of a new product or the modification of an existing product, such as disposable diapers and CD players; and the most recent version of Microsoft Office.

Definitions with a focus on the market consider customers' level of familiarity with a product when determining whether or not it is novel. Possible meanings include:

i. When just a tiny (predetermined) fraction of the whole market has bought a product, we consider it to be brand new.

ii. If a product has only been available for sale for a brief (described) amount of time, then we call it "new."

2.How we get our messages across

Communication between the marketer and customers, as well as communication among consumers (i.e., word of mouth), is crucial to the rapidity with which an invention spreads across a market. This means there will be two parts to this conversation:

a. Interactions between advertisers and their target audiences

b. Consumer-to-consumer communication, or "word of mouth."

As a consumer, you may choose from four distinct types of informational outlets:

- Individuals close to you, such as relatives, buddies, neighbors, and pals.
- Salespeople, advertisements, and other forms of commercial marketing all play a role in driving revenue growth.
- Mass media and consumer advocacy groups are examples of publicly available sources.

- Information obtained from actual experiments: showing off and playing with physical samples.
- Companies seek to establish a customer communication strategy that is both successful and economical, taking into account the nature of the innovation or new product and their target market.
- Progression Towards Broad Imitation

3. Structure of Society

The social context that facilitates the spread of a new product is sometimes referred to as a social system. The word "social system" is often used in diffusion studies, however the terms "market segment" and "target segment" may be more appropriate here. That which individuals are a part of and do their work inside, whether it be physical, social, or cultural, is referred to as a social system. All of the farmers in a certain area, for instance, may make up the social system for new hybrid seed rice.

It is crucial for marketers to keep in mind that the direction of a social system determines the environment in which their goods will be most likely to succeed. One such trend is the worldwide drop in demand for red meat that has occurred in recent years. Red meat has taken a back seat to other protein sources due to the rising awareness that it is higher in fat and calories than other options. At the same time, many people are opting to eat more chicken and fish since these items conform to their dietary preferences.

4. Time

Diffusion research is influenced by time in three different but related ways:

a) How long it takes for customers to make a decision on whether to buy a new product or service after becoming aware of it for the first time is known as "purchase time." For instance, Asha Chavan in Pune established the idea of the "Home Land" mega market, which, in addition to selling a wide range of high-quality goods, also offered free, same-day delivery of all orders placed through telephone, even those for a single item. In addition to its commercial services, Homeland also provides bill payment for utilities, telecommunications, and other personal expenses at no cost.

b) The determination of adopter categories: An adopter category is a kind of consumer categorization that identifies a customer's temporal position in respect to other consumers. We often divide adopters into five groups: pioneers, early adopters, early majority, late majority, and laggards. Let's return to these classifications in a while to talk about them.

c) The adoption rate: This concept investigates how long it takes for a new product or service to become widely used by people in a given social system.

If you are in the market for a second automobile but your current vehicle still serves your needs, you may hesitate to make a purchase for some time. This behavior fits into the "late adopter" category of the adopter categorization system, which reflects how far down the adoption curve a consumer is. Those who are innovators are the first to try anything new, while those who are laggards are the last to catch on.

The time it takes for people in a society to start using a new product or service is called its adoption rate. For example, black-and-white televisions were widely accepted by customers considerably sooner than their producers had anticipated, whereas garbage compactors lagged far behind.

Diffusion's Time-Dependent Characteristics

When releasing a new product, the goal of marketing should be to swiftly and widely accept it by the market. Both the Penetrating approach (low initial pricing to deter rivals from joining the market) and the Skimming strategy are used by marketers to get a large part of the market for their new products.

Dissemination Potential as Affected by Product Features

A number of the variables below affect how quickly innovations catch on:

1) Certain demographics, such as the young, well-off, and well-educated, tend to be more open to new ideas and concepts than their more conservative and economically-challenged counterparts. This demonstrates that the intended audience is a crucial factor in determining the pace of spread.
2) Changes in the pace of innovation dissemination are proportional to the perceived risk of making the transition to the new invention. The danger is in the possibility that the product won't work as advertised, in dealing with the fallout of the transition, and in going back to the tried-and-true option if one is dissatisfied with the new one.
3) Decisions may be made on an individual basis or by a group. Individual choices accelerate spread more than group decisions.
4) The dissemination rate may also be influenced by the marketing effort put out. More expensive marketing campaigns that run

constantly and at huge volumes spread more quickly than less intensive campaigns.

5) The experiment is low-risk and low-cost, allowing for quicker spread. There are ways to test out things before buying them, such as borrowing, renting, or trying them out for a trial period. The spread of pharmaceuticals and other low-priced goods is especially rapid. Even auto dealerships are offering test drives for free to spread the word about their newest models.

6) When a product successfully meets a consumer's perceived need, word of mouth spreads rapidly.

7) Compatibility: The more the product is consistent with the ideas, attitudes and values of the person or group the quicker the dispersion - veggies soup for vegetarians, conventional microwave no roasting.

8) Relevant advantage: The advantage might be of pricing, quality, convenience of handling, product quality. To achieve swift diffusion, the product must provide either a pricing advantage or a performance advantage. Although washing machines are costly, they save time and effort.

9) Diffusion is slowed down when a product is complicated (i.e., hard to comprehend and utilize). The product's complexity shouldn't prevent it from being simple to utilize. There are a wide variety of factors that might contribute to complexity (at-tributes complexity which are difficult to under- stand). The other may be the difficulty of making trade-offs. There is a give and take between purchasing power and cost. Microwave ovens are a good example of how convenience may come at the expense of either cooking area or food quality.

10) A product's diffusion rate and level of debate are both increased if its beneficial impacts can be readily noticed.

Adopters are divided into groups

There are five distinct categories of adoptees depending on their adoption times.

The first 2.5% of consumers that buy into a new technology are considered innovators. The first 13.5 percent of adopters are considered early adopters.

The next 34% to adopt are considered the early majority. The remaining 34% of the population is the late majority. This group accounts for the remaining 16% of adoptees.

Innovators

Entrepreneurial spirit is a hallmark of innovators. They are a more educated, socially mobile, and younger generation. They are able to take on risk connected with the launch of a new product. They have an open mind, are familiar with and receptive to commercial media, and are interested in learning about and trying out cutting-edge goods and services.

The pioneers

They use some degree of forethought before betting on cutting-edge technologies. As influential members of society, they are a valuable source of knowledge for others, but they are also very sensitive to the prospect of failure. As a result, people consider the product's benefits and drawbacks before making a final decision.

Prompt onset of adulthood

After the product has been proven successful by its early adopters and inventors, later users are more likely to utilize it regularly. They're seasoned, well-educated, and less mobile in their latter years. Interpersonal communication is crucial to them as a means of gathering information. There are 34% more of these people than there were before.

Inadequately-timed Majority

They have serious reservations regarding brand-new merchandise. Consumers are motivated to utilize a product less by the product's novelty and more by external factors, such as product scarcity and peer pressure. They are lower in social standing and less likely to move up the social ladder.

Laggards

Their values tend to be more time-honored. As a result, they have a hard time connecting with others and tend to live in the past. They're quite hesitant to embrace the changes. Only 16% of all shoppers are in this category. Adopter categories are often shown as if they followed the form of a normal distribution, as in the image below, which is a bell-shaped curve describing the overall population that adopts a product.

Personal Impact's Crucial Function

A person's personal impact is a crucial component in the rate of product acceptance. This questions how one person's comments on "a new product" may influence another's perspective shift or likelihood. This suggests that a person's choice to accept a new product or innovation might be influenced by the feedback they get from a close friend or acquaintance.

Generally speaking, it has been shown that customers, and particularly women, like to consult one another's friends and respect the comments offered by them on new items, the quality differences among the various brands, store at which to buy to enjoy shopping, and so forth.

Distribution in the Market: Diffusion-Related Tactics

There are distinctions between early adopters, sometimes known as innovators, and late adopters (Laggards). The "moving target market" technique has been embraced as the method for reaching the desired audience. After deciding on a broad audience, marketers may narrow their attention to certain subsets, such as first-mover adopters, early majority consumers, or even laggards. This happens when people continue to show interest in a product. After then, the media and advertising shift gears to appeal to a variety of demographics.

4

PERCEPTION AND CONSUMER BEHAVIOUR

Introduction

When we see anything, we are engaging in the cognitive process of choosing, organizing, and making sense of information inputs. Certain aspects of perception are highlighted in the definition provided above:

- To pick relevant facts or information from the environment, arrange it, and derive meaning from it is the mental process known as perception.
- An individual's actions, emotions, and sentiments, among other things, are grounded on the person's interpretations of the world around them.
- Since perception is a mental operation, it will always be open to individual interpretation.

There are three stages in the perceptual process.

1) Sensation - Paying attention to something using one of the five senses
2) Organization - The second skill is organization, which entails classifying things into groups based on similarities between them and the stimuli that we see, such as colors.
3) Interpretation - We interpret what we've experienced, giving it significance and assigning value and preference based on our observations.

There are three ways in which individuals' perceptions of an item might vary:

1. Focusing only on few details
2. Distortion upon selection and
3. Retention upon selection

One's focus is arbitrary. The typical individual may be subjected to more than 1500 advertisements per day. Since it is impossible to pay attention to everything that is happening at once, most of these impulses will be ignored. Marketers have to put in extra effort to catch customers' attention because of their tendency to pay just a portion of any given topic's merits. When a stimulus is associated with an event, meets immediate needs, or has varying input intensities, the brain is more likely to pay attention to it (sharp price drop).

Alteration of Some Details While Ignoring Others. Not all stimuli have the same effect on recipients. There is a propensity for people to engage in selective distortion, in which they interpret data in a manner that supports their existing worldview. However, there is nothing that marketers can do to combat this kind of distortion. Marketers that use comparison ads (those that set one product against another) must tread carefully lest customers misinterpret their message as having been paid for by the competition.

Retention bias. Although most of what they learn will be forgotten, people are more likely to recall evidence that confirms their own ideas and values. Selective recollection means that we are more likely to recall positive details about other items. Marketers use drama and repetition in their communication with their target market because of selective retention. Supportive information is retained, whereas contradictory data is forgotten.

Components of Observation

The term "sensation" refers to the sense organs' quick and direct reaction to stimuli (an advertisement, a package, and a brand name). Any discrete sensory input serves as a stimulus.

The parts of the human body that take in information about the external environment in the form of sight, hearing, smell, taste, or touch are collectively known as sense receptors.

The term "human sensitivity" describes the capacity of a human to feel things. The degree to which a person is affected by a given stimulus depends on both the quality of that stimulus and the quantity or intensity to which that stimulus is exposed.

The difference in input energy is what causes a shift in sensation. Therefore, there would be minimal feeling in a continuous environment, whether it is highly crowded and loud or relatively calm, due to the lack of change, the steady level of stimulation.

The capacity to identify shifts improves with diminishing sensory input. An organism's adaptability to changing environmental circumstances is shown by the human body. major repercussions for marketers, since it shields us from harmful, disruptive, or irrelevant bombardment when input levels are high.

The Completely Uncompromising Limit - Absolute threshold refers to the lowest possible intensity at which a person may detect a change in their environment. A person's absolute threshold for a stimuli is the point at which they can tell the difference between the stimulus and nothing. Due to the issue of sensory adaptation, many marketing strategies are often revised. To get their messages heard over the din of advertising customers are subjected to on a daily basis, marketers are increasingly turning to multisensory approaches. Some boost sensory input to help cut through the "noise" of marketing. Some ads are designed to draw in the viewer by reducing the number of sensory cues they are presented with.

At What Point Does the Differential Become a Dealbreaker? The difference threshold, also known as the Just Noticeable Difference (JND), is the smallest detectable difference between two stimuli (just noticeable difference). The JND between two stimuli is not an absolute but rather a relative quantity, as found by a German scientist called Ernst Weber in the 19th century. In accordance with Weber's rule, the higher the strength of the first stimulus, the greater the increase in intensity must be for the secondary stimulus to be regarded as distinct. For most individuals to notice a difference between the two stimuli, a further level of stimulation comparable to the JND must be introduced. Weber's law is universal, applying to all senses and almost all intensities. The idea is used by merchants to lower selling costs. Discounts of less than twenty percent are unlikely to attract much attention from buyers.

How and Why We Perceive

Processing information entails a chain of operations, from sensing a stimulus through converting it into usable data and storing it. According to the information processing paradigm, there are four distinct phases: exposure,

Focus, mental interpretation, and long-term retention. The act of perception consists of the first three. When a person's visual receptor nerves are activated by a stimuli like an advertising, this is called exposure. When the receptor nerves transmit a feeling to the brain, attention is triggered. The intended audience makes mental space, i.e., pays attention to, the advertisement. Meaning is ascribed to the experienced experiences via the process of interpretation. The recipient (in this case, the intended recipient) determines how the communication is understood.

Long-term memory is the preservation of meaning over time, whereas short-term memory is the utilization of meaning for instant decision making.

The advertising and message are committed to memory by the intended recipient.

Perceiving as a Process

Exposure to an object or situation often leads to a lasting memory. Experience, Focus, Analysis, and Recall Methods of perception

The perceptual process shown in Figure follows a linear progression from first exposure through long-term memory retention. However, it is obvious that these processes are interacting and take place almost simultaneously. It means that we are influenced by our memories in terms of what we pay attention to and how we interpret what we see. Also, the information being processed is shaping the very nature of memory. When the time comes to make a purchase, the person will be unable to access most of the translated information from active memory. There are several subprocesses that make up perceiving. Consideration of input-throughput-output analysis sheds light on this phenomenon. The premise of this method is that there is some kind of input that, once processed, yields some kind of output. Meaning, environmental stimuli will make up the bulk of your brain's sensory inputs.

Methods of Perception

The existence of stimuli such as people, objects, events, information, etc. is the initial step in the perceptual process.

The following part will be devoted to a discussion of the perceptual process. The results of perception: As for the perceived

The thoughts, sentiments, attitudes, etc. that emerge from people's activities are the outputs.

Imperfections in the Way We Perceive

Customers "zip" and "zap" through the majority of the 3,000 marketing messages they get every day, such as television advertising.

Customers engage in "selective attention," when they pay little mind to advertisements that do not pertain to their interests (e.g., by quickly flicking past them in a magazine).

Consumers engage in selective interpretation when they change their perceptions of a situation so that it conforms more closely to their preexisting views; for example, smokers and nonsmokers may have different interpretations of the health warnings printed on cigarette packages.

Perceptional Dynamics

Physical cues from the surrounding environment; a person's own expectations, motivations, and prior experiences; and b) the ability to learn from those cues. Due to the fact that every person is an original with their own set of life circumstances, it stands to reason that their perspectives will likewise vary.

Perceptions consist of:

a. selection, organizing, and interpretation of inputs.
b. People are quite picky about what kinds of stimuli they "recognize."
c. They automatically sort familiar stimuli in accordance with well accepted psychological concepts.
d. They subjectively assign meaning to such stimuli based on their own wants, expectations, and past experiences.

Selective Processing of Perception

As buyers, we unconsciously pick and choose the sensations we pay attention to. In addition to the stimulus's inherent properties, two important considerations determine which stimuli are chosen:

a. The influence of customers' prior exposure on their anticipations.
b. Their original goals (their needs, desires, interests, and so on).

A stimulus's likelihood of being perceived may be affected by the aforementioned variables.

The Stimulus's Composition

There are a plethora of factors at play in each given marketing stimulus.

Here are some illustrations:

a. The product's inherent qualities.
b. Its morphological characteristics
c. The aesthetics of the packaging.
d. The name of the brand.
e. The ads and adverts.
f. placement of an advertisement in a printed medium.
g. The context of editorial work

The goal of advertisers is to gain maximum contrast and break through the consumer's perceptual screen, therefore they resort to aggressive attention-getting tactics.

Advertisers utilize jarring colour combinations, large font sizes, and other techniques to grab readers' attention.

Expectations

What one anticipates is what one sees. They have some preconceived notions about what they will observe based on their level of exposure, their level of expertise, or both. In general, people pay greater attention to stimuli that starkly deviate from expectations than they do to stimuli that are more in line with those expectations.

Motives

When people look at something, they usually see something they desire or need. As the intensity of a need rises, it tends to override the brain's ability to process information from sources that are seemingly unrelated to the need. The perceptual system of an individual fine-tunes its sensitivity to the specific environmental cues that have the most significance for that person. Executives in charge of marketing understand the value of tailoring goods to customers' actual wants and requirements.

To perceive just what one wants to see

Consumers' "selection" (selective perception) of environmental stimuli depends on how those expectations and motivations play off of the input itself. Consumers engage in deliberate "selective exposure," intentionally seeking out messages they find appealing or to which they may relate.

There is a conscious effort to shield consumers from unpleasant or dangerous advertising.

c. Consumers' heightened awareness of stimuli that serve their wants or interests is a result of their ability to focus selectively.
d. Customers are less likely to notice non-essential stimuli.
e. People differ in terms of their preferred mode of communication and the content they are most interested in learning about.

Threatening or harmful stimuli are less likely to be perceived than neutral ones, as a kind of perceptual protection. Information that does not fit an individual's wants, values, or beliefs may be subconsciously distorted.

Consumers "tune out" massive volumes of advertising via a process known as "perceptual blocking."

Distinctive Perception

Selecting from a wide variety of environmental stimuli does not lead to the perception of distinct, individual feelings in the human mind. When people encounter a lot of information, they prefer to categorize it and think of it as a whole. Gestalt psychology is the branch of study that established the foundational theories of perceptual organization (Gestalt means "pattern" or "configuration" in German). The concepts of figure-ground, grouping, and closure are fundamental to perceptual organization.

Symbol and Substance

Stimuli that stand out from their surroundings are more likely to be acknowledged. The contrast between a figure and its background is the simplest possible illustration of this concept. There is often no trouble visualizing the figure. The conventional wisdom holds that ground is unbounded, nebulous, and unbroken. Since the figure looks to be dominating, the ground is subconsciously seen as secondary and less significant. Those working in advertising must take great care in their preparations to ensure that the stimulus they want to highlight is recognized as figure, rather than ground.

Sometimes advertisers don't make it obvious which part of the ad is meant to be taken literally and which is a statistic, leading customers to get confused.

Grouping

People have a tendency to process information by grouping it into larger "chunks" rather of processing it in its individual components. Marketers may benefit from grouping in order to convey connotations about their items.

Closure

Closure is something that people need sometimes.

a. So, in order to have a whole image, individuals arrange the pieces of their vision in a certain way.

b. They have a tendency to "fill in the blanks," or make up missing information, if the pattern of stimuli to which they are exposed is incomplete. Just the process of finishing it makes the recipient more invested in the message.

Interpretation Based on Perception

An individual's perception of a stimulus is certain to be different from everyone else's since it is based on their own prior knowledge and expectations. There is often a great deal of ambiguity around stimuli.

f. People tend to read meaning into extremely ambiguous stimuli in a manner that benefits their own wants, goals, and interests.

g. The degree of accuracy in a person's interpretations is influenced by a number of factors, including the nature of the stimulus, the person's prior experiences, and his or her current goals and priorities.

Vision Distortion

Several factors may affect a person's views.

- People have a tendency to project their own idealized versions of certain characteristics onto others who resemble them, regardless of whether or not they are really shared by the two individuals. For instance, studies have shown that models who are seen as beautiful have a greater impact on consumers' purchasing decisions than those who are just attractive.
- Stereotypes People have preconceived notions about what particular stimuli signify, or "images" of those meanings in their brains.
- First impressions are often long-lasting, yet they are created before the perceiver has sufficient information to determine whether stimuli are significant or predictive.
- Many individuals make hasty judgments without considering the whole picture, such as getting the wrong conclusion after hearing just part of an advertisement.
- The term "halo effect" is used to characterize instances in which an item or person is judged across several criteria based on the results of a single or small set of criteria.
- Consumers try to maintain or improve their idealized versions of themselves by purchasing and avoiding brands that they perceive to be at odds with their ideals. Buyer mental pictures describe this phenomenon. Shoppers are more likely to patronize businesses whose displays reflect their own sense of identity.

Mapping the Mind's Eye

Using perceptual mapping, businesses may see how their goods stack up against the competition across a variety of important dimensions. With the use of perceptual mapping, a marketer may understand where different products in a given category are failing to meet consumers' demands.

The Role of Perception in Advertising

The Strategic Placing of Services

Many of the challenges that manufacturers don't confront when trying to promote their products also affect service marketers. Being intangible, services rely heavily on their reputation to set themselves apart from other offerings. The goal of every advertising campaign is to get people to start thinking about a product whenever they see a certain symbol. Marketers of services have come up with several methods to help clients remember the services they've purchased.

Value As Seen By the Consumer

Whether a customer thinks a price is high, low, or fair has a significant impact on their propensity to buy and their level of happiness after making a purchase.

Prices Used as a Benchmark

What we mean by "reference price" is any price that a buyer uses as a yardstick against which to evaluate a different price. Internal or external pricing might be used as references. When advertising a product at a reduced price, advertisers will often include a higher external reference price ("sold elsewhere for...") to convince customers that they are getting a great deal.

Indications of High-Quality Perception

There are many different informational signals that consumers use to create their opinions about the quality of a product (perceived quality).

a) Size, color, taste, and smell are all examples of intrinsic signals that are part of the product itself.
b) Examples of extrinsic signals include: pricing, shop aesthetics, service atmosphere, brand reputation, and marketing copy.

Products' Perceived Quality

The size, color, taste, etc. of the product itself are all examples of intrinsic cues.

a) Although consumers believe they evaluate products based on intrinsic clues, they are often fooled in blind tasting tests.
b) When people haven't had a chance to try a product for themselves, they typically make snap judgments about its quality based on things like price, brand reputation, shop reputation, and so on.

Numerous buyers form opinions based on preconceived notions about a product's place of origin.

Quality of Service as Perceived

Consumers have a harder time gauging service quality than product quality. These features of services are: intangibility; variability; perishability; inseparability; concurrent production and consumption; and inseparability. Services are more subjective than tangible goods, thus customers often depend on extrinsic or surrogate signals to make decisions. To ensure quality and reliability, many businesses attempt to standardize their procedures. As a service is being created, it is being used by others. The consequent difficulty in resolving issues with subpar services is evident. According to the findings of this study, the quality of service a customer perceives is a consequence of the size and direction of the gap between the customer's expectations and their evaluation of the service provided.

Parity of Cost and Performance

There is an inverse relationship between the perceived advantages (or quality) of a product and the perceived cost to get it. Several studies back up the idea that customers use price as a quality gauge. According to other research, customers use brand recognition as a proxy for product quality. Because consumers typically regard price as a proxy for a product's quality, some brands intentionally set a high price for their offerings and their assurances of high-quality. Marketers have positioned their items as the best of their kind by exploiting the price-quality link.

- A favourable correlation between cost and quality exists.
- Customers who lack the knowledge or self-assurance to make an informed decision often resort to using price as a proxy for quality.

Pictures of Shops

The public's opinion of the value of goods sold in a business is shaped in part by the store's own image. According to research, customers are more likely to shop at a business that offers discounts on a wide variety of things if they believe the company's prices to be lower overall. Assortment depth also has a role in how customers perceive a store's legitimacy. The customer's appraisal of a product is often impacted by the knowledge of where it was purchased, and the consumer's opinion of a retail outlet is influenced by the sort of product the consumer intends to buy.

Impression of the Makers

The brands that consumers see themselves purchasing from go beyond the perceived pricing and shop look. New goods from manufacturers with a positive reputation tend to be more well-received by consumers than those from manufacturers with a negative reputation or even a "neutral" reputation. These days, businesses actively work to improve their public image via channels such as advertising, displays, and event sponsorship.

Information Acquisition by Customers

Marketers care about how people learn because they want to instruct customers on a wide range of topics, including but not limited to: where to acquire the product, how to use it, how to keep it in good condition, and how to dispose of it when it's no longer needed. Consumer communication is the foundation of marketing tactics.

a) The ultimate goal of every marketing campaign is to have its messages read, believed, remembered, and recalled.

b) This is why they are enthusiastic about every facet of the educational experience.

There is no one true theory of learning that applies to everyone.

Both cognitive and behavioral learning theories have contributed significantly to our understanding of how we learn. In contrast to behavioral theorists' nearly entire emphasis on visible actions (responses) that occur as a consequence of exposure to stimuli, cognitive theorists attribute learning to solely mental processes.

In-Store Instructions

The term "consumer learning" refers to the way in which people gain the purchasing and consuming expertise they will draw upon in their future actions. There are a few interesting tidbits in this definition.

a) To begin, consumer learning is a process, meaning that it is dynamic and ever-changing as a consequence of new information or experience.

b) An individual's behavior in comparable circumstances may be informed by both freshly learned information and personal experience.

Although experience is a key component in learning, this does not imply that all knowledge is actively pursued. A lot of what we know was picked up by chance or without any effort. The word "learning" refers to a wide spectrum of mental development, from the acquisition of highly ingrained behavioral patterns to the acquisition of highly abstract cognitive skills like conceptualization and complicated problem solving. c) Most learning theorists agree that there are many forms of learning, and they provide explanations for these variations by appealing to different models of education. While there is some disagreement among learning theorists, most believe that motivation, signals, response, and reinforcement are necessary for learning to take place.

In order to be motivated, one must first identify what it is that they want or need.

a) A consumer's propensity to look for details about a product depends heavily on how closely the product relates to the consumer's goals. Marketers have the challenging job of trying to convince different groups of people that their product is the best solution to their problems.

b) Motives are what drive learning, and signals are what point those motivations in the right direction.

c) Customers are guided in their purchases by a variety of signals including pricing, design, packaging, promotion, and placement in the shop. When cues line up with consumers' expectations, they help channel purchasing behaviour.

Individuals' responses to cues, or the actions they do as a result of receiving the signal, are known as responses. There is no direct correlation between a request and an answer. When someone has a need or a reason, they could react in many different ways. A consumer's reaction is significantly influenced by their prior knowledge, which is in turn influenced by the reinforcement they received in the past when displaying similar reactions.

Positive reinforcement is the process of increasing the probability that a previously elicited reaction will be repeated in the future in response to the same signals or stimuli.

Theories of behaviour change and instruction

Theories of behaviour change are often known as stimulus response theories. a) An individual is considered to have "learned" when their behaviour in response to a given stimulus becomes routine. The process of learning is less of a focus for behavioural theories than its inputs and outputs. Both classical conditioning and instrumental (or operant) conditioning have applications in marketing.

Conservative Training

a) Classical conditioning theorists from the past assumed that all living things just took what was given to them.

   Conditioned reactions to stimuli are learned behaviours that occur without conscious thought. Ivan Pavlov originally articulated the concept of conditioning and proposed it as a framework for understanding the learning process at large.

b) According to Pavlov, conditioned learning takes place when a stimulus that is associated with another stimulus evokes a known response and then elicits the same response when employed alone.

c) He utilized canines as examples to prove his points.

d) The dogs were starving and were eager to eat.

e) To get the dogs salivating, Pavlov rang a bell and then smeared meat paste on their mouths.

f) After hearing the bell sound often enough, followed so quickly by the meal, the dogs salivated at the sound of the bell alone.

When discussing consumer behaviour, an unconditioned stimulus may be a logo or icon for a well-known brand (like Microsoft's "windows" emblem) that communicates a sense of technical supremacy and smooth functioning (the unconditioned response).

To condition a person, you may expose them to novel items with well-known symbols on them.

Associational learning in the brain

According to modern conditioning theory, classical conditioning is the process by which an organism "represents" and "anticipates" its environment by forming mental representations of the relationships between events. The dogs' expectancies, and hence their behaviour (in this case, salivation), were affected by the proximity (i.e., contiguity) between the conditioned stimulus (the bell) and the unconditioned stimulus (the meat paste). Instead of learning new reflexes, classical conditioning is thought of as cognitive associative learning, where one learns new information about the environment.

For a strong association to form between the conditioned stimulus (CS) and the unconditioned stimulus (US), forward conditioning is necessary. This means that the CS must come before the US, that the CS and US must be paired multiple times, that the CS and US must be related in some way, that the CS must be novel and unfamiliar, that the US must be biologically or symbolically salient, and that the US must be presented repeatedly. Neo-Pavlovian conditioning characterizes the consumer as an inquisitive mind, one that draws on prior knowledge and experiences to construct an accurate mental model of the world.

Uses of Classical Conditioning in Military Strategy

Classical conditioning provides the basis for our understanding of three fundamental ideas: repetition, stimulus generalization, and stimulus discrimination.

One of repetition's benefits is that it reduces the rate at which information is forgotten while also strengthening previously formed associations.

a) There is a diminishing return on practice at a certain threshold of exposure.

This is known as advertisement fatigue, and it may be mitigated by switching up the ads.

Subtle or major changes to the messaging may help prevent wear and tear.

1. Classical conditioning theorists say that individuals' capacity for generalization is as important as repetition when it comes to learning.
2. "Me-too" imitations are successful because buyers mistake them for the genuine, marketed goods due to stimulus generalization.
   a) It explains why private label producers want to mimic the look of popular name companies' packaging. Marketers use the stimulus generalization concept while expanding product lines, forms, and categories.
   b) In product line extensions, a marketer introduces new items under an existing brand name, hoping that consumers would buy them because they are familiar with the name.
   c) Businesses provide variants of their products in dimensions, hues, and even tastes.
   d) Extending an existing product category often aims for untapped market niches.

Marketing a company's whole product range under the same brand name, or "family branding," is another tactic that takes advantage of consumers' propensity to extrapolate their positive brand experiences to new offerings. Private labelling in retail typically has the same impact as "family" labels.

Third, in contrast to stimulus generalization, stimulus discrimination involves picking a single stimulus out of a group of candidates that are otherwise visually indistinguishable.

a) Positioning strategy, which aims to create a distinct identity for a brand in the minds of consumers by distinguishing it from competitors, is grounded on the fact that consumers can tell the difference between several identical stimuli. Positioning your stimuli strategically gives you a distinct edge over the competition.
b) A product's or service's reputation is very important to its overall success in the market.
c) In contrast to the imitator, who seeks customers who would generalize their impressions and assign unique qualities of the market leader's goods to their own, the leader in a given market seeks customers who will see their products as uniquely consumer's capacity to recognize the difference between varied stimuli. The goal of most approaches to product differentiation is to set one product or brand apart from its rivals by emphasizing some aspect that those customers will find more interesting, useful, or desirable. Once stimulus discrimination has taken place, it may be very difficult to displace a market leader.

d) The longer a consumer spends learning to differentiate between products, or identifying a brand name with a particular one, the less likely they are to generalize the stimulus. Many marketing practices may be seen as extensions of the concepts of classical conditioning.

e) Major applicable principles that may explain consumer behaviour are stimulus repetition, stimulus generalization, and stimulus discrimination.

Tool-Based Conditioning

a) Just as in classical conditioning, instrumental conditioning calls for some kind of association between a cue and an action. In instrumental conditioning, however, one learns to respond to the stimulus that produces the greatest positive outcome. Those who subscribe to the theory of instrumental learning believe that knowledge is acquired by trial and error; routines are established when individuals are rewarded for previously successful actions.

b) Although classical conditioning may provide light on how consumers pick up on very elementary forms of behaviour, instrumental conditioning is more beneficial in understanding more complicated, goal-directed actions. American psychologist B. F. Skinner proposed the idea that most learning takes place in a structured setting where students are "rewarded" for making the right decisions.

c) In the realm of consumer behaviour, instrumental conditioning proposes that shoppers learn via trial and error, with certain purchasing patterns leading to more positive outcomes (i.e. rewards) than others.

d) A person is more likely to engage in a conduct again after a positive experience. Similar to Pavlov, Skinner's concept of learning was created via study of animal behaviour. To use a marketing example, a customer who tries on many pairs of jeans before settling on one that works for her (via positive reinforcement) has participated in instrumental learning.

Behaviour Reinforcement

Two distinct forms of reinforcement (or reward) effect were identified by Skinner, each of which increased the probability of a response being produced again.

a) In the first category, called "positive reinforcement," the occurrence of events increases the probability of a certain reaction.

b) An unpleasant or unfavourable event that helps to reinforce a certain behaviour is known as negative reinforcement (or "negative reinforcement" for short).

c) You may get the desired behaviour by using either positive or negative reinforcement.

To discourage conduct, punishment is intended, but negative reinforcement is not.

Demise and oblivion

The term "extinction" refers to the process by which a learnt reaction fades to nothing when it is no longer reinforced, at which time there is no longer any association between the stimulus and the anticipated reward.

a) The process of forgetting, also known as degradation, is commonly linked to the passage of time.

b) Repetition is a powerful tool for marketers to overcome forgetfulness, and purposeful improvements to customer pleasure may help them fight extinction.

Marketers have learned that maintaining the intended consumer behavior requires a continuous high level of product quality and the happiness of customers with each usage. Total (or continuous) reinforcement, Systematic (fixed ratio) reinforcement, and Random (variable ratio) reinforcement are the three kinds of reinforcement programs recognized by marketers. High rates of the desired behaviour are generated by variable ratios, and they are rather resistant to extinction, maybe because consumers have an insatiable appetite for optimism. The term "shaping" refers to the practice of reinforcing customer actions that come before the intended behaviour. Consumer behaviour may be shaped to improve the likelihood of it happening.

It's either a kind of modelled or observed learning....

Researchers in the field of learning theory have shown that a significant amount of instruction is absorbed by what psychologists refer to as "modelling" or "observational learning," even in the absence of direct reinforcement, either positive or negative (also called vicarious learning). People learn by emulation; they watch how others react to stimuli, take note of the outcomes (reinforcement), and then mimic (model) the actions that lead to reinforcement. a) In behavioural terms, modelling refers to the process by which a person picks up new habits by watching the actions of others and the results of those actions. b) The individuals they look up to are often those who inspire them in some way, whether it via their physical attributes, their achievements, their abilities, or even their social status. c) Kids pick up a lot of tips on how to act among others and how to spend money by watching their parents and elder siblings. Marketers use observational learning to cast their models, whether they are famous faces or fresh faces. Ads often show unfavorable outcomes for those who engage in specific activities. d) Public service announcements, which may detail the hazards of smoking, speeding, or drug use, fall under this category.

Theoretical Framework of Cognitive Learning

The results of practice aren't necessary for all kinds of learning. Learning also occurs a) as a by-product of the critical thinking and problem-solving of consumers. Mental work is the foundation of cognitive learning. As to cognitive learning theory, humans are uniquely adept at problem-solving learning, which gives them some measure of agency over their surroundings.

Processing of Information

Like a computer, the mind processes data that is fed into it.

The intricacy of the information being processed and the consumer's cognitive capacity are both factors in the information's processing. People vary greatly in their capacity to conceptualize and retain knowledge. More familiarity with a product category means a more informed customer.

Information Keeping, Retention, and Retrieval Practices of the General Public

It is generally accepted that the memory has three distinct tiers, or "stores," for storing information: a sensory store, a "working memory," and a "long-term storage" tier. This is due to the fact that information processing happens in phases. All of the knowledge we have comes to us through our senses, however our sensory organs don't provide information as complete pictures.

a) Individual data points are brought together to produce a coherent whole.
b) The sensory buffer stores an impression of a sensory input for no more than a few of seconds.
c) This shows that marketers may easily insert data into consumers' sensory memory, but struggle to leave a lasting impression.
   When data is transferred from the sensory store to the short-term storage, it is assumed to have survived.
d) Working memory is what we have available to us at any one time.
e) Information is transmitted to the long-term storage if rehearsal, the quiet, mental repeating of content, occurs.

f) Information is instantly lost if it isn't practiced and shared.

Data stored in a long-term repository might remain accessible for days, weeks, or even years after being first uploaded. A person's ability to transfer information from their working memory to their long-term storage space is influenced by how much time they spend practicing the transfer process, or encoding.

g) Selecting and associating a word or picture with a perceptual item is called encoding.

h) As an added bonus, visual information may be absorbed faster than words.

i) The amount of information that consumers encode is influenced by a number of factors, including their gender and the level of cognitive investment in the information intake process. If a person is given too much data to process, they may experience information overload.

j) It seems to depend on the depth and breadth of the data.

k) The research on what amounts to overload is conflicting.

l) It's tough to know when something has become too much. Information is retained when new associations are formed between previously unrelated pieces of data.

m) Many theorists in the field of information processing see the long-term store as a network with nodes (i.e., ideas) connected by connections.

n) As people learn more, their social circles grow, and they look for new sources of data.

o) This is called "activation," and it entails connecting previously unrelated pieces of information to create a more cohesive whole.

p) A schema is the comprehensive set of memories triggered by a certain stimuli.

q) The elderly, contrary to popular belief, rely more heavily on schema-based information processing processes than do younger persons, according to the available research.

r) The degree to which newly offered items are related to previously learned product categories influences the depth and breadth of consumers' information searches.

s) After encoding something, consumers recode it to incorporate more information (chunking).

t) The amount of background knowledge is a crucial factor.

Consumers with greater expertise in the area can process larger and more intricate pieces of information.

u) There are two types of long-term storage: episodic (in the sequence of acquisition) and semantic (according to significant concepts).

v) A large number of learning theorists hold that the frameworks we use to integrate new information with our existing knowledge are based on the semantic organization of our stored memories. Information retrieval refers to the act of recovering previously stored data.

w) There has been a lot of study on the process of recalling information from memory.

x) Benefits, not features, are what customers remember long after making a purchase, according to the literature.

y) Consumers who are highly motivated to make a purchase will likely spend more time evaluating and expanding upon information they have found to be relevant to their requirements, as well as retrieving this knowledge from their long-term memory.

When relevant to the advertising message, incongruous (e.g. surprising) elements seem to break through consumers' perceptual filters and make an ad more memorable. However, irrelevant or incongruous aspects in an advertisement might nonetheless get through to the consumer's conscious mind, even if they do nothing to make the product stand out in their mind. Interference effects occur when one advertisement causes misunderstanding with another, leading to a failure to get the intended message.

- A consumer's capacity to remember information about a promoted brand may be impaired by exposure to advertisements for rival brands or for other items offered by the same manufacturer. In reality, two distinct forms of interference exist.
- It is possible for newly acquired knowledge to impede one's ability to recall previously acquired facts.
- Prior knowledge may cloud one's ability to remember new information.

Processing Data in Both Small and Large Quantities

In the past, academics studying consumer behaviour assumed that everyone went through the same mental and behavioural steps before making a purchase (extensive information processing).

This process included being knowledgeable about something (being exposed to it), thinking about it (forming preferences and attitudes), acting (making a purchase), and reflecting on the experience afterwards (adoption or rejection). The consumer adoption process often follows this similar pattern of phases. Some theorists came to see that not all buying scenarios needed lengthy information processing and review, and that occasionally customers moved straight from being aware of a need to making a habitual purchase.

- Lack of extensive research and introspection (limited information processing).
- Low involvement purchases were those of little emotional consequence, whereas high involvement purchases required extensive research.

Perspective on Participation

The study of lateralization, or split-brain hypothesis, led to the development of involvement theory.

a) It is assumed here that the right and left hemispheres of the brain are divided in terms of the types of data they handle.
b) Cognitive tasks like reading, talking, and processing knowledge about causes and effects are left to the left hemisphere of the brain.
c) The right cerebral hemisphere deals with abstract, timeless, visual, and global knowledge.

Theory of Participation and Methods for Communicating with the Public

a) Right-brained information is passively processed and stored by individuals.

Viewing television, for example, is thought of as a right hemisphere activity since it is so visually oriented.

b) It was previously believed that passive learning occurred after being repeatedly exposed to material that required little cognitive effort.
c) High-involvement data is often processed in the left hemisphere.
d) New studies imply that visual cues aid in memory and familiarity, whereas verbal signals activate cognitive processes and inspire examination.
e) The visual aspect of advertising, especially the imaginative use of symbols, is emphasized by the right-brain processing hypothesis.
f) Visual signals are better at evoking product recognition and memory, whereas verbal cues (which engage left-brain processing) prompt the kind of mental activity that leads customers to weigh the pros and drawbacks of a given purchase.

The split-brain hypothesis has several serious flaws.

The hemispheres of the brain may not always function separately, but rather, as recent studies have shown, they often coordinate their efforts to process information. There is evidence to suggest that both hemispheres of the brain can engage in low- and high-level tasks. It does seem that the right half is more geared toward cognition and the left side toward emotion.

Relevance to the Consumer and Involvement Theory

How invested a customer becomes in a product is directly proportional to the product's perceived value to the buyer.

When it comes to the level of personal importance and level of risk associated with a purchase, "high-involvement" transactions are the ones that stand out.

Low-involvement purchases are those that don't need much thought from the buyer, don't have much of an impact on the buyer's life, and don't pose much of a threat.

Consumers who are highly invested in a purchase are known as "narrow categorizers" because they are more selective about the brands they'll buy. In contrast, consumers who are less invested in a purchase are more responsive to advertising and are more inclined to explore more brands (they are broad categorizers).

Dissuasion's Central and Peripheral Paths

There are two ways to persuade someone: directly, by appealing to their interests in the product, and indirectly, by appealing to their emotions or rationality.

a. It's more successful to advertise to those who are more invested in the purchase when using the core route to persuasion.
b. As a corollary, low-involvement purchases benefit more from the peripheral path to persuasion. According to the elaboration likelihood model (ELM), the engagement of the receiver in the message processing is the most important component in identifying the most persuasive strategy to use.
c. Therefore, when consumers are highly invested, they tend to choose the "middle road" and rely their judgments on the message's supporting evidence when making a decision.
d. When people aren't invested, they take a more passive approach to forming opinions and selecting products.
e. There is no mistaking the elaboration likelihood model's applications in marketing:

f. When trying to convince a customer to make a high-involvement purchase, it's best to employ the centre (i.e. highly cognitive) method, where the marketer emphasizes the product's robust, sturdy, and high-quality characteristics.

g. Marketers should choose the "peripheral road to persuasion" for low-involvement transactions, meaning they should concentrate more on the presentation style than the substance of the message itself (e.g., through the use of celebrity spokespersons or highly visual and symbolic advertisements).

Participation Quantifiers

The term "involvement" has been defined and conceived in a wide range of ways by researchers. These include: ego involvement; commitment; communication involvement; buy significance; the depth of information search; individuals; product scenarios; and purchasing choices.

a) There have been several studies that attempted to separate consumer loyalty to a brand from that of a specific product.

b) Some people see a distinction between continuous participation and response participation. The difficulty in measuring participation stems from the fact that it is not well defined.

c) Ego participation, risk perception, and purchase priority are areas of focus for researchers who see involvement as a cognitive state.

d) Researchers that study the psychological and behavioural components of engagement track actions like product research and assessment.

e) Some would have us gauge customer engagement by how much the product means to them. Rather than trying to quantify a single degree of engagement, it makes more sense to create an involvement profile that takes into account the many various aspects and interpretations of the term.

The Use of Participation in Marketing

Multiple marketing strategies may benefit from the insights of involvement theory. f) It seems that the content, duration, and presentation of print and TV commercials are strongly influenced by the left-brain (cognitive processing)/right-brain (passive processing) paradigm. Marketers may do more to engage customers with their commercials if they grasp the dynamics of low-involvement information processing. Predicting Consumer Knowledge using

Metrics One of the main purposes of consumer research is to increase brand loyalty and market share.

a) Stable and expanding market share can only be achieved with the support of devoted brand followers.
b) Brands that command a bigger percentage of the market tend to have a more devoted customer base.

Tests of Recall and Recognizability

Consumers' recollection of ads, their familiarity with them after reading or seeing them, their impressions of the advertised product and brand, and their propensity to make a purchase are all measured through recognition and recall tests.

a) Recollection tests employ unassisted recall, whereas recognition tests rely on recall with prompts.
b) In recognition tests, consumers are shown an advertisement and asked whether they recall seeing it or remembering any of the ad's key features.
c) In recall tests, consumers are asked whether they have read a certain publication or watched a certain program, and if so, whether they can recall any advertisements they may have seen, as well as the product itself, the brand it was associated with, and any key features or benefits of the advertised brand.

Nature of Perception

- Perception refers to the process of interpreting and organizing sensory information in order to understand and navigate the environment.
- It is a fundamental aspect of human experience and plays a crucial role in guiding behaviour and decision making.
- Perception allows individuals to identify objects, recognize patterns, and make sense of the world around them.

Importance of Perception

- Perception enables individuals to navigate their environment and make decisions.
- It plays a crucial role in our ability to understand and interact with the world around us.
- It enables individuals to interact with others in a meaningful way.

Limitations of Perception

- Perception is inherently subjective and can be influenced by factors such as past experiences, cultural background, and individual biases.
- It can be prone to errors and illusions due to the way that the brain processes sensory information.
- Perception can be influenced by factors such as attention, expectation, and context, which can lead to errors or distortions in how we interpret sensory information.

Sensation

Sensation and perception were first differentiated by Scottish philosopher Thomas Reid (1710-1796). It was defined that a feeling is the mental representation of sensory organ activity. Perception, on the other hand, is distinct from sensation in that it involves conscious awareness of external things and events. Therefore, sensation is the conscious awareness caused by activation of a sense organ, while perception is the cognitive process through which sensations are arranged and interpreted. All humans possess six senses: vision (eyes), audition (ears), touch (skin), taste (mouth), and proprioception (body position awareness) (proprioception and kinaesthesia). A wide range of visual, tactile, auditory, and olfactory data is sent to our brain by our sense receptors. Transduction occurs in every sense, with inputs being recognized by receptor cells, transformed into electrical impulses, and then sent to the brain.

As a result, we call the mental processes that allow us to become aware of external stimuli — sensation and perception — respectively. Humans get information about their surroundings through sensory nerves that carry electrical impulses generated by specialized receptor cells. The field of research known as "sensation" is concerned with how living things react to and respond to sensory stimulus from their external environment (e.g. the eyes, ears, nose, tongue and skin). The term "perception" refers to the mental process through which incoming sensory data is processed, interpreted, and organized into a coherent whole that forms our conscious understanding of the world around us. Sense organs convert external physical energies like light, sound, and thermal radiation from an object into a code that is then sent to the brain, where it is processed. Therefore, the boundary between the concepts of sensation and perception is fuzzy at best. When we talk about sensation, we usually mean the act of taking in and relaying information, but when we talk about perception, we mean the act of consciously integrating and organizing this information.

Sensation is the process through which different types of sensory stimuli (electro-magnetic, pressure, sound waves) are registered by sense organs (eyes, tongue, skin, ears). The following elements make up this conception of sensation:

1) The participation of the organism's sensory apparatus.
2) The Existence of Stimuli in the Real World
3) Putting together information from scratch; and
4) The First Point of Contact, Also Known as Meaningless Contact

Say, for instance, you smell the alluring aroma of a rose. The 'nose' is the sensory organ through which the scent is experienced. There is a rose bush in the yard, and it serves as a stimulant. What you're sensing is the process of knowledge creation from unprocessed sensory data. Only the first touch has occurred, and you have no solid evidence that it came from a rose. Up until this point, all you've been feeling are sensations. Attempt to put yourself in the shoes of someone experiencing something similar and try to grasp what it means. The first step in recognizing an object's existence is a sensory experience.

Powers of Perception and Motion

Everything from the breath-taking sunrise to the jarring "crack" of starting an old motorcycle, from the silky feel of one's own skin to the sweltering heat of summer to the biting cold of winter, from the sour to the sweet, we experience it all. That begs the question, how? All of them rely on various sensory channels. The five senses we experience with our eyes, ears, skin, nose, and tongue are sight, sound, touch, smell, and taste. Things like light, sound, heat, and touch all give out physical energy. When these physical energy are used as stimuli, several feelings may be experienced. You now know I our senses include sight, sound, touch, smell, and taste, and (ii) objects emit physical energy like light, sound, heat, and touch. Sensation often does not occur until it is stimulated by some kind of physical energy.

Void Area

Blindness occurs at the point where the optic nerve originates from the retina. There's absolutely no visibility in the blind zone. These optic nerves go along the inside of the orbital ceiling to the brain. People unconsciously shift their head position or shift their focus to the other eye to counteract the effects of a blind spot. By now, you should have a firm grasp on the relationship between visual acuity and the subjective experience of seeing clearly.

The ear is the organ of sense through which sound is detected and processed. You can listen to the world around you thanks to the two ears located on either side of your head. Sound is created when a vibrating or moving object alters the air pressure around it. One's ears are the first to pick up on and register this. Pitch, volume, and timbre are the three most distinguishing features of every sound. The frequency of the oscillation of waves defines the pitch, or the high or low quality of a sound. Pitch increases as vibration speed increases. The expansion and contraction of sound waves, their amplitude, is what makes sounds loud. Turning up the volume on the TV raises the amplitude of the vibrations, making the sound louder. The timbre of a sound depends on the nature of the sound generator. A note performed on the shehnai, for instance, will have a different tone when compared to the piano. The term "timbre" is used to describe this variation in opulence. Hearing is characterized by pitch and loudness, whereas sound waves are characterized by frequency and amplitude. The outer ear, the middle ear, and the inner ear all contribute to the ear's ability to hear.

Smell

Our five senses—sight, sound, smell, taste, and touch—provide information about the world immediately around us. Our receptive abilities, such as sight, sound, and scent, allow us to take in more of the world around us. Smell is the most basic of these senses. An individual's ability to smell is triggered by the activation of receptor cells in the nasal passages. Chemicals in the air activate receptors near the top of the nasal cavity, and this information may be gathered by olfactory perception. As opposed to canines' around 200 million olfactory receptors, humans only have roughly 50 million. Dogs are used by the police to sniff out criminals and other suspicious activity because of their heightened sense of smell. Even more so, our olfactory receptors have a restricted spectrum of stimuli to which they are sensitive. The atomic weight of all the atoms in an odorous molecule should be between 15 to 300, according to Carlson (1998), therefore only such chemicals will be detected by human olfactory receptors. This explains why a molecular weight of 46 alcohol in a mixed drink may be detected, but a molecular weight of 342 sugar in a single teaspoon cannot. In many respects, the human sense of smell predates all others. Other animals, however, rely on their sense of smell more heavily. Pheromones are chemical compounds secreted by some animals that cause responses in others of the same species. An ancient means of communication, olfaction may be used in certain circumstances. Humans' varying responses to olfactory receptors and the location of stimuli allow for a wide range of olfactory experiences.

Taste

Smell and taste are connected senses. There are taste buds all across the top and sides of the tongue, and they are responsible for interpreting flavours predominantly. In fact, there are several receptor cells in each taste bud. We have around 10,000 taste receptors each person. Catfish have the most taste buds of any animal, at 175,000, whereas chickens have the fewest, with just 24. You could believe, based on your past encounters, that you can identify a wide variety of tastes in food. Obviously, that's not the case. There are just four flavours that your taste buds can register: sweet, salty, sour, and bitter. But if your palate is so sophisticated, why do you think there are so many more flavours to your experience than these four? The reason for this is because there are numerous other senses that come into play during eating besides taste, including scent, texture, warmth, and pressure on the tongue and mouth. However, taste buds are essential for the experience of flavour. The areas of your tongue closest to the tip and the sides are often the most sensitive to salt. Both sour and bitter flavours are picked up by different parts of the tongue. According to this theory, various types of taste receptors are responsible for each of these fundamental tastes. In addition, there is no conclusive response to the issue of what stimuli create these four fundamental taste attributes. Sweetness may be created not just by sugars but also by saccharin, a chemical molecule that is structurally significantly distinct from sugar. It is yet unclear what properties these drugs have that cause them to activate the same taste receptors. As people become older, they lose taste buds from their tongues. This means that, on average, adults are less sensitive to flavour than youngsters.

Skin Sensations

Take this as an illustration: Keep a cold water bucket, a warm water bucket, and a lukewarm water bucket on hand. Now, dip your hands into the chilly water and the warm water. Only the part of your hands that comes into contact with both water and air will feel hot or cold. Put your hands in the third bucket, which should be filled with warm water. Feelings will reverse when you put one hand into cold water and the other into warm water. The current experience will vary from person to person according on the average temperature to which their skin has acclimated. When the skin is stimulated, the organism learns about its immediate surroundings. Pressure, heat, cold, and pain are the four basic perceptions that make up what we call "skin senses." Because of how dissimilar these sensory attributes are, it's often assumed that they're generated by separate receptor systems. The hands, fingers, lips, and tongue are particularly sensitive since they are used to immediately interact with the environment around us. Sensitivity to the stimuli that trigger various feelings varies throughout the skin. Feel your skin in a new way right now. Do yourself a favor and blindfold yourself. Gently prodding your skin with a ballpoint pen will cause you to feel pressure just at the spots where the pen makes contact. A cold wire, a hot wire, and a pin all go through the same motions. Certain areas of your body will experience cold from a cold wire, warmth from a warm wire, and pain from a pin's tip. Such a feeling is the result of receptors in the skin responding to various stimuli at various locations. Pressure or touch refers to the sensation one feels while being gently prodded with a sharp item. As a general rule, certain regions of the body are more sensitive to touch than others. Extreme sensitivity may be seen in the lips, fingers, palms, and tip of the tongue. The trunk of the body, arms, and legs are the least sensitive parts of the body. Various areas of the body need different accounts of touch or pressure to generate the same feeling. Understanding the underlying receptor systems for temperature and pain is more limited. Heat and cold receptors may be found in the skin as well. The extremities of the hands and feet can withstand higher temperatures than those of the body as a whole, yet the core of the body is where these temperature sensors are located. There are 6 times as many cold receptors as heat receptors. There's been a lot of back and forth over how we feel pain. It has been hypothesized by some researchers that these cells are specialized pain receptors that are set off by tissue damage. Some people think that when a skin receptor is overestimated, pain results. A wide range of sensory organs, not only the skin, seem to be involved in the processing of painful stimuli. Pain may be caused by the overstimulation of any sensory system, for as by intense light, sound, or temperature.

Sensation via Touch

Your body's kinaesthetic senses reveal how your muscles and joints are positioned and moving. Put your finger to your lips and close your eyes. You have a firm grasp of the physical location of both limbs. The ability to move and perceive where our bodies are in space is called kinaesthesia. Muscles have kinaesthetic receptors that provide information to the brain about the weight being applied to the muscle and the intensity with which it is contracting. Joints house additional receptors. Kinaesthetic receptors detect motion and relay that information to the brain. One other function of the kinaesthetic senses is to help maintain a healthy feeling of physical equilibrium. If you lose the ability to discriminate between things of various weights while lifting, you may find it difficult to keep your equilibrium. These senses monitor the subject's orientation in space and time, as well as their movement with respect to the force of gravity.

Cognition's organizing principles, or the Gestalt law

The Gestalt concept was introduced in the early 20th century by Max Wertheimer, Wolfgang Köhler, and Kurt Koffka, three German psychologists. Gestalt theory is also known as the study of forms. Gestalt theorists argue that during perception, rather of interpreting a collection of inputs as a single entity, we look for commonalities between them. Gestalt may be defined as "shape" or "configuration" in its most basic form. In Gestalt theory, the 'whole is distinct from the sum of its parts,' as the saying goes. This suggests that the perception takes on new significance depending on the level of organization (or organized whole, as in Gestalten). This ability to perceive complicated patterns as single shapes or things is a direct result of the structuring that goes into them. It's possible that the arrangement of things is what constitutes organization. Gestalt psychologists began with this assumption and developed a set of rules and principles to describe how humans interpret parts of stimuli as constituting a whole. The term "laws of perceptual organization" is used to describe these rules of thumb.

Figure-Ground Relationship Law

We prefer to divide reality into separate "figure" and "ground" components, according to this idea. Always, the picture (or person) stands out against the backdrop. The "figure" of a stimulus is the portion of it that draws our eyes, while the "ground" is the rest of the scene. A figure's distinct form makes it easier to recall it in detail, but a background's limitlessness and lack of definition makes it less so. Take a peek at Figure 2.11 now. So, tell me, what do you see? If you had to choose between a human and a chess piece, which would you choose? Both the chessboard and the players fade into the background depending on whether attention is focused on the pieces or the players. In both cases, you'll arrange the figure (picture) in relation to the backdrop.

Law of Proximity (b)

This term describes the clustering of things that are physically near to one another. Stimuli that are spatially near together are automatically interpreted as belonging to the same category, allowing us to make sense of the world around us. This is why Figure 2.12 depicts a cluster of circles rather than a series of individual circles. The human brain has a natural inclination to lump together significant components for the sake of clarity and simplicity.

The Law of Pragnanz, the Law of Symmetry, or the Law of Good Figure entails the following.

Good figure is the original meaning of the German term Pragnanz. Thus, the "rule of excellent figure" is a synonym for this idea. This principle states that humans have a preference for arranging stimuli such that the result is symmetrical or balanced. As a result, we prefer to organize stimuli in the most basic and consistent manner possible. We may thus conclude that our perception favours shapes that are less complex. Figure 2.13, for instance, is often seen as an Olympic sign rather than five individual circles.

It's the rule of continuity

What this means is that we have a natural inclination to see figures as a whole rather than a collection of separate elements. The perception of lines is a good example of this concept in action. We tend to see the line in Figure 2.14 rather than the individual circles and black squares.

Common Fate Law

Movement is essential to this rule of law. Stimuli travelling in similar directions are interpreted as belonging to the same group, according to this theory of group organization.

Law of Completion

The rule of closure is the glue that holds all our impressions together. The perceptual processes arrange the information we get about the stimulus by completing any sensory gaps. The law of proximity and this one are not interchangeable.

This is what we mean by the Law of Similarity

According to this theory, classification should be done on the basis of shared characteristics.

For convenience's sake, let's say we're watching a cricket match and the players are all wearing different colours of jerseys.

Affective conditions

Opinions may be shaped by a number of different factors. Intervening variables include things like one's preconceived notions, one's own values, one's basic need for survival, and so on. The importance of such factors has been underlined by Helmholtz and other Gestaltists.

Perception and its Relation to Drive and Objectives

When it comes to perception and other psychological functions, motivation is always a crucial factor. Surely you've noticed that when you're hungry, the fragrance of food is more enticing than when you're full. The same result has been seen in several controlled laboratory experiments. Sanford (1936) conducted a famous experiment showing that people who were hungry were more likely to associate ambiguous cues with food than those who weren't hungry. To a similar extent, a subsequent research by Changizi and Hall (2001) showed that thirst also impacts perception. Participants were more likely to attribute transparency to unclear stimuli, a trait often associated with water.

Influence of Anticipatory or Anticipatory Perception

The ability to anticipate how something will be perceived is called perceptual expectation. The influence of preconceptions on human vision was shown in an iconic experiment by Bruner and Minturn (1955). A 13-shaped ambiguous stimulus was shown to participants in two different contexts: first, in the context of numbers, where it was interpreted as the numeral 13, and second, in the context of letters, where it was interpreted as the letter B. The individuals in both scenarios were exposed to the same confusing stimuli, but their interpretation of it differed because of their prior knowledge and expectations.

The Influence of Feelings

Do you believe that moods may alter one's perceptions? McGinnies (1949) used a word list consisting of eleven emotionally neutral terms (apple, kid, river, music, sleep) (raped, whore, penis, bitch). McGinnies discovered striking variations between the unaffected terms and the essential ones. Anxiety-avoidance responses in the form of perceptual defence mechanisms were hypothesized to explain why the threshold was higher for emotional words, why the galvanic skin reaction was stronger, and why there were more distortions for emotional words. Feelings don't always cloud judgement. According to the research, your performance suffers when the perceptual task has nothing to do with your feelings. However, it improves efficiency when it is emotionally meaningful.

Influence of Stimulus Variables

Heavy vehicles often utilize horns with a high frequency, high pitch, and a high volume. Why? Simply to get your focus. Different stimuli, whether they be auditory, gustatory, visual, or haptic, are more likely to pique our interest and subsequently alter our interpretation of their meaning, according to research. The evolutionary psychologist asserts that there is a selective advantage to possessing this trait. Humans' ability to use it to detect threats is a testament to its usefulness.

Implications of Experience

The way you perceive inputs is heavily influenced by your prior experience, which in turn molds your perspective. In the dark, you can mistake a rope for a snake because of your prior knowledge.

Cultural Influence

This gesture means "beautiful" or "perfect" in India, while in Brazil it is seen as an insult.

This scenario exemplifies how cultural shifts may alter one's perception of a stimuli.

Experience of depth

The capacity to see three-dimensional space, or depth perception, is what allows us to determine how far away an item is. Without the ability to judge depth, doing tasks like walking, driving, etc. would be very difficult. This talent doesn't come pre-wired but rather develops at a young age. This means that although some of it may be inherent, most of it is acquired via one's upbringing and environment. Distance perception is the mental process through which we estimate the physical distance to an item. Our ability to assess depth and distance relies on both monocular cues (information from just one eye) and binocular signals (information from both eyes).

Single-Eye Cues

These are the signals or cues that can be picked up by the brain from only one eye. These signals aren't as reliable as binocular cues. Painters employ these indicators to create the illusion of depth in two-dimensional works.

The following are examples of frequent monocular cues:

Size in Relation to Something Else

This clue tells us how far away an item is by comparing its size to that of something else of a comparable size. This cue is applicable to both flat and 3D pictures. If two things are about the same size, the one that seems bigger to the human eye is the one that is physically closer.

Gradient of Texture

The shift in the perceived gradient or degree of texture provides this indicator. Objects closer to our eyes have a rougher, more distinct texture than those farther away, implying a greater distance. This variation in texture is proportional to the separating distance.

The Atmospheric View from Above/Haze

Haze makes things seem further away than they really are. Atmospheric dust particles, fog, or water vapor can contribute to the appearance of haze. It's not always easy to tell how far away things are when there's haze around. Dependent on the density of the haze, the same peak might seem either closer or farther away.

View from a Straight Line

This indicator relies on the meeting of two lines at a vanishing point on the horizon. Convergence of rail lines or a road that seems to converge from a distance is a good illustration of such a cue. It's implied by this clue that the closer the lines are, the less the gap will be.

Interposition/Occlusion

When two objects overlap, the one that is veiled or occluded seems farther away than the one that isn't.

This cue uses both eyes, yet it is still classified as a monocular cue. Because our lenses change size depending on the viewer's distance, this phenomenon is called accommodation. Generally speaking, the lens of the eye is thicker when an item is up close to the eye and more narrow when the object is farther away.

Movement Parallax

J.J. Gibson coins the phrase "motion perspective" to describe the progression of visual data around a moving observer. As the observer travels through the environment, the speed with which distant objects move changes depending on their distance from and location in relation to the observer. Because of this, complicated motions occur, which is called motion parallax.

Multiple Senses Input

Binocular cues are information gathered from both eyes. When compared to monocular cues, they are far more effective. Stereopsis is the brain's ability to use two eyes together to form a three-dimensional image. The two primary categories of binocular cues are:

An Inequality of the Eyes (binocular parallax)

Left eye = L O=Left eye

The average distance between a human being's two eyes is 6.3 centimeters. As a result, the retinal picture of the identical object might seem somewhat different depending on the observer's perspective. Objects that are closer to the eyes provide a more distinct retinal picture. To determine an object's depth, height, and breadth, our brain combines the information from the two pictures captured by the retina.

When we concentrate our eyes on anything, our eyes produce what is called a "convergence angle." It's important to note that the convergence angle varies depending on how far away or how close an item is. We establish a narrower convergence angle while looking at an item far away, and a wider one when looking at something up close. Any shift in convergence provides the perceiver with information about the depth and range of the scene.

Sense of motion

When a vehicle approaches, how can we tell whether it's heading in our direction or going the other way? An individual's capacity to perceive motion allows them to accurately determine the course and velocity of an item in motion. Psychologists have used the following four considerations in their effort to address problems about movement perception:

1. Movement of the retina: When an object is in motion, the picture of that object on the retina also shifts. The retinal image's mobility is picked up by motion- and direction-sensitive visual neurons. Movement is sensed in this manner.
2. If you look at a moving item for a while (a few seconds to a few minutes) and then look at something still, you may experience motion aftereffect (MAE). As a result, the still item will seem to be moving in the opposite direction as the one that is really in motion. The term "motion adaptation effect" (MAE) describes this occurrence.
3. Thirdly, induced motion occurs when a smaller, stationary body is encircled by a bigger, moving body, causing the smaller, stationary body to seem to move in the opposite direction of the larger, moving body. When the moon is surrounded by slowly

moving clouds, we believe the moon to be moving due to this optical illusion.

4. Apparent motion: Wertheimer, a Gestalt theorist, initially introduced this concept, also known as perceptual motion (1912). This effect occurs when a series of static stimuli is delivered to the brain, leading to an impression of movement. There is no transfer of energy from source to receptor for there to be a sensation of motion. That is, even if the eyes, head, and body remain still and the item itself remains still, the perception of motion will persist.

For example, if you switch on a string of decorative lights one at a time, you'll notice that the light seems to move across the room as if it were really traveling from one bulb to the next. This is the phi-phenomenon. As the lights flash on and off in rapid succession, the illusion of motion is created.

The cinematic use of the strobe effect. To illustrate, consider a movie projector, which, in order to create the illusion of motion, displays a series of still images of the scene. Even though each frame is taken by itself, the resulting image is distinct from what came before. When the frames are shown at the correct rate, the impression of motion is continuous and unbroken.

To illustrate the autokinetic effect, imagine a totally black environment with a single, fixed point of light. The shift seems to be unrelated to eye movements but may affect up to 20 degrees of the viewer's field of view. The term "autokinetic illusion" describes this phenomena.

The perception of one's own size

Systems for evaluating stimulus magnitude will be discussed here. The size-distance invariance theory, the familiar size hypothesis, and the direct perception hypothesis all attempt to explain how we are able to accurately evaluate the size of stimuli despite a change in distance.

1) The "size-distance invariance" (SDI) hypothesis: This theory assumes that there is a direct correlation between the magnitude of a stimulus and how far away it is (Kilpatrick and Ittelson, 1953). It also claims that the retinal picture is used to infer stimulus size if distance information is available. In the absence of this distance cue, however, we must rely on ocular angle alone to create an estimate of an object's size. This connection may be expressed mathematically as:

$S`/D` = f \square \theta \square$

S' = S' percieved size

Perceived distance, denoted by D'
= Perceptual Axis

At this juncture, it's necessary to define the phrase "visual angle" before continuing. This is the inclination our eyes make after taking in an object's image.

2) The familiar size theory or cue is utilized to determine not just the size of the stimuli, but also their distance and depth. As the distance from a stimulus decreases, the visual angle for that stimulus also lowers. Together, our prior knowledge of the size of the targeted stimulus and this new information (visual angle) allow our brain to calculate the true size, distance, and depth of the object. This idea suggests that familiar size affects our impression of size, which in turn affects our perception of distance.

An egocentric reference distance is used to estimate the size of a known item under unconventional viewing conditions.

3) Third, there is Direct Perception Theory, which was proposed by Gibson in 1979. Epstein (1982) summed up his thoughts on the topic of size perception on page 78 as follows:

(i) there is no perceptual representation of size correlated with the retinal size of the object,

(ii) perceived size and perceived distance are independent functions of information in stimulation, and

(iii) perceived size and perceived distance are not causally linked, nor is the perception of size mediated by operations combining information about retinal size and perceived distance. The exact variables of stimulation that influence these precepts in the given settings are responsible for the relationship between perceived size and perceived distance.

Mistakes in perception: illusion

Can one's own viewpoint be taken as gospel? Of course not! It is possible to misunderstand or abuse the perception process. Mistakes and incorrect interpretations of stimuli are common, whether they are intentional or not. To'misinterpret' sensory data is to experience an illusion. As another definition goes, an illusion is "a difference between one's consciousness and some input". Seeing a rope as a snake at night, or a ghost in a tree. These are also common illusions. We'll discuss several frequent types of illusion below.

The Muller–Lyre Illusion

This optical illusion makes it seem like two parallel lines of the same length are really varied in length from one another. In contrast to lines that extend outward, those that point inward seem to be shorter. Also called the arrow-head illusion, this phenomenon occurs when the perception of a line's length changes depending on the form and location of the lines that encircle it.

Illusion, Ponzo

This is an example of an optical illusion in which the size of two parallel lines drawn across the image seems to be different than it really is because of the convergence of the lines. Both the top and bottom yellow lines are the same length, despite the higher one seeming to be longer (see Figure 2.33). Because we use the liner's perspective cue to assess the size of the yellow line, we often get it wrong. It's a common optical illusion called "the train."

The Ebbinghaus Illusion

It's a trick of the eye that makes things seem bigger or smaller than they really are. Titchener circles are a kind of optical illusion that was first discovered by Hermann Ebbinghaus but became well recognized because to the efforts of Edward B. Titchener. Right, time for a response. Determine which of the magenta circles below is the smallest.

Ames Room Illusion

This optical illusion causes a misperception of size and is named after its inventor, American ophthalmologist and perceptual psychologist Adelbert Ames, Jr. A person in one corner of a room seems much bigger than someone in another corner to an onlooker. This optical illusion is a spectacular illustration of depth perception signals.

The Moon Illusion

When the moon rises over the horizon, does it ever strike you as unusually large? Those who have seen it must agree that it seems larger on the horizon than it really is as it passes above. However, the moon's actual size remains unchanged. The term "moon illusion" describes our tendency to see the moon as being of different proportions at the horizon and the zenith. The illusion arises because our brains are conditioned to think of the sky as a flattened dome, causing them to artificially shrink the size of the moon when it is in the sky at zenith. This means that a spatial illusion is being created.

Poggendorff's Illusion

This is because the Zollner illusion served as an inspiration for the Poggendorff illusion. Two segments of an oblique line do not seem to be in a straight line when the line is intersected by a blank region defined by two vertical parallel lines.

Determining consumer buying Behaviour-Consumer purchase decision

Determinants and Features of Perception Affecting Consumer Behavior

With the knowledge you gain from this lesson, you will be able to: • recognize and explain the stimulus factors determining one's perception; • investigate the individual response factors determining one's perception; • understand the marketing significance or implications of the factors determining consumer perception; and • comprehend the features of perception affecting consumer behavior.

Introduction

As we discussed in the last unit, perception is the way in which we take in, analyze, and make sense of the world around us. The factors and characteristics of perception that shape consumer behavior will be emphasized in this course. What follows is a condensed version of a conversation we had earlier.

Analysis of Perception Factors and Their Role in Promotion

There are a lot of distractions out there for consumers, both in the commercial and social spheres. The media, things available in shops, and even the habits of others in the same socioeconomic class as you may all serve as influences. However, it's possible that we miss some of the information that's being sent to us. In other words, we only pay attention to and seek out the things that pique our own interests. To put it another way, we do not pick up on every detail of our environment. Ideas, thoughts, and information that go counter to our already acquired worldviews are either ignored or reworked. We recall just the details that we choose to recall. The implication is that not everyone is influenced by marketing. Factors such as the stimuli's characteristics, our own wants, and the cognitive architectures we've developed all play a role in shaping our perceptions. In general, we may classify the elements that shape people's perspectives into two groups. First, there are the stimuli, and second, there is the individual's own reaction to those stimuli. There is a lot of overlap between these two categories, and each contributes greatly to an individual's perception. Now, let's take a look at each one individually:

Affective Factors

When a stimulus stimulates sensory receptors and those sensations are interpreted by the brain, we have perception. The moment of every day, our senses are bombarded with many stimuli, not all of which are registered. Perceptions are founded on the specifics of the stimulus themselves. It follows that our interpretations are based on the stimuli we encounter. To be more specific, they are the material properties of the relevant stimuli. This category includes just those aspects that may be directly attributed to the physical stimulus itself. Gestalt psychologists argue that an individual's perception is mostly governed by physiological processes happening in the nervous system in response to stimulus by physical things. A person's perception is determined by the properties of the stimuli that attract his attention. These traits, or stimulus elements, are very important for marketers to consider since they have a major impact on the results of their campaigns. Features of stimuli such as (a) color, (b) contrast, (c) size, (d) loudness, (e) brightness, (f) placement, (g) movement, (h) directionality, (I) isolation, (j) introductory questions, (k) novelty, (l) the use of an attractive spokesman, etc., all play a role in how consumers interpret those features. The next few paragraphs will be dedicated to a brief overview of these topics.

(a) Colour: is used to grab the viewer's eye fast. We all know that things with bold colours stand out more than their more subdued counterparts. It's no secret that colour ads are more effective than black and white ones in grabbing people's attention. There are a variety of factors at play that contribute to the way in which we each individually interpret objects that are mostly black and white or lacklustre in colour. Reasons are listed below. Coloured objects are more likely to catch and keep the viewer's eye than black-and-white ones. The second explanation is that individuals in today's metropolitan society value products that are vividly coloured because they wish to incorporate more colour into their life. Many items, it seems, really do better when shown in colour as opposed to monochrome. Moreover, colour may be employed to produce mood, which secures our attention, and as a consequence alter our perceptions.

Marketers should keep in mind that people have different reactions to different colors before settling on a scheme. Some people may associate a certain shade of color with happy emotions, while others may associate it with negative ones. Again, some things, like garment materials, come in a wide variety of appealing hues, while others, like hair-dye, have a narrower palette from which to choose.

(b) People are more likely to focus on stimuli that stand out against their surroundings than on ones that blend in. You learned that customers had a quicker and more positive reaction to brightly colored products. But studies show that our attention is drawn more readily to objects that stand out from their surroundings. The human attention is drawn to stimuli that stand out from their backdrop if their hue is inconsistent. You may have observed that a black-and-white advertising stands out more and is easier to understand when placed against a colorful backdrop. One more time, a radio commercial that is louder than others stands out immediately. The uniqueness of the stimuli plays a role in causing this effect. This argues that in order to attract the attention of their target audience, marketers should use the notion of contrast in the design, packaging, and advertising of their products.

(c) The magnitude of the stimulus has an effect on the amount of focus it receives from consumers. It's common knowledge that things of greater size attract more attention than those of lesser size. When it comes to commercials, you've probably seen that people pay more attention to the bigger ones. As for the dimensions of the product, the same holds true. Items with a larger surface area get more attention than their smaller counterparts. Although expanding the size of a stimulus may be effective, it is important for marketers to remember that doing so has to make sense in relation to the magnitude of the stimulus to begin with. For the price hike to register with buyers as an actual price hike, it must be commensurate with the pre-boost level of the product or service.

(d) Loudness: The intensity of a stimuli will frequently impact attention. A loud stimulus will be more likely to be perceived than one of less intensity. The purpose of the first blast of sound in television and radio commercials is only to grab the attention of the audience. Marketers should notice that, double the loudness of sound always does not guarantee twice the perception. You know that human ears are sensitive to noises originating in a frequency of 12,000 to 20,000 cycles per second. Therefore, while deciding on the volume level for their commercials, businesses should take the audible perception threshold in mind.

(e) Color vibrancy: vivid colors attract the eye more than muted ones. Because of this, commercials in print and on air tend to be more visually striking than they formerly were. Similar to how size and volume work, the brightness of colors may have an effect.

(f) Position, or where something is in relation to the viewer's line of sight, is the subject of this clause. Perception isn't the only thing that position affects. Multiple studies have indicated that people tend to pay more attention to things that are in the middle of their field of vision as opposed to those on the edges. It's been observed that people are more likely to notice anything kept or exhibited on a shelf at or near eye level than something stored or shown below. Advertisements in print publications tend to attract greater attention when placed on the left side of the page and in the top half of the page due to the natural reading order of most individuals. Based on their research, Starch has determined that magazine advertisers that place their advertisements near the rear of the publication are more likely to reach their target audience. Thirty percent more people are likely to read a publication if advertisements are placed on the inner front and back covers. The answer to this question once again differs from nation to nation. The inverse trend should be seen in nations where people read from right to left.

(g) Stimulus motion: a moving stimulus will be recognized more quickly than a still one. Attracting attention via the appearance of movement is another viable strategy. In general, things that are in motion are more conspicuous than those that are at rest. This is due to the fact that modern marketers place a high priority on video commercials and interactive point-of-purchase displays that may be seen while the consumer is shopping. It's likely that we've all seen a great deal of outdoor advertising using moving elements, such as vertically rotating neon signs and in-store displays with similar elements. The purpose of these is to draw the target audience's focus more intently on the offered goods. It is important for advertisers to remember that relocating billboards, signs, and other outdoor advertising may cause serious or even deadly traffic accidents. Therefore, care should be taken when deciding where to position such advertising so that they do not pose a threat to passing cars.

(h) Directional cues, such as arrows or pointing fingers, attract greater attention than random or non-directional ones. Ads that use directional arrows or other indicators and symbols that draw attention to a certain region or piece of information are more likely to be seen.

(i) As a first step, we may isolate the item in question from the rest of the stimulus set. Maybe you saw an ad the size of a matchbox in the midst of a newspaper page that otherwise had nothing on it. Conceptually, we want to draw the reader's attention to the stimulus ad by setting it out from the rest of the ads. Commercials on television might also benefit from the isolation concept.

(j) A question at the beginning of an ad may attract more readers than a statement would. Ads that pose questions to the target audience (such as "what do you think about cleanliness?") have a far higher chance of being read or noticed.

(k) Novelty: Audience members have a rapid reaction time to stimuli that they find novel or surprising. Several research have looked at how people's attention is affected by an advertisement's collative qualities. Ads that were deemed startling, odd, or humorous were more likely to have been read or viewed, according to research by Holbrook and Lehmann.

Advertisements featuring beautiful models or celebrities tend to stand out to viewers and leave a lasting impression. Marketers should be cautious in picking models or celebrities for their commercials, because wrong usage of such may provide unfavorable image to the customers that would severely influence their sales.

Consumers' impressions may also be influenced by additional stimuli elements, which have been uncovered via studies. Findings suggest that consumers' attention might be influenced by a message's perceived tempo. Advertisements that appear in compressed form are determined to be more intriguing to the audiences that affect their impressions of the promoted brands. It is also observed that stimuli or information that are tangible rather than abstract, picture evoking, emotionally appealing, comprising a large lot of detail and precision regarding things, activities, results, and situational context are received better by the consumers. Ads that use precise, detailed, and particular language do better than those that use more generic language in getting people to pay attention.

Individual Differences in Reaction Factors

Perception is determined by more than just the stimuli that are presented to the brain. Personal traits are what drive an individual's focus and attention. To influence how customers see a product or message, marketers must first identify this collection of criteria and then tailor their approach accordingly. Individuals' (a)curiosity, (b)focus, (c)needs/motives, (d)life experiences, (e)personality, (f)attitudes, (g)values, and (h)mindset are all important in determining their responses. Pay attention to them now:

(a) When considering the factors that influence one's perspective, the first one to consider is interest. It is the product of both long-term and short-term objectives and reflects one's general way of life. Achievable short-term objectives and plans shift and change as circumstances demand. As a general rule, people pay more attention to stimuli and information that piques their interest. The topics in which they are actively engaged also pique their curiosity. They care mostly about themselves and their own unique manifestations. Since people have various hobbies and pursuits, the same thing might have varying meanings to them. Furthermore, there is a difference between the sexes that plays a role. It has been observed that males have a propensity for a variety of pursuits that mostly bore women. Studies have shown that people feel a need to keep an eye on the items in which they've emotionally invested. People tend to read articles about topics in which they have an interest, such as events in which they participated or products they have purchased. Similarly, smokers are much more likely to read articles supporting the link between smoking and lung cancer than they are to read articles disproving the link. Therefore, it stands to reason that individuals are more likely to pay attention to and recall information on topics in which they are already engaged.

(b) Focusing one's cognitive resources on a particular set of stimuli. One's impression of a stimulus item is based on how much attention he pays to it. We're well aware that the focus of people's attention is always shifting. According to studies, people's focus on any given task varies every five seconds. Removing focus from a stimuli reduces the likelihood that it will be seen. In order to keep customers interested, businesses must come up with items that are novel, practical, and exceptional. This might help people quickly understand the message being conveyed.

(c) Needs/Motivations: We are aware that our physical and psychological requirements influence the perception of the item we experience. Take, for instance, two guys who are sitting at a lunch counter and looking over the menu that has been put on the wall. One is starving to death while the other is only thirsty. While both are presented with the identical physical object, one will focus on the burger and sandwiches while the other focuses on the tea, coffee, and cola. The second guy's response will be exactly the opposite. If you ask either man what they saw on the menu, you'll get a list of food items followed by "and other stuff" from the first man and a list of drinks followed by "and other things" from the second. Whereas in the first scenario, the food items were viewed and arranged against a backdrop of non-differentiated "other things," in the second scenario, the roles were reversed. This means that even a purely visual signal might be interpreted differently depending on the individual's demands, incentives, and punishments.

(d) Perceptions are also shaped by (d) our recollections and experiences from the past. The method through which we assign meaning to incoming inputs is influenced by our prior experiences. As a result of one's prior exposure to identical stimuli, that person is more likely to assign those stimuli to the same perceptual category and respond in the same way in the future. If you have a bad experience with one product from a firm, it's probable that you'll have an unfavorable impression of all of the things they sell. You probably feel that way because of a bad encounter you had with one of the company's goods in the past.

(e) One's personality and the traits that make up that personality have a role in how that person interprets the world around them. Due to individual differences in perspective, the same stimulus might evoke a wide range of interpretations from each observer. Those who have trouble dealing with uncertainty are more likely to be swayed by official certifications, according to a single research.

(f) In addition to the stimulus itself, the consumer's attitude has a role in how the stimulus is perceived. Consumers evaluate inputs from different sources based on their preexisting attitudes and worldviews. As a result, people tend to react to and interpret events in ways that are in line with the beliefs they already have. If their attitudes are favorable, they will have a favorable impression of the stimulus. If you have a bias towards a certain brand of ball point pen, for instance, you will read and understand any marketing for that brand through the lens of your bias.

(g) Values: The standards by which we measure right behavior. How we interpret external events is also affected by the values we have. Many types of groups in society teach their members morals and ethics. It doesn't take long for the principles you instill in them to stick. As a result, they affect how a person perceives the world around him. In general, we form unfavorable impressions of stimuli that go counter to our own beliefs and ideals while trying to maintain a positive self-image.

(h) Our mental set, or the way we think about the world, is a crucial factor in shaping our perspectives. Everyday life is rife with examples that apply here as well. "Cognitive set accounts for the selectivity of perception in that the same objective event is perceived very differently by different observers," writes author David Brooks. "It is the "map" one makes of the world, through which some people, skills, experiences, needs, values, and goals are elevated and others flattened." 3 In light of our new mental set, we are able to choose for perception a wider variety of items, resulting in more nuanced and complex cognitive structures. The perceptions of a police officer, a social worker, a ward politician, and a tourist from another country all varied greatly when strolling through the same slum. That's because various people's unique mental make-ups cause them to interpret the identical physical phenomenon in vastly diverse ways.

Consumers' Decision-Making and How Perception Plays a Role

Several aspects of perception influence how a person interprets a given input or piece of information. The traits or characteristics of perception have a significant role in how a person processes, evaluates, and explains specific information.

One's sensitivity to stimuli, two's ability to filter out irrelevant data, three's ability to organize that data, and four's ability to ignore irrelevant data are all aspects of perceptual cues. The following paragraphs will provide a quick overview of these aspects:

- Perceptual Cues: are essentially stimuli that cause individuals to feel curious or interested. The signals a someone receives have a significant role in shaping their perception of a stimuli. People utilize all sorts of hints to figure out what a certain circumstance, item, shop, or other entity is like. Consumers benefit from cues in order to arrive at optimal purchasing judgments. Two sorts of signals, as shown by several research, are used by consumers to make purchasing choices. There are two types of cues: those that are "relevant" and those that are "irrelevant." Relevant cues are the primary drivers of consumer behavior at the point of purchase. The size, shape, color, packaging, and pricing of a product are all examples of relevant signals. They serve as prompts or indicators to customers, guiding them toward a final buying decision. Consumers often rely on pertinent indications while making purchases. A customer will rely on irrelevant signals when they have a difficult time making a purchasing choice based on information that is directly relevant to them. When making a purchase decision, it's important to put aside any clues that aren't directly related to the product or service at hand. In the absence of clear information, buyers may make irrational purchases based on less important factors.
- Perceptual Selectivity: As you well know, customers are continually subjected to a plethora of environmental cues. The amount of information bombarding a person at any one moment is much more than his cognitive capacity. They are so overwhelmed by the sheer volume of information that they are forced to pick and choose which stimuli they really pay attention to. Every person only pays partial attention to advertisements and other forms of communication. A research indicated that people only pay attention to around 5-25% of the things they see or hear. While browsing the aisles of a supermarket, you may see hundreds of products, but you'll only pay attention to the ones you need. As a result, you only pick and choose which stimuli to

register as real, while being constantly bombarded by them. That said, the key to selective thinking is how you go about doing it. We've already spoken about how your needs, past experiences, beliefs, worldview, and so on all play a role. Marketers strive for commercials that stand out from the crowd since they cannot afford endless ad exposure.

• Perceptual Organization This is another property of perception that affects consumer behavior. Having been exposed to new knowledge, a person may develop an interest in it. His focus will be drawn to whatever piques his curiosity. When someone is interested in something, the next step is to attempt to figure out what it means to them. It is via the process of perceptual structuring that the input is understood. Using his own worldview, he will attempt to organize the many aspects of the stimulus in a way that minimizes its ambiguity. You attempt to make sense of a commercial you watch on television, for instance, by connecting its many parts in your mind and drawing conclusions about its intended message.

Threshold is the minimum amount of energy in a stimulus needed to elicit a certain experience. It's the level of stimulation required to elicit a perceptual response. Since you already know that our senses are the most fundamental perceptors, you already know that the word "threshold" refers to anything linked to our sensory systems. There are three distinct thresholds for each of our five senses. Lower threshold, terminal threshold, and difference threshold are these three. A stimulus's lower threshold is the level at which it must be presented to the senses for them to register its presence. The terminal threshold is the level of sensory intake beyond which further increases have no perceptible effect on human perceptions. A person's difference threshold, also known as the Just Noticeable Difference (JND), is the minimum change in stimulus strength that elicits a perceptible shift in experience. Note that in order to induce a perceptual response from consumers, the intensity of a marketer's stimuli must be greater than both the lower and higher thresholds. It's also important to remember that these thresholds seldom stay constant over time. A consumer's lower threshold level for a stimulus may shift as they get used to it. As a result, marketers need to keep tabs on the intensity of the stimuli required to elicit the responses they want. According to Weber's Law, the higher the strength of the first stimulus, the greater the extra intensity required for the secondary stimulus to be recognized and interpreted as different from the primary stimulus (also known as the difference threshold or J.N.D.). A price rise of Rs. 5 on a pen that used to cost Rs. 10 is going to be seen as quite a bit by most people.

However, if the price of a single unit in a building with twenty apartments is decreased by Rs. 10,000, nobody would notice. Therefore, for a change in stimulus intensity to be perceived by consumers as an increase or reduction, it must be proportional to the starting intensity of the same stimulus. This idea has potential for usage by marketers in two different sectors. First, to avoid customers seeing any changes, such as smaller packaging, higher prices, or worse quality. Second, to guarantee that customers easily recognize and appreciate any changes in quality, size, packaging, or pricing.

As we have shown, in order to affect consumers, a stimulus has to be presented at a level of intensity over their lower threshold. Many research disproved this theory. Based on the results of these research, it seems that certain stimuli may be detected even when they are offered at levels below the lower threshold, also known as the limen. Subliminal perception is a notion born from this. It's possible that people may be influenced by stimuli that lie just below their threshold of conscious awareness. Sometimes one of our five senses may pick up on these stimuli even when we aren't consciously aware of them. This kind of knowing happens in the background, or subliminally. To sum up, subliminal perception occurs when a stimulus is provided at a level below the lower threshold at which it may be detected. Consumers may be influenced by subliminal messages, according to a number of studies. After every five seconds throughout a six-week period in a certain theater, the advertisement "DRINK Coca Cola and EAT Popcorn" was presented for 1/3000 of a second, according to one research conducted in the mid-1950s. Researchers found that throughout the advertising time, sales of both Coke and Popcorn grew by 57.7 percent and 18.1 percent, respectively. It's strong evidence that customers may be influenced by subliminal cues, something that marketers should take carefully.

Decision-Making Styles

As a general rule, customers evaluate things based on how well they meet their own requirements. To develop a strong enough desire for a product to actively seek it out in stores, one must first become aware of the product's availability as well as the product's suitability to one's needs. As a general rule, we pay more attention to and form opinions about things that have personal significance to us and that align with our prior knowledge and understanding. Businesses usually do not count on customers paying attention to every item on display as they browse the aisles. Their goods need to stand out from the hundreds of others on store shelves, so they create custom packaging and even display cases. Experts in the field of marketing understand that consumers often exercise discretion while making purchases. Because of this, it remains a topic of inquiry for academics studying consumer behavior and, indeed, for all marketers. Businesses invest a lot of time and money into trying to get customers to notice their goods and read their ads. When a consumer is interested in a product, they are more likely to pay attention to related marketing materials. Because of this, marketers put forth significant effort to win over the hearts and minds of customers. Once a consumer becomes familiar with a brand, they are able to put a price on it. He researches other companies' costs, makes comparisons, and thinks about whether or not the brand he's contemplating is worth the money. One buyer may associate a greater price with better quality, while another would not. In this way, people have different perspectives on what a fair price is. If the cost is acceptable, the customer researches any potential downsides to purchasing that specific brand. To put it another way, he may attribute varying degrees of danger to a given transaction. Others may react differently to what you see. The way in which, say, quality is perceived may have an effect on how much something costs. Once again, the way a brand's pricing is framed might influence how consumers evaluate the potential downsides of making a purchase of that brand. As a result, consumers' perceptions influence their actions in a variety of ways. Marketers may increase their messages' likelihood of penetrating consumers' minds and having the intended effect by learning more about how people form and process information in general.

Exactly What Role Does Process Play In How People Think About Brands?

A marketer's ability to generate brand sales hinges on whether or not his product is well received by his intended demographic. In the eyes of the public, how does a certain brand stand out? However subjective it may be, there are a lot of elements that go into how a brand is perceived. The social and physical environment in which the individual is seeing the brand, as well as the social and physical context of the stimuli associated with the brand, all have a role in shaping the individual's perception of the brand. Size, color, form, quality, service, qualities, uniqueness, advertising, and packaging, as well as the name / image of the manufacturing firm and retailers where the brand is sold, all have a role in shaping how consumers see the brand. The marketer has to determine what kind of impression he wants to make with his brand. If he wants his brand to be associated with quality or worth in the eyes of customers, he shouldn't give discounts or other price-related incentives.

Sensitivity to Cost

Many marketeers fret about how customers evaluate prices. It's more likely that a brand will do well in sales if its target clients think its pricing is fair. As one would expect, larger effective costs are indicative of greater monetary dangers. Therefore, knowing how customers evaluate pricing is of paramount importance to marketers. A marketer may query a consumer with inquiries like "is there a correlation between the price and the quality of this product?" to get a sense of the customer's perspective on pricing. Do consumers see product pricing differently if they finish in an odd number as opposed to an even number? Different client segments may react differently to price-related incentives, therefore a marketer may get conflicting responses to these kinds of inquiries. Research has been done to address these and similar issues about how prices are perceived. In the following paragraphs, we will discuss some of the most significant results on pricing perception that have emerged from various research. These results may be used as guidance for businesses as they decide which pricing incentives to provide consumers.

Conclusion 1: First, there isn't a unified body of research on the topic of price-awareness. Neither the types of customers who are price-conscious nor the categories of goods where this mindset is most likely to emerge are immediately apparent.

Conclusion 2: There seems to be a positive association between price and judgments of product quality at least within certain product categories, however this relationship needs more study. When faced with uncertainty, when lacking in self-assurance, or when lacking in other signs of product quality, consumers seem to place more weight on pricing. When there is a certain image of the brand, that is more essential than the price as a gauge of quality. When there are more informational cues to consider, consumers tend to place less weight on price.

Conclusion 3: The third finding suggests that customers have higher and lower price limits, or "absolute thresholds," respectively. Therefore, customers look for products whose prices fall within the ranges presented.

Conclusion 4: Monroe asks a crucial, though mostly unanswered, issue in his fourth finding: "When and under what conditions are differently priced but identical items seen as separate offers?" There's a notion called "difference threshold" at play here; it refers to how much of a shift must occur before customers take notice. It's possible that customers are more sensitive to a price increase than they would be to a decrease of the same magnitude, at least for certain items.

Conclusion 5: The link between the perceived price and the reference price plays a significant role in how customers value a product or service. It's possible for shoppers to form a reference pricing system based on past experiences across a variety of product types and quality tiers. You can average prices or look at the cost of the most popular brand to get an idea of what the going rate is, but they are only two of many possible starting points for determining the standard pricing. In order to determine how much a certain brand or product should cost, shoppers refer to this reference price.

Researchers conclude that, despite a plethora of literature, little is known about how price influences a shopper's evaluation of competing offers and, ultimately, his propensity to make a purchase or consumption.

Perceptions of Danger

Marketers evaluate the level of risk that customers are willing to take in order to make a purchase, in addition to presenting them with information about the product. Each potential buyer will have their own unique set of concerns about a product. When customers are unsure of what they want to achieve with a purchase, perceived risk enters the picture. Consumers' actions are influenced by the perceived level of danger connected to making a purchase. Buyers' level of assurance that a choice will result in a satisfying end and the expenses associated with the decision determine the level of risk they are willing to assume. The inability to fulfill an arousal leads to losses in many areas, including time, money, and pride. It's possible to have reservations about potential adverse outcomes even after a choice has been taken. If any of these things hold true, the buyer must face the worry that their purchase will have unintended repercussions if they don't get it just right. The degree of perceived risk is often higher when considering a large purchase. A person's sense of risk may rise, for instance, if they finance the purchase of a new automobile during a time when interest rates are very high. Perceived danger, whether actual or imagined, may be a significant factor in consumers' final choices. The doubt that the product will serve the purchase purpose, or the dread of repercussions related to the product's performance, quality, and capacity to satisfy social and psychological demands, both contribute to the impression of risk. Actual or potential danger might be of the physical, monetary, or social kind. In various purchasing scenarios, two distinct types of risk might be seen. The inherent risk of a transaction is the first and most obvious danger. Another kind of risk is one that can be managed. This is the risk that appears after the data has been analyzed, and the buyer often employs a variety of strategies to mitigate it. A purchaser may, for instance, see firearms as very risky. On the other side, he could feel safe purchasing a name brand. There is a significant level of inherent risk, but the level of managed risk is acceptable.

When making a purchase, customers face a number of unknowns and potential drawbacks, and marketers are cognizant of this fact. Multiple methods of minimizing potential harm are used by shoppers. It is also the marketer's responsibility to mitigate or get rid of any unfounded fears or doubts their target audience may have. Here, we'll talk about what shoppers and sellers can do to mitigate or eradicate worries about a product's safety.

Methods for Lessening or Doing Away with Potential Dangers

A customer may take steps to mitigate or remove perceived dangers, or marketers can provide assistance in this area. Businesses may assist customers feel safer by providing options like refunds or replacements in the event of product dissatisfaction, as well as by sending messages that highlight the benefits of their products. Marketers may use these strategies to lower customers' sense of danger.

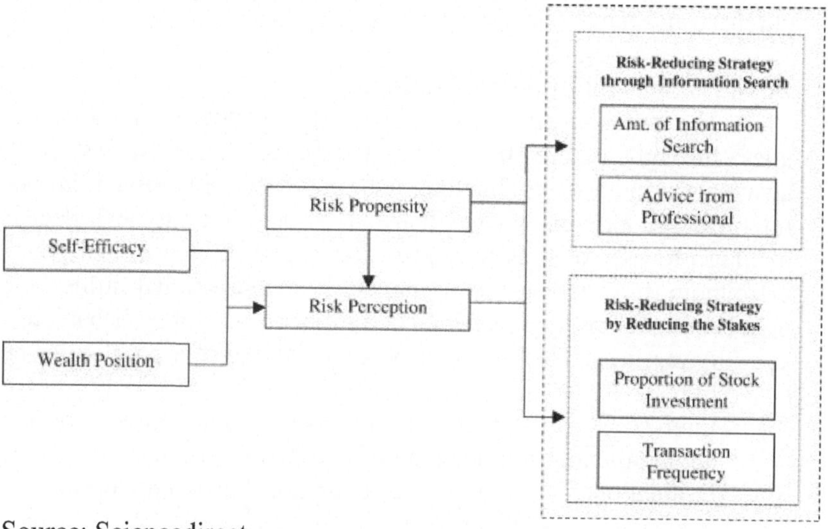

Source: Sciencedirect

Focused promotional efforts emphasizing quality and reliability become an important marketing strategy in helping consumers reduce their perceived risks. Marketers may also provide enough relevant information to the consumers, and should take special efforts to increase consumer confidence in such information. This is possible using testimonials taken from credible people and transmitting them through reliable media.

Consumers themselves may also take number of measures to reduce their perceived risks. To reduce risk related to quality, they may buy expensive items as an assurance of quality. The financial risk may be minimized by purchasing least expensive items. Consumer may engage himself in word-of-mouth communication to reduce perceived risk. He may talk to someone who has already bought or used a particular brand, which will help him reduce or eliminate risk involved in the purchase of a particular brand of a product. Developing loyalty toward specific brand or store may also help a consumer reduced his perceived risk. One may also reduce or eliminate perceived risk by reading articles on use tests, and by reading or listening to advertisements. Perceived risk may also be reduced by a consumer by examining a product in a store display or buying and using sample of a product before he goes for regular purchase. Consumers may also seek reassurance from the sellers in the form of guarantee or warranty and thus can minimize their perceived risks. It is obvious that the less risk involved in purchase, the more likely that the consumer will make the purchase and remain happy.

Buying stage and situational influence

The buying stage refers to the different phases that a customer goes through before making a purchase. These stages include awareness, interest, evaluation, and purchase. Situational influence refers to the external factors that can impact a customer's decision-making process, such as time pressure, social influence, and physical surroundings. Together, the buying stage and situational influence can help businesses better understand and influence customer behaviour.

1. Awareness: The customer becomes aware of a problem or need they have.
2. Interest: The customer starts to research and gather information about potential solutions to their problem or need.
3. Evaluation: The customer compares different options and evaluates the pros and cons of each.
4. Purchase: The customer makes a decision and purchases a product or service.

Situational influence refers to the external factors that can impact a customer's decision-making process at each stage of the buying process. For example:

- Time pressure can impact a customer's decision to purchase quickly or delay the purchase.
- Social influence can impact a customer's decision by the opinion of family, friends, and online reviews.
- Physical surroundings can impact a customer's decision by the location, atmosphere and layout of the store.

By understanding the buying stage and situational influence, businesses can create more effective marketing campaigns, improve the customer experience, and increase the likelihood of making a sale.

Models of consumer behaviour-Economic model. teaming model. sociological model

1. The economic model of consumer behaviour is based on the theory of consumer choice, which states that consumers make rational choices based on their budget and preferences in order to maximize their utility or satisfaction. According to this model, consumers have a certain budget and a set of preferences, and they will choose the combination of goods and services that gives them the most satisfaction for the money they have to spend. This model assumes that consumers have complete information about all the products and services available to them and that they make rational decisions based on that information.

2. The psychological model of consumer behaviour, on the other hand, focuses on how consumers perceive and process information and how this influences their decision-making. This model emphasizes the role of emotions, attitudes, and motivation in consumer behaviour. For example, emotions such as fear, desire, and trust can influence the way consumers perceive and evaluate products and services. Attitudes, on the other hand, are a consumer's overall evaluation of a product or service, and they can influence the consumer's behaviour towards it. In addition, motivation is another key aspect of this model. It is the driving force behind consumer behaviour and can be influenced by factors such as needs, wants and desires.

3. Finally, the sociological model of consumer behaviour examines the influence of social factors, such as family, friends, reference groups, and culture, on consumer behaviour. This model emphasizes the role of socialization, norms, and values in shaping consumer behaviour. For example, family, friends, and reference groups can influence the consumer's beliefs and attitudes towards

products and services, while culture can shape the consumer's values and norms related to consumption. Socialization also plays a major role in shaping consumer behaviour as people learn about products, services, and consumption through their interactions with family, friends, and other groups.

All of these models have their own strengths and weaknesses, and they offer different perspectives on how consumers make decisions and what influences their behaviour. In reality, consumer behaviour is influenced by a combination of factors, including economic, psychological, and sociological factors.

The public's perception of the quality of a company's goods is a major challenge that must be addressed head-on. Perhaps nowhere is this more of a worry than in the automotive business, where brand recognition is so crucial to sales.

U.S. manufacturers began taking serious measures in 2007 to incorporate technology and developments whose goals were to improve the quality image of domestic vehicles in an effort to counteract the negative stereotypes about the reliability of American automobiles compared to those of cars built elsewhere. Many newer models of cars now come standard with advanced safety features like automatic navigation and parking systems, lane-departure warning, collision avoidance mechanisms, side blind-zone alert, and hands-free communication systems (including calling, radio tuning, climate control, and a concierge service). For example, over the last three years, General Motors has spent over $7 billion per year on R&D, with a significant portion of it going into autonomous driving technology. With the 2017 Cadillac CTS, General Motors hopes to break ground in the automotive industry by introducing vehicle-to-vehicle communication, or "cars talking to each other" to prevent accident.

To compete with and even outdo the imported vehicles, American automakers like Chrysler, GM, Ford, and Tesla have been working tirelessly in recent years. Clean Fleet Report lists many 2016 models from GM, Ford, and Tesla as among the top ten vehicles available for purchase. However, despite the exceptional quality of these vehicles, domestic manufacturers still seem to be fighting an uphill battle to overcome what appears to be a national prejudice against American-made cars.

Automakers inside the United States have made efforts to change buyers' perceptions of the quality of domestic automobiles by highlighting the place where these vehicles are really being manufactured. For instance, Toyota assembles its best-selling Camry in the USA with 90% American-made components. However, 80 percent of the components of a Ford Fusion are made in countries other than the United States. On top of that, the Envision, Buick's most recent SUV concept, is assembled in China from the ground up. Several Japanese and European brands, including as Honda, Toyota, Subaru, Nissan, BMW, and Volkswagen, are also assembled in the USA, a fact that is heavily promoted by the industry. Accordingly, the prevalent belief that vehicles manufactured elsewhere are of higher quality may be unwarranted.

Do you agree with the claim that quality perception is not a "generalized" idea, but rather relies on which particular brand or model is better suited to what an individual happens to be searching for in a vehicle, as the discussion over the quality of import vs domestic automobiles continues? Provide an instance that illustrates your argument. Check out J. D. Powers and Associates at http://www.jdpower.com/ autos/articles/2016 to read up on automobile quality ratings, and check out Clean Fleet Report at http://www.cleanfleetreport.com/ to read up on hybrid and electric vehicle ratings. In regards to the aforementioned advancements in vehicle technology, the question then becomes how well customers will interact with and enjoy all this technology. Will it really aid them, or become an unnecessary hassle for vehicle enthusiasts?

We also keep talking about how perception is affected by things like stimuli, personality, and context.

Limiting principles

The range of perception that a human being is capable of is not infinite. A dog's ability to hear and react to a high-pitched whistle is one example. Psycho- physics is the study of the relationship between external physical stimulus and the subsequent subjective experience. The book delves at how our minds and bodies are connected.

One's absolute threshold, one's terminal threshold, and one's differential threshold (also known as the just-noticeable difference) are the three thresholds that make up one's senses (JND). The lowest possible concentration at which a person may detect a change in their environment is called the absolute threshold. It's the level at which we stop registering the presence of a physical stimulus. In theory, there exists an absolute upper limit for each and every conceivable sensory experience.

When a stimulus's intensity is increased over the terminal threshold, no further increase is felt. Would it improve the flavor of Kellogg's Raisin Bran if I added a third scoop of raisins to the bowl? How would the aroma of Hugo Boss aftershave change if additional perfume were added to the bottle? Do you think Maxwell House Coffee would benefit from having a different blend of coffee beans added to it? An obvious reason why such alterations would be unnecessary is if they increased costs without noticeably improving either quality or flavor.

The differential threshold, also known as the just-noticeable-difference (JND), is the lowest change in stimulus intensity that may be observed by a person and yet be regarded as an increase or decrease. The link between stimulus intensity and the change in intensity needed to make a perceptible difference was first measured by Ernst H. Weber, a pioneer in the study of psychophysics, in 1834. Weber claims that the amount of the JND, the smallest detectable change in stimulus intensity, depends on the intensity at which the stimulus was first presented. If the bulb in your desk lamp is 200 watts, for instance, you probably won't be able to see the difference if you turn it up or down by one watt. The light from a second candle would be readily noticeable in a room lit by a single candle. Similarly, the market would not likely notice a $200 refund for buying a $60,000 BMW, but it would notice a $200 rebate granted by Sears for the purchase of a $500 washing machine.

Insights for Marketers from the JND

Within the realm of marketing, the JND has a variety of possible uses. All of them have to do with how a thing is priced, how big it is, and how it is packaged. Whether or whether a change (such as smaller or larger packaging, a higher or lower pricing, or a different product quality) is intended to be noticeable to customers, marketers still need to estimate the JND.

Discounts of less than 20% off the original price of an item have minimal impact on increasing sales, according to merchants in the clothing industry. Customers will see a discount of 20% or more as substantial. In contrast, if the goal is to sneakily increase prices, businesses may hope consumers won't notice any change. Because of the ever-increasing price of raw materials, this is especially true for manufacturers. There is discussion of raising pricing, which might hurt the company's competitive standing, or switching to a different ingredient set (thereby reducing the quantity or quality of the product). In either situation, the goal is to shift below the JND so as to have the smallest possible negative impact on the firm's ability to compete.

As a means of dealing with price inflation, several businesses have resorted to downsizing (reducing package size while keeping the same price). Philip Morris reduced the volume of their Brim coffee from 12 to 11.5 ounces while maintaining the same can size and retail pricing. Kimberly-Clark has also reduced the quantity of diapers in a package from 88 to 80. These changes effectively increased unit pricing without notifying customers of the increase. 18

Manufacturers and merchants that use the pricing strategy of "price lining," in which just a small range of prices is made available for a given category of goods, are guided by the same underlying principle. Stores catering to female customers may have many pricing points for the same item, such as three lines of dresses with varying levels of quality and detail at different price points. By increasing the price difference between the lines, marketers give the idea that they are vastly different. Customers are less likely to confuse the lines, even if they are quite similar, because of this strategy.

From a moral standpoint, several JND strategies have been called into question, particularly those that require achieving imperceptible decreases in pack-age contents. It is the expectation of the M&Ms candy company that customers would notice the difference between the standard-sized and the bonus-sized packets, hence the company periodically runs sales campaigns in which the latter boasts of 10 percent more candy at the usual selling price.

Perception and its situational influences

In addition to our own traits and the attributes of a product or advertisement, the context in which we make a purchase or utilize a product has a significant influence on our final decision. There are a wide range of emotions that may permeate our being, from elation to depression, from a sense of calm to a sense of urgency. It's not uncommon for us to modify our purchases to fit our current mood and life circumstances. Such actions are manifestations of our present selves, both in terms of our bodily and mental health. A person who is dealing with stress may turn to unhealthy habits like smoking, drinking, or overeating.

Contextual factors are the broader set of conditions that influence consumer behavior and the nature of interactions with brands. Physical environment, social environment, job description, time, and antecedent states are the five types of situational variables. They, together with the stimuli and the individual's own characteristics, affect our interpretation of and reaction to whatever it is we're looking at or experiencing.

Conditions of the Real World

All of the things we can see, hear, touch, smell, taste, and smell at a location make up its immediate physical environment. Midtown Manhattan's Macy's department store, with its ornate fittings and eye-catching displays, is a prime illustration of a certain kind of physical setting. Location, parking, and product selection are all examples of the store's immediate physical environment. Retailers create the impression they want customers to have of their stores by carefully orchestrating the layout (the visible arrangement of merchandise and promotional materials), atmospherics (decor, sounds or music, lighting, aromas, temperature, humidity), customer services, and many other factors, such as employees' dress, presentation, and demeanor. Shoppers' impressions may also be affected by things like store layout, sales, stockouts, and return policies, as well as by external factors like bad weather.

This factor makes the most sense for brick-and-mortar establishments, but it is also relevant to the internet shops that customers frequent.

Individuals' purchasing habits might be influenced by their social environments

To get the intended impact in a digital setting, one has to have a website that is both innovative and appealing. This includes things like a unique logo, digital photographs, print collateral, a rich interactive media presentation, music, Flash, and smart graphic design.

Environments with Other People

The social context is another another set of circumstances to consider. These include the presence of other people in the business, such as family members, employees, or customers, as well as the level of congestion that exists. It's common for young children to beg their parents for junk food when shopping with them, for instance. Salespeople's personalities and demeanor, as well as any nearby human interactions, are also parts of the social environment.

Determining the Role of a Task

A third contextual variable is how a person defines their position throughout the shopping experience, or the tasks they want to do. When it comes to things like clothes for the kids, one parent could step up and take charge. The shopper's motivation for an action may be rooted in the task specification itself. The bottle of wine we bring as a present to the hosts of a dinner party may be quite different from the bottle we would choose for ourselves. Marketers may use the idea of task definition as a foundation to boost revenue. Stores like those do their best to get engaged couples to create wedding gift lists. This service makes it easier for friends and family to contribute to a couple's nuptials by buying presents online.

A View from the Past

As a fourth contextual element, time perspective is essential to consider. Both absolute and relative time frames are possible. Absolute time dimensions include things like time of day, weekday, and season. The passage of time might be considered in connection to a past or future occurrence (such as time since or until meals or a paycheck). Many goods' selling points stem from the time they'll save consumers. It's important to note that customers' actions in the market are affected by both absolute and relative time. Consumers who have to work during the day tend to do their shopping then. After receiving a paycheck, many people feel more financially secure and spend more freely than they do during the interim between paychecks. Similarly, the situation for those who put off their Christmas shopping till the last minute is considerably different from that of those who get it all done in plenty of time.

The advent of internet shopping has caused a dramatic shift in the traditional shopping experience, particularly with regards to the amount of time spent doing so. Consumers may find a wide range of items and information on where to obtain them at the cheapest prices on the Internet, making online shopping a fast, easy, and handy option. In addition, unlike in traditional shops, the consumer need not waste time getting to the store, negotiating with salespeople, and standing in long checkout lines.

Condition Prior to

The individual's physical or mental condition just before the present state is called the antecedent state and is the fifth situational component. Conditions in the past are transient. Conditions and emotions like these are short-lived and easy to categorize. The availability of funds is a condition of the present moment. Transient emotions include joy, sadness, calmness, anger, relaxation, and elation. Consumers' propensity to shop, the items they purchase, and the amounts they spend are all susceptible to their immediate emotional and environmental states.

Whether acting alone or in concert, contextual elements may have a significant influence on consumers' final decisions. Moreover, they might interact with other product or customer attributes to have an impact on sales. For their anniversary, a newly promoted CEO may choose to splurge on her ecstatic spouse rather than get him a shirt.

Knowing a customer's emotional state and having some idea of the context in which their purchase or use of a product will occur may help marketers better anticipate their customers' preferences.

Gestalt psychology

Gestalt psychologists advocate re-framing how one looks at the world. Instead of focusing on the parts of a stimulus, as is the case with the conventional view, this one encourages the observer to generate holistic perceptions based on the entire.

The German term gestalt means "whole impression" or "whole feeling." When we take in information, it is as a whole, or Gestalt, rather of noticing and seeing individual pieces. In reality, we prefer to take in unified wholes and straightforward, whole patterns rather than partial ones.

Also, the marketing team places a higher value on the integrated marketing mix than on the individual components of the marketing mix, such as product features, pricing, channels, and advertising. A consumer's overall impression of a certain business, brand, or corporation is the sum of their experiences with that establishment, acquired via exposure to advertising and other means. Marketers are also aware of how even a little change may have a dramatic effect on the reception of a product, its packaging, or an advertisement. Coca-Cola famously tried to alter the recipe of their most popular product in 1985. Over the course of 190,000 blind tasting tests, participants were asked to choose between the original Coke formula, the new Coke recipe, and Pepsi. It turns out that the new Coke recipe always comes out on top. 22 Because of the public outcry that ensued when the original recipe was discontinued, Coca-Cola has once again made Coke Classic available.

As a rule, consumers' interpretations of environmental stimuli adhere to a set of Gestalt principles known as closure, grouping, proximity, context, and figure and ground. Let's examine their implications for our marketing plans and our customers' opinions.

We have a psychological phenomenon called closure, which causes us to see things as whole even though they are incomplete. When presented with a partial input, our minds automatically fill in the gaps. By engaging with this stimuli directly, we improve our ability to recall its details later on. Soap operas, for instance, thrive because viewers need closure. Fans of a program can't stop watching until the plot is resolved. Similar to how advertisements sometimes employ half-finished images, phrases, or tunes to catch listeners' ears, increase their retention, and ultimately their sales.

Grouping is relevant to a number of Gestalt ideas. Humans have a natural inclination to group information rather than receive it in discrete pieces. We combine data into coherent wholes, allowing us to compare products across several dimensions. Prospective students' impressions of the colleges they are considering attending sometimes require categorizing the institutions into several categories. In evaluating these institutions, it is common practice to focus more on the schools' worldwide rankings and reputations as a whole than on the particulars of each one.

According to the Gestalt principle of proximity, two objects may come to be associated with one another just by being physically and temporally close to one another. The proximity of two objects gives the impression that they are linked or belong together. If nuts are located in the same aisle as other high-calorie meals like snack foods or baking supplies, we may subconsciously associate them with fatty treats. Nuts may not seem like a protein-rich snack when we buy them from the grocery store, but when they are stocked beside the health foods, we may think otherwise. Similar to how proximity is related to product placement. Marketers try to make a favourable connection between their products and good icons or scenarios. They also make an effort to link the product or service in question to a positive result.

Similarly, our reactions to stimuli are coloured by the conditions in which they are presented. An piece in the Wall Street Journal would be read and understood quite differently from the identical topic in a supermarket tabloid. A picture of a four-wheel drive car set against a rocky backdrop might convey an idea of the vehicle's toughness. In the same way, a hybrid, electric, or tiny automobile is seen favourably in this age of environmental awareness, fuel scarcity, and skyrocketing gas costs.

The term "figure and ground" implies that things are seen in relation to their ground. The object's interaction with its context is crucial to establishing the intended impression. Gestalt psychologists observe that when putting together a collection of disparate inputs, individuals are more likely to separate those that are more salient from those that are less so. The figure often takes centre stage in advertising formats such as print advertisements, television commercials, and websites, while the text and other visual components take a more subservient role. If the figure is more prominent than the backdrop, the viewer's attention is more likely to be drawn to the figure. This is especially true if the background is out of focus.

So far, we've spoken about the physical and mental processes that work together to create an impression. Consumers' propensity to group items into logical groups or classes is another interesting phenomenon that deserves further investigation. By doing this, the process of purchasing and processing information becomes easier.

Perception classification

Instead of focusing on the specifics of an item, we are more likely to react to it based on the class it belongs to. As a result, we are able to swiftly and easily digest the vast array of stimuli to which we are constantly exposed. A shopper, for instance, encounters an unusual product while grocery shopping. The shopper learns that the product is pasta from its location on the shelf and the design of the packaging. The term "perceptual categorization" describes this mental step. Weighting clues from the stimulus item against potential matches in long-term memory allows us to classify items. Typical responses to items in a certain category may be expected. We may eat pasta if we think it's a healthy and delicious alternative to high-fat meals, but if we don't like it, we won't.

People create both broad categories of products (such as detergents, snacks, and cereals) and specific subsets within those categories (dishwashing detergents and laundry detergents). Quality, durability, prestige, economy, and use occasion are sometimes used to further subdivide the larger group. Filet mignon and ground beef, for instance, are both regarded as foods by customers. However, filet mignon is more costly and is usually saved for exceptional occasions, whereas hamburgers are more commonplace. Retailers make an effort to ensure their wares are properly sorted. Toyota's Lexus and Nissan's Infiniti, for instance, were both designed to compete with and be compared to other luxury automobiles. Both manufacturers created newspaper advertising and commercials featuring the new models next to high-end automobiles like BMWs and Mercedes-Benzes to achieve this goal. Both the Honda Civic hybrid and the Toyota Prius were heralded as progressive green technologies when they were first debuted.

We learned in the chapter before this one about market segmentation that modern-day product marketers don't strive to please everyone with their wares. Even while it's crucial for customers to identify a brand with the category in which it belongs, marketers don't want their products to be mistaken for those of competitors. Positioning strategies, on the other hand, aim to place brands in their proper categories while also emphasizing what makes them stand out from competitors. Manufacturers of analgesic medicines, for instance, would want for their wares to be appropriately categorized as pain relievers, but they don't want customers to mistakenly believe that all pain treatments are equivalent.

The goal of marketing research is to learn how consumers arrive at conclusions about the qualities they want in a given product. They also make an effort to provide customers explicit clues that help them place things in the right categories. Antiseptic hue, medicinal flavour, and tingling feeling are all characteristics of the original formulation of Listerine, which give the impression that it effectively eliminates bacteria. A new jar of peanut butter or container of margarine may be identified by the swirl at the top. One tell-tale sign of quality in a brand new automobile is the satisfying bang of the door.

Variables Used as a Stand-In

Complexity has increased dramatically in recent years, especially in technologically advanced consumer goods. Wi-Fi, high-definition, and three-dimensional televisions, digital cameras, cell phones, and tablets all have dozens, if not hundreds, of uses and capabilities. In many circumstances, consumers have difficulty appraising and evaluating the features and benefits of such products. It takes a lot of effort and expertise for the average user to keep up with the latest features of such items. Consumers simplify their decision-making by relying on replacement cues to classify the brands or their qualities since the general public typically lacks the technical understanding and the time necessary to study, assess, and compare between these brands. In the case of a smartphone purchase, for instance, a shopper may utilize indicators like price and brand name as criteria to help make a final decision. We refer to signals like price and brand as surrogate indications. Surrogate indicators are used to classify products into groups or differentiate across brands of the same kind. For instance, one research found that buyers consider surrogate indications such manufacturer reputation, brand diversity, merchant reputation, and product warranty while making purchases. Brand name, price, and outward appearance are also often used stand-ins for quality. 25 When buyers are given information about a product's quality via things like packaging or a guarantee, such things might act as surrogate indications. Consumers often rely on the product's country of origin as a stand-in for other indicators. An item's perceived worth changes depending on the country of origin. A consumer's propensity to buy a product from a certain country is heavily impacted by their past exposure to the product, as well as their knowledge and impressions about that country. Products from certain nations, such toys or seafood from China, may not fare as well as others, like Japanese automobiles, French perfumes, or Swiss watches.

Consumers often substitute cost for quality, as implied by the proverb "You get what you pay for." When faced with uncertainty, when we lack trust in our ability to judge quality directly, and when we suspect major quality or price fluctuations across brands, we often use price as an indication of quality. As shoppers, we create preconceived views about the going rate for various products, which we then use as yardsticks to evaluate actual market pricing. There is some wiggle room in these projected costs over time. We readjust our pricing expectations in response to changes in the market and to our own past experiences with purchasing decisions when selling prices fluctuate.

While cost is certainly a factor, it is not usually the deciding factor when evaluating quality. Price-quality correlations are not always as strong as one would expect because of other variables such brand names, store visuals, consumer expectations, and past experiences with the brand, as well as particular product-quality qualities. As a result, our overall impressions of a thing are a synthesis of our reactions to its price, to many other exterior signals, and to our evaluations of its inherent qualities.

Conformity to Prototype

Prototype matching describes the human inclination to evaluate product brands by holding them up to the category's exemplar or ideal brand, a phenomena strongly connected to perceptual categorization. Different baggage companies, for instance, may be judged against an industry standard bearer like Samsonite. Accordingly, the degree to which a specific piece of baggage has characteristics with the category exemplar would be used to determine its acceptability. The ability of a dominant brand to influence the industry as a whole may be attributed to prototype matching.

Conclusions forged from perceptions

People are able to link many stimuli in their minds. As a result of this knowledge and their personal experiences with the stimulus, they generate opinions about items, brands, shops, and enterprises. Perceptual inferences are the beliefs that a person subconsciously or consciously assigns to items, brands, or businesses based on various types of past information and experience. Consumers may, for instance, have learned to equate a higher purchase price with a better quality product, leading them to expect greater happiness with their purchases of more costly brands and models.

Marketers may include suitable sensory signals in the design of their products to trigger conclusions about product quality. For instance, the antiseptic scent of Pine-Sol gives the impression that it also kills germs when cleaning. Clive Christian of London's Imperial Majesty perfume is available at Nordstrom for $869 per ounce and comes in a Bac-carat crystal bottle with an 18K gold-plated bottle collar embellished with diamonds.

Insights may be categorized into three distinct categories based on how they were derived from the senses. Inferences drawn from evaluations are those that lead to a generally favourable or unfavourable opinion of the brand in question. If you have a nice time with a Magnavox TV, you could think that everything the company does is top-notch. The halo effect describes this phenomenon. A person's perception of all Magnavox products might be negatively impacted by a single unpleasant encounter with a television (a negative halo effect). A lot of deductions rely on resemblance. By associating novel items with known ones, we may form impressions about the brand they represent. A consumer may think of ketchup when they see a new condiment sold in a tall, skinny container. Other inferences are correlational, based on extrapolating from a broader context to a narrower one. When looking for a headache treatment, for instance, a shopper may assume that a larger pain reliever dose means a quicker acting product. In light of this, it follows that the pain must be alleviated the quickest by the strongest of the brands.

Plans and Programs

Shoppers mentally file away data about products they've sorted into several categories. Those with more shopping under their belts have a more streamlined shopping process because of the more systematic way in which they recollect information. A schema is a mental map that helps you make sense of the world by providing a framework for interpreting and making sense of incoming information. One of the world's largest food manufacturers spent a lot of cash to perfect a method of making ketchup that keeps the tomato's original scent and taste intact. But the ketchup bombed when it hit shop shelves. Why? As a result of the new method, the ketchup no longer has the overdone, burned taste that permeates traditional ketchup. This is the taste that most people associate with authentic ketchup, which is a shame. The company overcooked its ingredients by adjusting its machinery, and the result was a new and superior ketchup that was successfully returned to the market. Many people's expectations of what ketchup should taste like were not met by the original recipe.

Consumers operate under overarching conceptual frameworks that include a variety of specialized schemas. Some people, for instance, have overarching schemas about the various automotive manufacturers, while others have more detailed schemas regarding the many options available to car owners, such as four-wheel drive, convertible tops, manual and automatic transmissions, and so on. Similarly, a person may have overarching store-related schemas and more specific store-specific subschemas, such as those for specialty shops, discount merchants, grocery stores, and corner stores.

We all have mental "scripts" that guide us in acting appropriately in response to situations that are likely to arise again and again. When we buy something online, return an item to a retailer, or negotiate the price of a new automobile, for instance, we follow a script, a predetermined series of actions that is designed to achieve a certain goal. For instance, while purchasing a new automobile, we may

(1) place an order specifying the make, model, style, colour, and other options;

(2) settle on a delivery date;

(3) discuss and settle on a price; and

(4) finalize the terms of a financing arrangement.

Our expectations of where we will be, what will happen, who will be there, what we will do, and what will happen as a result all make up our scripts. They allow us to predict the results of our actions in common scenarios by organizing our prior information about what to do in certain situations. A script, once triggered, directs most relevant behaviour automatically, saving us from having to make numerous conscious judgments in comparable situations. Shopping is made easier using scripts. Instead of systematically categorizing data, we learn habits that eventually lead to the purchase and usage of a product.

Assumptions and visions

Image, in its simplest definition, is a customer's overall perception of a business, product, brand, or shop. Suits from Armani, for instance, project a distinct image than ones from Sears. Images may originate from a variety of sensory inputs, such as media, personal experience, and culturally recognized symbols.

Inspired by Levy's previous writings, Martineau defined image as "the whole collection of attitudes, the halo of psychological meanings, the connections of emotion, the permanently etched aesthetic signals beyond plain physical features."

In other words, consumers' mental pictures of a stimulus's practical and psychological effects are evoked by the term "image." It's the image, character, and emotions that a product evokes in the minds of its buyers.

Manufacturers and merchants that want to attract clients must provide an image that is acceptable to that market. Customers often choose one business or brand over another simply because they have a more favorable mental picture of it in their head. Sometimes, the reputation of a company and the message it sends to customers are more significant than the quality of a product or the price at which it is sold. As a result, it is crucial that businesses understand the myriad of aspects that go into creating a brand's and a store's reputation.

A mental image has numerous components, including perceptions of product features, sorts of individuals who use a brand, and scenarios surrounding brand usage, making image creation a difficult task for marketers. Images may be constructed around concepts such as cost-effectiveness, safety, dependability, enjoyment, social standing, and uniqueness.

The perceived qualities of a thing aren't always the same as its actual qualities. As an example, our preconceived notions of certain foods and drinks heavily influence our actual tastes. Customers often have a hard time believing that brands in the same market segment are so similar. Customers develop brand loyalty less because of actual distinctions between products and more because of image-building efforts put forward by marketers via branding, packaging, price, and advertising. Blind wine tastings at a California vineyard make the importance of brand image immediately obvious. Participants in the study were given blind taste tests of red wines like Merlot and Cabernet Sauvignon. It included wines from Charles Shaw's own winery, as well as pricey competitive California brands and rare French labels. Charles Shaw's wine, which retails for only $2.49 a bottle, has been consistently rated better than similarly priced wines sold by competitors who charge far higher rates. The idea is that the higher pricing and well-known names on the labels of designer wines gave the impression to buyers that they were of superior quality and flavour.

Retail establishments may be pictured in the same way that goods and labels can. When compared to discount retailers like Target, Kmart, Walmart, and Ross, upscale department stores like Bloomingdale's, Saks Fifth Avenue, Nieman Marcus, and Crate &

Barrel present a radically different image. Consumers seek for retailers that reflect their own sense of identity while making purchases. When shopping, certain shops might be intimidating, while others are welcoming. For some shoppers, a certain retailer is reliable for acquiring some products but not others. Sears may be seen as a great site to purchase appliances and home decor, but apparel may not be. Though its clothes has a reputation for being less than beautiful, Sears is hoping to change consumers' minds by stocking the Lands' End brand.

Stores can't cater to everyone, so they try to portray themselves in a way that's consistent with the way their target demographic sees itself. The goods selection, customer service, pricing policies, promotional activities, reputation for honesty, community participation, and store atmosphere of a retailer all contribute to the establishment's overall impression. Everything from the interior and exterior layout of the business to the music playing in the background and the scent of freshly baked goods all contribute to the company's "atmosphere," which is intended to evoke a positive emotional response from consumers and encourage them to make a purchase. Store fixtures, retail displays, wall and floor coverings, lighting, colours, noises, aroma, cleanliness, crowd levels, staff, and customers are all examples of interior atmospheric aspects. Location, storefront aesthetic, display windows, entrances, and traffic congestion are all examples of external atmospheric components.

Consumers, interestingly enough, build mental pictures of shops regardless of whether or not the stores themselves want to transmit a certain image to them.

Customers' perceptions of a store's quality were most affected by the number of salespeople per department, even though brand recognition was the most salient factor.

Visuals for Advertisement

Imagination is the mental visualization of sensory data stored in short-term memory. The term "working memory" is used to describe a person's mental capacity to temporarily store and modify information. When giving verbal directions to a friend from out of town, for instance, we often utilize mental imagery to envision the streets, exits, traffic lights, and stop signs in order to better convey our recollection of the trip. There are two main ways in which customers benefit from imagery. This aids in the process of retrieving and articulating previously learned material. Pictures and diagrams of items or circumstances can help customers understand them better.

As a perceptual tool, imagery is crucial in advertising. Advertising is only one industry where drawings play a crucial role in the creation of visuals. You may use images to show the proper way to utilize a product if you want. According to studies, people are more likely to remember a brand name if it is shown in a photograph with the product itself (a technique known as "dual coding"). It is believed that this improved memory recall is due to our exposure to the material in both verbal and visual formats.

Advertising, in particular, plays a vital function in the marketing mix with the other elements, helping to build and maintain a positive reputation for a company, its products, and its retail establishment.

Advertising, due to its visual nature, has been called the "industry of image management," or the process of establishing and sustaining mental representations of a brand or product among consumers.

Alteration of Appearance

Having a good reputation in the eyes of the public is critical to a business's survival. Images might be crystal clear or hazy, very positive or downright unpleasant. Maintaining a good reputation is crucial to the success of any business, thus it's important to take care of the image your company presents to the public. When a company has a poor reputation, it may hinder its capacity to conduct business and possibly put its existence in jeopardy. So, efforts for preserving and restoring youth might be either proactive or reactive, or even defensive.

Until something bad happens and executives are presented with a poor image to fix, management may take a company's good reputation for granted. Changing one's reputation takes time because of how slowly people's opinions may shift. There is no shortage of firms in business history that have had to deal with the problem of improving their public image. Target's massive customer data security breach, Volkswagen's diesel emission scandal where the company intentionally masked true emission levels of diesel-powered cars, Johnson & Johnson Baby Powder containing talc for feminine hygiene that contributed to ovarian cancer in women, Takata's controversy over defective and potentially lethal airbags that inconvenienced millions of American car owners, and Toyota's cover-up of a safety recall involving faulty and potentially lethal accelerator pedals all come to mind.

Howard Sheth model of buying

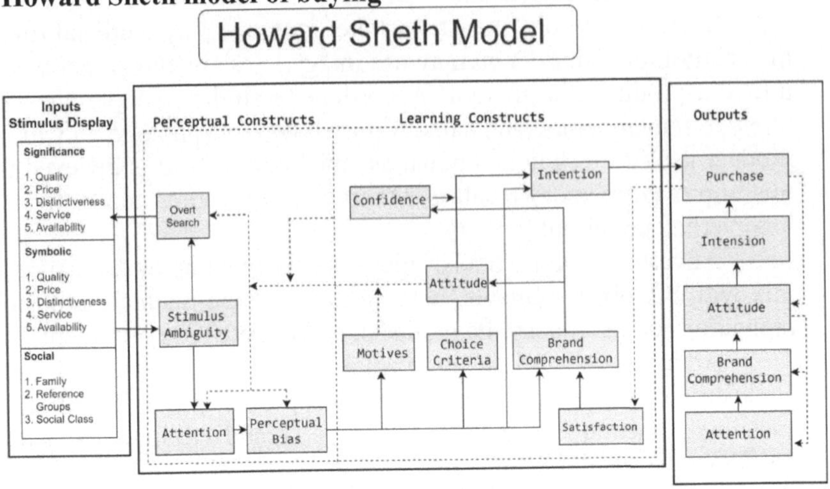

The Howard Sheth model of buying is a widely recognized model of consumer decision-making that describes the complex process that individuals go through when making a purchase. The model was developed by John Howard and Jagdish Sheth in the late 1960s and early 1970s, and it has since become a fundamental framework for understanding consumer behavior.

The model describes a dynamic, non-linear process that involves multiple stages, each of which is influenced by a wide range of factors, including psychological, social, and cultural influences. The stages of the Howard Sheth model of buying include:

1. Problem recognition: This is the stage at which the consumer becomes aware of a need or want that they would like to satisfy. This stage is triggered by internal or external stimuli, such as a change in lifestyle or a marketing campaign.
2. Information search: After recognizing a need or want, consumers will begin to search for information to help them evaluate potential solutions. This can include searching for information online, talking to friends and family, or consulting experts.
3. Evaluation of alternatives: Once the consumer has gathered information, they will begin to evaluate the various options available to them. This stage involves weighing the pros and cons of different alternatives and determining which one best meets the consumer's needs and wants.
4. Purchase decision: After evaluating the alternatives, the consumer will make a final decision about which product or service to purchase. This decision is influenced by a wide range of factors, including price, quality, and brand reputation.

5. Post-purchase evaluation: After making a purchase, the consumer will evaluate their decision to see if it met their expectations. If the product or service did not live up to expectations, the consumer may return it or seek a refund.

The Howard Sheth model of buying emphasizes the importance of psychological and social factors in the decision-making process. For example, the model suggests that consumers are influenced by their beliefs, attitudes, and values, which can shape their perceptions of different products and services. Additionally, the model suggests that consumers are influenced by the opinions and behaviors of those around them, such as friends and family members.

In addition to its theoretical contributions, the Howard Sheth model of buying has practical applications in marketing and consumer research. For example, it can be used to guide the development of marketing strategies, such as how to best target different segments of the population and how to create effective advertising campaigns. Additionally, the model can be used to evaluate the effectiveness of different marketing tactics, such as how well a particular advertising campaign resonates with consumers.

Overall, the Howard Sheth model of buying is a widely recognized framework for understanding consumer behavior. It describes a complex, dynamic process that is influenced by a wide range of factors, including psychological, social, and cultural influences. It has practical applications in marketing and consumer research and is important for understanding the consumer decision-making process.

5

ATTITUDE AND CONSUMER BEHAVIOUR

Attitude and consumer behaviour- Meaning of attitude

From the beginning of the field, attitude has been one of social psychology's primary foci of inquiry. Attitude is a term used to describe how we feel about and react to other people, topics, events, circumstances, etc. Attitude is one of the most overused words in popular culture and in our regular conversations. It is often said that:

"I can't decide whether I like Rohan or not."

When asked, "Do I have good or bad thoughts and sentiments regarding dogs as pets?" or "Does my co-worker, Anand, have an attitude problem?"

People often support worldwide nuclear non-proliferation and the death penalty for sexual predators.

These comments all touch with attitudes in one way or another. The purpose of this lesson is to define and explicate the concept of attitude. The parts, varieties, and roles of attitude will be further upon. Moreover, we will discuss the theory and method behind how attitudes are first formed and how they evolve over time. The problem of how one's outlook affects one's actions will also be addressed. Lastly, we'll grasp the idea, procedure, and importance of persuasion.

WHAT DOES "ATTITUDE" MEAN?

Although the word "attitude" appears often in everyday speech, social psychologists adopt a narrower definition. Several social psychologists have attempted to provide their own expressions of what attitude is, but Gordon Allport's (1935) definition remains one of the most widely accepted and widely cited. Allport defined attitude as "a mental and neural state of readiness, organized through experience, exerting a directive or dynamic influence upon the individual's response to all objects and situations to which it is related." There are three facets of attitudes that are described in the definition.

First, attitudes are mental and neurological states of readiness, as defined by Allport. By implication, this view holds that other people's opinions and perspectives are irrelevant and unobservable. Attitudes can only be accessed by the person who has them. Attitudes can only be measured indirectly via the use of social psychological instruments.

Second, the definition stresses that attitudes are formed and structured via life experiences. This suggests that the experiences we have with our families, neighborhoods, peer groups, workplaces, and wider societies serve as the seedbed from which our perspectives towards different individuals, topics, events, and circumstances emerge. This theory, however, disregards the influence of genetics in favor of social learning when it comes to shaping one's worldview.

Last but not least, the definition argues that an individual's attitude acts as a directive or dynamic impact on how they react to everything associated with that attitude. Attitudes, therefore, aren't only the things we feel or believe about other people, topics, events, or circumstances; they also shape and foretell how we'll react to them in the future.

AN ANALYSIS OF THE COMPOSITION OF PERCEPTIONS

There are three interconnected aspects of an attitude:

The cognitive aspect of an attitude consists of the person's mental representations and interpretations of the attitude's object. The cognitive aspect of an attitude further directs how we take in data about the object of that attitude. Attitudes are formed first by 'factual' assessments of the qualities of the attitude object, leading to either a positive or negative judgment of the object. Once an opinion is formed, it influences how we take in, process, and act upon data from the external world.

Each attitude has a good or negative emotional underpinning, or affective component. Emotional reactions, whether positive and negative, are triggered by this affective sensation in response to the attitude abhorrent. This is where feelings of approval or disapproval of the attitude object come from.

We are predisposed to react to the object of our attitude in a way that is congruent with our attitude, as shown by the behavioural component.

Although these three elements are separate actions, they work together as one to convey the mood. Since they are all part of the same mindset, they act in the same way. A person with a preconceived notion that polythene bags are harmful to the environment is more likely to actively seek for evidence to back up that belief. They will find the consumer products bundled in polythene bags to be offensive. Even more so, he or she refuses to use polythene bags for personal items. This ensures internal coherence within the attitude framework. Attitude changes in one component cause shifts in the other two because of the feedback loop established by their mutual effect. The attitude becomes dynamic as a result of this process.

STATEMENTS OF MIND

Typically, we voice our opinions as we see fit. We are self-aware of the impact of our beliefs and values on our actions. Those views are said to be "explicit" in the field of psychology. Because of their conscious nature, the cognitive processing and behavioral effects of the explicit attitudes are readily apparent to us. The process of evaluating and carrying out decisions within your control activates your explicit attitudes. Consider the case of our awareness of our opinion and sentiments regarding a certain brand of toothpaste.

How One's Attitude and Oneself Alter

The way we think about other people and the actions we do as a result of it is called social cognition (buying or not buying toothpaste of that brand).

Many other attitudes, however, operate entirely subconsciously. An implicit attitude describes these kinds of beliefs. Implicit attitudes, in contrast to explicit ones, are governed by unconsciously triggered appraisal and carried out in behaviour without the holder's knowledge. Therefore, implicit attitudes naturally influence behaviour, with no need for intentional thinking or awareness.

It is considered that as individuals create new attitudes, they often replace their old ones. A new attitude does not replace an older one when it is formed, according to a model of dual attitudes given by Wilson, Lindsey, and Schooler (2000). However, the two perspectives do not conflict with one another. When a person adopts a new viewpoint, that viewpoint comes to be known as their "explicit attitude," whereas their "implicit" viewpoints are retained in memory but are no longer actively used. According to research, 'subconscious' level implicit attitudes are manifested in behaviour when the old attitude finds an appropriate setting or is "primed" by the situation.

Nature and characteristics of attitude

As with skills, attitudes may be taught and then remembered for a long time. And in many situations, they become fundamental to who we are. There are several ways in which they benefit the user.

As an adaptive and instrumental mechanism, the formation of favourable attitudes toward rewarding items and unfavorable attitudes toward those that obstruct or punish us goes hand-in-hand. Attitudes, beliefs, and points of view that are considered acceptable in a given society are taught in this way. Therefore, once formed, attitudes offer us with a straightforward and effective method of assessing items. When students are rewarded for appropriate behavior and disciplined when they are not, they learn to develop a favorable attitude toward school discipline.

Attitudes help us grasp and explain the complexities of the social world by providing us with simpler categories for a wide range of social stimuli (people, events, circumstances, and so on). The social world acquires significance and credence for our conclusions about its members based on our beliefs and expectations about the object category. Such functions of attitudes include, for instance, our strong biases and stereotyped ideas about a certain ethnic group. As a result, we may use these attitude schemas to anticipate the actions of individuals who fall into these groups with minimal mental effort.

As a form of self-expression, attitudes help people establish, strengthen, and improve their sense of self-worth. Attitudes often serve as an expression of the holder's core beliefs and a source of affirmation for the holder's sense of identity. Some beliefs are manifestations of a person's group membership. Attitudes have a dual purpose in this way. In the first place, our attitudes and the actions we do in the world reveal our deepest values. And we prefer to adopt a perspective that agrees with our own self-image.

The ego-defensive function of attitudes relates to the ways in which we defend our sense of self-worth or rationalize behavior that leaves us feeling bad about ourselves. Psychoanalytic concepts are in play here; in this role, people use a variety of defensive mechanisms—including denial, repression, projection, rationalization, etc.—in order to prevent emotional distress. A player whose pride has been bruised by a loss in an interscholastic badminton competition could, for example, acquire a negative attitude toward the match referee as a means of self-protection.

Types of attitude

1. Positive attitudes: Positive attitudes are characterized by feelings of favor or approval towards a certain object or situation. These attitudes are associated with positive emotions such as happiness, contentment, and satisfaction. Examples of positive attitudes include having a positive attitude towards a new job, a person, or a particular activity. People who have a positive attitude tend to see the good in things and tend to be optimistic about the future. They are more likely to have a better quality of

life and tend to be more successful in their personal and professional lives.

2. Negative attitudes: Negative attitudes are characterized by feelings of disfavor or disapproval towards a certain object or situation. These attitudes are associated with negative emotions such as anger, frustration, and dissatisfaction. Examples of negative attitudes include having a negative attitude towards a particular political candidate, a certain type of food, or a particular activity. People who have a negative attitude tend to focus on the negative aspects of things and tend to be pessimistic about the future. They are more likely to have a lower quality of life and tend to be less successful in their personal and professional lives.
3. Ambivalent attitudes: Ambivalent attitudes are characterized by having both positive and negative feelings towards a certain object or situation. These attitudes are associated with mixed emotions such as confusion, uncertainty, and indecision. An example of an ambivalent attitude would be someone who is moving to a new city and has mixed feelings about it. They may have heard good things about the city, but also have heard negative things, making them unsure about whether they will like it or not. People with ambivalent attitudes may have a harder time making decisions and may be more likely to change their minds.
4. Latent attitudes: Latent attitudes are attitudes that are not currently active or being expressed, but are likely to be activated in certain situations. They are attitudes that a person has that they may not be aware of and that they may not be able to express. For example, someone may have a latent attitude about a certain political issue that they have not yet formed an opinion on. They may not be able to express their attitude until they are faced with a situation that requires them to do so. Latent attitudes can be difficult to measure and are often inferred from other attitudes or behaviors.
5. Behavioral attitudes: Behavioral attitudes are characterized by observable actions or behaviors towards a certain object or situation. These attitudes are associated with the actions that a person takes in response to a particular object or situation. For example, someone may show a behavioral attitude by choosing to boycott a certain company's products. Behavioral attitudes can be measured by observing a person's actions and can be a more reliable indicator of attitudes than self-reported attitudes.

6. Cognitive attitudes: Cognitive attitudes are characterized by the thoughts and beliefs we have towards a certain object or situation. These attitudes are associated with the way a person thinks about and interprets a particular object or situation. For example, someone may have a cognitive attitude that all politicians are corrupt. Cognitive attitudes can be measured by asking people to explain their thoughts and beliefs about a particular object or situation.
7. Affective attitudes: Affective attitudes are characterized by the emotions we feel towards a certain object or situation. These attitudes are associated with the way a person feels about a particular object or situation. For example, someone may have an affective attitude of anger towards a company that has mistreated its employees. Affective attitudes can be measured by asking people to describe their emotions about a particular object or situation. Affective attitudes are considered more direct and less influenced by cognitive process than cognitive attitudes.

Learning of Attitude

When we are socialized, one of the most significant things that happens is that our attitudes are formed. As we interact with diverse parts of the social environment, we develop opinions about them. These beliefs further influence how we act in various social contexts. The formation of such opinions has been the subject of much study by social psychologists. As a result, social learning is a crucial part of this trajectory of attitude development. These perspectives are acquired via either firsthand encounter or secondhand observation of what is considered to be the "correct" or "wrong" way of thinking by others around us. Below is a brief overview of many mechanisms via which we learn or shape our perspectives.

Simple Disclosing

Just being around something—food, photos, language, advertising slogans, etc.—can trigger favorable emotions. Repeated exposure of research participants to nonsense syllables and Chinese characters resulted in more favorable judgments of both.

This suggests that familiarity may not automatically lead to contempt. People, concepts, and catchphrases that are constantly recycled become like old acquaintances. All one has to do is look at the advertising slogans to see this process at work. Over time, hearing these catchphrases often causes us to warm up to the promoted product. To take it a step further, this preference is reflected in a rise in retail spending. Recent research suggests that the impact of simple exposure is at its strongest when it happens at unpredictable intervals across time, and that repeated exposures may have the opposite effect (Bornstein, 1989). Furthermore, Bornstein (1989) claimed that frequent exposure to neutral or positive stimuli builds liking. However, frequent exposure to what were originally upsetting stimuli may cause that feeling to grow.

Direct Experience

Personal experience is another important means through which people create their opinions and beliefs. A single formative or formative direct personal event may either fortify an already-firm mindset or completely reverse its orientation. Certainly, the devastating effects of the atomic bombs dropped on Hiroshima and Nagasaki during World War II contributed to a widespread and deeply held distaste for such weapons. A person's beliefs and values are more likely to be shaped by their experiences and to influence their actions after they have been internalized. Such beliefs are more resistant to change because people are more prone to look for evidence to back them up.

Conditioning in the Classical Tradition

The process of socialization is the primary means through which we acquire our attitudes. According to the theory of classical conditioning proposed by Pavlov (1927) and used in Social Cognition, learning takes place when a neutral stimulus (conditioned stimulus, CS) is repeatedly paired with a natural stimulus (unconditioned stimulus, UCS), and eventually the CS alone learns to elicit the response (conditioned response, CR) that naturally occurs (unconditioned response, UCR) after the natural stimulus. The ring of a bell, for example, was used in an experiment by Pavlov to demonstrate that dogs could be trained to salivate in response to the stimulus of food. Marketers and PR operatives rely too much on this method to sway public opinion.

Watson, an early proponent of behaviourism, showed how a conditioned negative reaction (fear) might be learned. Little Albert, an 11-month-old child, was conditioned to dread a white rat by Watson and Rayner in 1920. At first, the youngster didn't seem to be bothered by the rat. The researchers used a loud (unpleasant and aversive) sound immediately behind the boy's head throughout the training phase, as he approached the rat. Little Albert developed a conditioned response after being exposed to the loud sound in the presence of the rat on several occasions, and he eventually learnt to show negative feeling (fear) in reaction to the rat on its own.

However, this process may cultivate more than just bad feelings; it can also foster good ones, like a desire to try new things. Over and over again, advertisers will pair their goods with personalities they believe would make their core demographic feel good. Based on the assumptions of classical conditioning, this should result in a preference for the once neutral brand that has been repeatedly linked to a favorable outcome. Many studies have shown that attitudes may be shaped by the classical conditioning process even when individuals are exposed to stimuli below the threshold of conscious awareness. This is referred to as subliminal conditioning.

Training Using Operant Means

Reflexive salivation in dogs in reaction to the stimuli linked with food, as well as negative emotional responses (fear) to stimuli that have been coupled with unpleasant or aversive sound, may be explained using the principles of classical conditioning. Classical training, however, cannot explain more nuanced behaviours like attitude change. B. F. Skinner, a renowned behaviourist, because they act on the environment to create effects or consequences and labelled these complicated behaviours as operant responses. Responses are learned and reinforced via the use of reinforcement in which are conditioning. In other words, the process of operant conditioning holds that behaviours with subsequent reinforcement are reinforced and more likely to occur. However, the frequency and strength of the behaviours that result from negative consequences are diminished.

As part of the socialization process, parents will often provide youngsters with treats or verbal praise if they make a good point or show good behaviour. When children behave inappropriately, they too face consequences. Even little incentives (praise) and punishments (scolding or neglect) from our parents, extended family, classmates, school, job colleagues, etc., have a significant impact on our behaviour. Once we've joined a group, we adopt its values and norms in order to reap the benefits and avoid the drawbacks of membership. In this manner, we acquire our fundamental beliefs about God and government. Sometimes our prior beliefs and values don't mesh well with the new community we've joined. Therefore, we tend to modify our old attitude and develop a new one similar to that of the newly joined group in order to satisfy the need to fit in with others in the new group and to obtain reward for having the same attitudes as others in the new group.

Understanding Through Observation

Attitudes are typically formed in the absence of immediate positive or negative reinforcement in the social sphere. It's very uncommon for us to pick up prejudices, bigotries, and other attitudes from our parents or friends just by witnessing how they handle similar situations. Our ability to pick up new habits just by seeing and mimicking the actions of others around us in a given situation is known as observational learning or modelling.

Attitudes are formed by a process of observational learning, which is explained by the mechanism of social comparison (Festinger, 1954). In point of fact, the social world is not black and white, such that we may confidently declare one viewpoint to be correct while dismissing the opposing one as incorrect. Accordingly, we assess the appropriateness of our own worldviews by contrasting them with those of other people. When our perspectives align with those of other people, we tend to feel validated in our own thinking that we are on the correct track. When we don't think for ourselves, we tend to adjust our demeanour to fit in with that of others around us.

Contrary to popular belief, we do not compare our opinions with members of any random group, but rather with individuals with whom we have a same identity. Therefore, we only have these communities to gauge our own beliefs and values against. According to this theory, we shape our opinions to reflect our desire to be like the people we like and different from the people we don't. Disagreement with individuals we care about causes us discomfort, therefore we often adopt the viewpoints of those we like or those who serve as a reference group in order to escape that unease.

Factors Related to Heredity

Recent research have provided actual data that shows there is more similarity of views among identical twins than between fraternal twins. This supports the idea that our strong sentiments, likes and dislikes, have their origin in our genetic makeup. There was no difference in personality between identical and fraternal twins raised in the same environment. These results imply that certain dispositions are innate and based on our genetic make-up. He speculated that our innate physical, sensory, and cognitive capacities, as well as our temperament and personality characteristics, are the sources of these inclinations.

Alter your perspective.

Elections are held in democracies like India's to choose which political party would serve as government. However, it is not uncommon for the opposition party to gain support from voters and unseat the incumbent. As a result, even entrenched opinions may be altered. A person who formerly had a favourable view on nuclear weapons may come to oppose them. Changing one's attitude is the act of switching one's emotional valence from positive to negative.

In order to understand this phenomenon, social psychologists suggest two distinct models. The two strategies contrast in terms of how they bring about a shift in perspective. One theory places the onus of attitude shift squarely on the individual (cognitive consistency approach). The other viewpoint, however, places more emphasis on exogenous factors in influencing behavioral shifts (persuasion).

Consistency Theory

There are three parts to a situation, as seen through the lens of balance theory: the subject (P), the object (O), and the attitude (X). As far as Heider is concerned, there are two distinct kinds of connections between components: emotional and structural. Examples of sentiment relationships include Rohan's fondness for coffee, Sandhya's advocacy for a cashless economy, and Nitesh's enthusiastic support of the Mumbai Indians in the Indian Premier League. Examples of unit relationships include Ritesh's collaboration with Omkar, Gaganhas's preparation of a proposal for a cashless economy, and Mukesh's ownership of the Mumbai Indians. The presence or absence of a positive (+) or negative (-) sign indicates a positive or negative (-) signs. Heider suggested that people classify these partnerships as either balanced (constant) or imbalanced (inconsistent). Example: "my enemy's enemy is my friend" is a well-balanced concept since there is a logical reason to like someone who has attacked your opponent. Multiplying the signs together yields a solution for triad balance. A balanced (consistent) cognitive structure results in a beneficial outcome; otherwise, it does not.

One of the main tenets of balance theory is that individuals would want to return to a state of equilibrium if they find themselves in an imbalanced one. According to Heider, this is how society finds its footing again in terms of interpersonal harmony. By exposing participants to the triads "Jim doesn't like Bob, but he enjoys the poetry that Bob wrote," Heider (1958) was able to illustrate this. In light of the circumstances, over 80% of respondents felt it necessary to alter their relationships in some way. Participants were almost unanimous in their recommendation that Jim alter his attitude toward Bob. Three-quarters of respondents advocated for Jim to reconsider his position on the poem. Approximately 5% of respondents proposed altering the unit connection between Bob and the poem by claiming that Bob did not write it.

While Heider's balancing theory may make sense at first glance, it cannot account for the complexities of real-world interactions. The balance theory considers the connection between the triad parts, but it doesn't elaborate on the strength of that connection. While both simple dislike and hostility have a negative connotation, the intensity of each is quite different. Only three-part scenarios are explained by balance theory, although in reality, social interactions are far more complicated. Despite these criticisms, balance theory has found application in a variety of contexts, including research on how people make friendships, respond to criticism, and comply to social norms.

The Concept of Cognitive Dissonance

Numerous opportunities arise in the course of a day for us to display incongruous worldviews and practices. Many individuals, for instance, continue to engage in the behavior of smoking despite being aware of the link between this activity and increased cancer risks (cognition).

This cognitive dissonance causes emotional distress, which in turn motivates a shift in perspective or practice to alleviate the tension and restore equilibrium in one's life. Festinger's theory of cognitive dissonance proposes that we have a psychological force (an inner drive) that works to keep all of our attitudes and beliefs in sync with one another and to prevent discord.

According to the hypothesis of cognitive dissonance, people experience emotional pain anytime they become aware of a contradiction between their own beliefs, values, and behaviours. We have a strong tendency to resolve dissonance, and the greater the dissonance, the more motivated you will be to resolve it. The degree of dissonance may vary according to the relevance and importance of opinions, attitudes, and actions and corresponding to the degree of incongruence between belief and behaviour. It has been proposed that one of three main strategies may be used to alleviate dissonance:

Make a shift in your worldview: Beliefs are often the root cause of inconsistencies between what you do and what you say you believe. When an individual's perspective is deeply held and fundamental to their worldview, it is very improbable that they will change their mind. More importantly, we tend to be resistant to altering our most fundamental worldviews. As a result, the easiest method of easing cognitive dissonance is seldom used.

In many cases, the dissonance may be eliminated by simply altering the offending behavior. Someone who continues to smoke after learning that tobacco usage increases the risk of developing cancer may decide to quit in order to lessen the cognitive dissonance brought on by this contradiction.

The dissonance may be resolved with the aid of a more sophisticated mode, which we can achieve by altering our interpretation of your behavior. So, we may make excuses for our behavior. People who smoke while knowing it causes cancer may justify their habit by saying things such, "I only smoke when I'm around my friends" or "I smoke to relieve the stress of the day." To put it another way, individuals justify their behavior by re-imagining it in a way that makes it compatible with their behaviors.

Many important social behaviors, including forced compliance, decision making, and effort justification, have been studied and included into the cognitive dissonance hypothesis.

Constraint-Based Conformity

There are numerous moments in our social lives when we are expected to act in a manner that goes against our private or personal beliefs (often due to the pressure of social standards, etiquettes, or duties). If a close friend, for instance, sings horribly, we have to shout his or her praises. Dissonance between belief and conduct is produced by such coerced compliance behaviors (action). Now that you've done something that goes against what you believe, the only way to lessen the cognitive dissonance is to change your mindset.

An experiment was done by Festinger and Carlsmith to check this theory. In the study, participants were asked to describe how engaging they found the activity of rotating pegs in a peg board to their fellow participants waiting in line after they had completed the work for an hour. For their time, they received $20 or $1. According to the study's authors, most participants praised the novelty of the experimental task to those still in line for payment. Participants given $1 rated the boring work as more fascinating than those paid $20, when asked to assess how entertaining the experiment was.

Based on their findings, the researchers concluded that individuals who were compensated $1 had a larger conflict between their beliefs and their actions. This cognitive conflict was addressed by revising the perception that the work was stimulating and rewarding. On the other hand, those who were paid $20 had a compelling motive to see the work positively and experience little to no cognitive dissonance as a result.

Making Choices When There Is Mental Discord

There are many of tough choices to be made in life, and some of them may really mess with your head. For a girl brought up in a traditional Indian family, the choice between getting married and pursuing a job, for instance, might be quite tough. Both options in a dilemma contain drawbacks and benefits, and choosing one eliminates the potential of enjoying the benefits of the other option. Whichever option is chosen, the benefits of the other option will be missed, and this will cause dissonance.

If the individual experiencing dissonance is able to simultaneously increase the appeal of the alternative he or she has selected while assigning less attractiveness or benefits to the rejected choice, dissonance may be lessened. 'Spreading apart the possibilities' is how Brehm (1956) described it.

A Defense of Effort

It seems to reason that individuals would place a higher value on accomplishments that require significant effort. According to Aronson and Mills (1959), this contradiction is amplified when we put in a lot of work for what amounts to nothing. In order to lessen this dissonance, it may help to pretend that the time and energy spent getting there wasn't really all that significant. It is challenging to eliminate dissonance in this manner, however, since such an assumption is unreasonable. To lessen cognitive dissonance, individuals prefer to rationalize their actions by exaggerating the significance of their accomplishments.

Persuasion

As soon as we turn on the TV, we are bombarded with commercials for a wide variety of goods, from clothing to sunglasses, sweets to dental hygiene products, vacation packages to consumer electronics, and so on. An abundance of studies shows that commercials like this have a major impact on our purchasing decisions. The way we feel about specific businesses and goods is altered as a direct result of these commercials. The term "persuasion" is used to describe the process of altering one's beliefs or opinions via such extrinsic communication, whether face-to-face or through textual or visual means.

Persuasion Models with Two Processes

Obviously, certain compelling arguments and advocates are going to have greater success than others. It's also true that some individuals are easier to convince than others. There are two competing explanations for this phenomenon, the elaboration-likelihood model and the heuristic-systematic model. Despite their subtle differences, both models suggest that successful persuasive communication involves a two-step procedure that use distinct channels for conveying the message. The two methods (central/systematic route and peripheral/heuristic approach) need different amounts of brainpower or mental elaboration.

When the receiver is highly motivated and has a high processing capacity to process the content of the message, the communication takes the central/systematic route; however, when the receiver is less motivated and has a low processing capacity to process the content of the message, the communication takes the peripheral/heuristic route, where attention is paid to cues unrelated to the content or quality of the message (refer the figure given below). Attitudes formed through the peripheral path are weaker, more susceptible to counter persuasion, and less accurate predictors of behavior than those formed via the core route.

Numerous elements are taken into account while deciding how to analyze an argumentative communication. When the persuader talks too quickly for thorough and methodical processing, listeners often opt for the more indirect, peripheral approach. The recipient's disposition also plays a significant impact in determining which of the two options is chosen. When the target is in a bad mood, they tend to look for danger everywhere around them, which causes them to digest information in a highly methodical fashion, favoring the center path. Conversely, those who are contented rely on indirect pathways, making them more receptive to subtle signals like the beauty of their source. In addition, the information is digested systematically via the central channel when the attitude is more relevant to the target and has direct influence on him or her. When it comes to less crucial attitudes, however, the peripheral pathway is used to process persuasion efforts. The path of persuasion is also influenced by a variety of personal characteristics. Those who score well on these traits are more likely to process arguments through the central nervous system.

To begin, if the persuader is using the center path in his or her communication, the success of the endeavor to persuade will depend largely on the quality and persuasiveness of the argument advanced by the persuader. The effectiveness of an effort at persuasion depends on the quality and strength of the argument's substance. However, in the case of the peripheral route, numerous characteristics of the message's origin become crucial. Attractiveness, similarity (in terms of shared attitudes, appearance, or social categories), and believability in the problems relevant to the specific attitude are the primary factors in the effectiveness of persuasion attempts.

Model of attitude- Tricomponent attitude model

The Tri-component Attitude Model is a psychological model that aims to explain the nature of attitudes and how they influence behavior. This model suggests that attitudes are not simply feelings, but rather a combination of different elements that can influence behavior. According to this model, attitudes are composed of three distinct components: affective, behavioral, and cognitive.

The affective component refers to an individual's emotional reaction to an attitude object. This could be a positive or negative feeling, such as liking or disliking something. For example, a person who has a positive attitude towards a brand of chocolate may have a good emotional feeling when they think about it or consume it. On the other hand, a person who has a negative attitude towards a particular political candidate may experience feelings of anger or frustration when they think about that person.

The behavioral component refers to an individual's actions or tendencies towards the attitude object. This can include things like avoiding or seeking out the attitude object. For example, a person who has a positive attitude towards exercise may make a point to go for a run or hit the gym regularly. On the other hand, a person who has a negative attitude towards smoking may avoid places where people smoke and may actively try to quit the habit.

The cognitive component refers to an individual's beliefs and evaluations about the attitude object. This can include things like facts, stereotypes, or other information that the person has learned or formed an opinion on. For example, a person who has a positive attitude towards recycling may believe that it is good for the environment and that it is something that should be done regularly. On the other hand, a person who has a negative attitude towards a particular race may believe that members of that race are lazy or criminal.

The Tri-component Attitude Model suggests that attitudes are not simply feelings, but rather a combination of different elements that can influence behavior. Affective, behavioral and cognitive components are interrelated and influence each other. The affective component can influence the behavioral component, for example, a positive feeling towards a brand can influence the behavior of purchasing that brand. Similarly, a cognitive component can influence the affective component, for example, having a knowledge about the environmental benefits of recycling can create a positive feeling towards recycling.

It's also important to note that attitudes are not always consistent with behavior and cognition, for example, a person may have a negative attitude towards smoking but still smoke. This is known as attitude-behavior gap. Attitudes can change over time, as new information, experiences, or other factors can influence the affective, behavioral, or cognitive components.

In conclusion, the Tri-component Attitude Model is a psychological model that describes attitudes as a combination of three components: affective, behavioral, and cognitive. This model suggests that attitudes are not simply feelings, but rather a combination of different elements that can influence behavior. It helps to understand how attitudes are formed, how they influence behavior and how they can be changed. Understanding the components of attitudes can also be helpful in developing effective strategies for attitude change.

Multi-attribute attitude model

A multi-attribute attitude model is a theoretical framework used to understand and predict how individuals form attitudes towards a particular object or concept. It is based on the idea that attitudes are formed based on the individual's evaluation of multiple attributes or features of the object. These attributes can include things like the object's perceived benefits and drawbacks, the individual's personal values and beliefs, and the social context in which the attitude is formed.

One of the most widely used multi-attribute attitude models is the Fishbein model, which suggests that attitudes are formed by the weighted sum of the individual's evaluations of the object's attributes. In this model, attitudes are represented as a function of the individual's beliefs about the object (i.e., their perceptions of the object's attributes) and their evaluations of those beliefs (i.e., the extent to which they find the object's attributes to be desirable or undesirable). The Fishbein model also incorporates the idea that the individual's beliefs about the object are influenced by their personal values and the social context in which the attitude is formed.

Another popular multi-attribute attitude model is the multi-attribute utility theory model, which suggests that attitudes are formed by the individual's assessment of the relative importance of the different attributes of the object and their evaluations of those attributes. This model is similar to the Fishbein model in that it also incorporates the idea that the individual's beliefs and evaluations are influenced by their personal values and the social context.

Multi-attribute attitude models have been used to explain and predict a wide range of attitudes and behaviors. For example, they have been used to understand and predict consumer behavior, such as how individuals evaluate and choose products, or how they form attitudes towards different brands. They have also been used to understand and predict attitudes towards social issues, such as how individuals evaluate and respond to different political candidates or policies.

One of the main advantages of multi-attribute attitude models is their ability to provide a comprehensive and detailed understanding of how attitudes are formed. By taking into account multiple attributes and factors that influence the attitude, these models can provide a more complete picture of the individual's attitude than models that focus on a single attribute or factor. Additionally, multi-attribute attitude models can be used to design interventions that aim to change the attitude in a desired way, by manipulating the various attributes and factors that influence the attitude.

However, there are also some limitations to multi-attribute attitude models. For example, these models can be complex and difficult to use, particularly when they involve a large number of attributes and factors. Additionally, these models can be difficult to test and validate, since they often involve multiple dependent and independent variables. Despite these limitations, multi-attribute attitude models remain an important tool for understanding and predicting attitudes, and continue to be widely used in a variety of fields.

In conclusion, multi-attribute attitude models are theoretical frameworks used to understand and predict how individuals form attitudes towards a particular object or concept. They are based on the idea that attitudes are formed based on the individual's evaluation of multiple attributes or features of the object, such as its perceived benefits and drawbacks, personal values and beliefs, and the social context in which the attitude is formed. These models have been used to explain and predict a wide range of attitudes and behaviors and can provide a comprehensive and detailed understanding of how attitudes are formed. However, these models can be complex and difficult to use, and there are some limitations to them.

The consumer decision making process

The consumer decision making process refers to the steps that a consumer goes through in order to make a purchase. These steps include:

1. Problem recognition: The consumer recognizes a need or want for a product or service.
2. Information search: The consumer seeks out information about potential products or services that could fulfill the need or want.
3. Evaluation of alternatives: The consumer evaluates the different options available, taking into account factors such as price, quality, and features.
4. Purchase decision: The consumer makes a decision to purchase a specific product or service.
5. Post-purchase evaluation: The consumer evaluates the product or service after using it, determining whether they are satisfied or dissatisfied with their decision.

It's worth noting that not all consumers go through all these steps, and the process may be different depending on the product or service, the consumer's prior knowledge or experience, and the buying situation.

Levels of consumer decision

The five levels of consumer decision making are a model that describes the process that consumers go through when making a purchase. These levels are problem recognition, information search, evaluation of alternatives, purchase decision, and post-purchase evaluation.

Problem recognition is the first step in the consumer decision making process. This is when the consumer realizes that they have a need or want for a product or service. This need or want may be triggered by an internal or external stimulus. For example, a consumer may realize that they need to buy a new pair of shoes because their old ones are worn out, or they may see an advertisement for a new pair of shoes that catches their attention.

Once the consumer recognizes their need or want, they will begin to gather information about potential products or services that can satisfy that need or want. This is known as the information search stage. Consumers may gather information from a variety of sources such as advertisements, word-of-mouth, and personal experience. They may also use the internet to research products and services, read reviews, and compare prices.

After the consumer has gathered all the information they need, they will then evaluate the various options available to them. This is the evaluation of alternatives stage. Consumers will use the information they have gathered to compare the different products and services, and determine which one best meets their needs or wants. They may also consider factors such as price, quality, and brand reputation when making this decision.

Once the consumer has evaluated the alternatives, they will make a purchase decision. This is the stage where the consumer decides which product or service to buy. They may also decide not to make a purchase if they do not find a suitable option.

The final stage in the consumer decision making process is the post-purchase evaluation. This is when the consumer evaluates their satisfaction with the product or service they have purchased. They may also compare their satisfaction with their expectations, and if they are not satisfied, they may decide to return or exchange the product.

It's important to note that not all consumer decisions go through all five levels, and some consumers may jump through these stages or may go back and forth between them. For example, a consumer may recognize a need or want, evaluate the alternatives and make a purchase decision, all in one step. Or, they might have bought a product before and based on their post purchase evaluation they might decide to stick with the same product in future. Additionally, the consumer decision making process can be influenced by various factors such as personal, psychological, social and cultural factors which may vary from person to person.

Marketers and businesses can use the five levels of consumer decision making to better understand their target market and create effective marketing strategies. By understanding the different stages that consumers go through when making a purchase, businesses can tailor their marketing efforts to address the needs and wants of their customers at each stage. They can also use this understanding to create a positive post-purchase experience, which can lead to repeat business and customer loyalty.

Consumer information processing model

The Consumer Information Processing (CIP) model is a framework that describes the way consumers process information when making decisions. The model consists of five stages: exposure, attention, comprehension, attitude formation, and behavior.

1. Exposure: This is the first stage of the CIP model, in which the consumer is exposed to a marketing stimulus, such as an advertisement or product. This stage is important because if the consumer is not exposed to the stimulus, they will not be able to process it further.
2. Attention: In this stage, the consumer pays attention to the stimulus and selects which information to process further. This

stage is important because the consumer has a limited amount of cognitive resources and can only process a certain amount of information at a time. Factors such as relevance, personal interest, and repetition can influence which information the consumer chooses to attend to.

3. Comprehension: In this stage, the consumer interprets and understands the meaning of the information. This stage is important because if the consumer does not understand the information, they will not be able to form an attitude or take action.
4. Attitude formation: In this stage, the consumer forms an attitude or opinion about the stimulus. This stage is important because the consumer's attitude can influence their behavior. Factors such as the consumer's prior knowledge, beliefs, and emotions can influence the attitude they form.
5. Behavior: In this stage, the consumer takes action based on their attitude, such as making a purchase or taking no action. This stage is important because it represents the ultimate goal of the marketing effort.

It's worth noting that this model is not a rigid or linear process and it's subject to change based on the context and the individual's personal characteristics. Additionally, it's important to note that not all five stages may be present in every decision-making situation, and the order of the stages may vary depending on the individual and the situation.

The Hierarchy of Effects model

The Hierarchy of Effects model is a theoretical framework used in marketing and advertising to describe the stages a consumer goes through when making a purchase decision. The stages of the model include:

1. Awareness: The consumer becomes aware of the product or brand. This is the first stage of the Hierarchy of Effects model and it's where the consumer first becomes aware of the product or brand. This can happen through advertising, word-of-mouth, or other forms of promotion. The goal of this stage is to make the product or brand known to the consumer.
2. Interest: The consumer develops an interest in the product or brand. Once the consumer is aware of the product or brand, they may start to show interest in it. This can happen if the product or brand is relevant to the consumer's needs or interests, or if it is

unique or innovative. The goal of this stage is to get the consumer to want to learn more about the product or brand.

3. Evaluation: The consumer evaluates the product or brand and compares it to alternatives. At this stage, the consumer is considering purchasing the product or brand and compares it to other similar products or brands. They may look at factors such as price, features, and reputation. The goal of this stage is to convince the consumer that the product or brand is the best choice.
4. Trial: The consumer makes a small purchase or uses the product to test it out. After evaluating the product or brand, the consumer may decide to try it out. This can happen through a small purchase, or by using a sample or trial version of the product. The goal of this stage is to provide the consumer with a positive experience that will lead to a full purchase.
5. Adoption: The consumer fully adopts the product or brand and continues to use it. If the consumer has a positive experience with the product or brand during the trial stage, they will adopt it and continue to use it. This is the final stage of the Hierarchy of Effects model, and it's where the consumer has fully made the decision to purchase and use the product or brand. The goal of this stage is to create customer loyalty and repeat purchases.

It's worth noting that the Hierarchy of effects model is a simplified version of consumer decision making process. Consumers might not go through these stages in a linear fashion, different consumers may have different journey and the decision making process can be influenced by many factors.

What Influences People's Decisions

There are four parts to every successful persuasion process: the origin, the content, the delivery method, and the target demographic. The persuasive effort's success or failure depends on the characteristics of a number of these factors.

The Origins

First and first, it's the communicator's abilities that make all the difference in persuasiveness. It's common to observe that the reception of essentially identical arguments delivered by various speakers varies widely. Sources high on the credibility scale have greater sway than those low on the scale. When we see a communicator as knowledgeable and trustworthy, we are more likely to believe what they say. At first, Hovland and Weiss (1951) asked participants to rate how they felt about nuclear submarines. Each participant in the study was given the same message about nuclear submarines to read a week later. But in one group, they were informed that the communication came from the renowned physicist Robert J. Oppenheimer, who would be a very trustworthy source. However, the remaining participants were informed that the message originated from Pravda, the journal of the Soviet Union's Communist Party at the time. The study's researchers may have unfairly assumed that the U.S. participants would see this as a low-credibility source. After the message was read, participants' opinions on nuclear submarines were reassessed immediately. According to the findings, those whose beliefs were influenced by a message from an apparently reliable source shifted their views more than those whose beliefs were influenced by a message from a less plausible source.

People's opinions are more easily swayed when the persuader is charismatic and likeable. As a general rule, we agree to purchase a product because we like the beautiful model used to market it. Fast talkers are more persuasive, according to certain studies. Speaking quickly gives the appearance that one is knowledgeable and fluent in the subject matter being discussed.

What It Says

One of the most significant aspects of a persuasive message is the emotional investment the audience has in it. Attaining one's goal via persuasion is aided by the presence of positive emotions, whether they are artificially created by the message or naturally existing in the surroundings. Researchers Dabbs and Janis (1965) found that when students were given peanuts and Pepsi to snack on while reading the message, they were more receptive to the persuasive argument. In reality, when people are in a good mood, their brains process information differently, and they pay less attention to the details of the messages they receive.

Messages encouraging people to quit smoking, refrain from engaging in risky sexual behavior, not drink and drive, etc., often include fear-inducing language. The dire repercussions of engaging in such behavior are made very clear in these warnings. When the target audience is made to feel a little uneasy, the message sinks in much more deeply. Extremely frightening communications, they said, actually scare listeners, prompting them to respond with robust rebuttals and denial.

There are communications whose whole structure is to give counterexamples. In contrast, some communications are crafted to offer just one side of an issue. Many academic studies have shown that two-way communication is more persuasive than one-way communication. The audience is more likely to be persuaded by such efforts if they believe that the two-sided communications were not purposely structured to alter the attitude. On the other hand, audiences react more negatively to one-sided communications since they seem to have been crafted with the intention of influencing the recipient's viewpoint.

The Strait of Gibraltar

Some efforts at persuasion essentially relay the speaker's words to the listeners. However, persuasive messages may also be delivered via more hands-on, experienced methods. Research shows that although some degree of persuasion may result from just receiving the message, this effect diminishes as the importance and relevance of the topic grow. An issue's potential for effectiveness as a tool of persuasion increases when it has personal significance to the target audience.

Research shows that direct, one-on-one communication with an audience is more effective than mass media in influencing behavior. Eldersveld and Dodge (1954) conducted research on the influence of several factors on political voting behavior and found that direct, personal contact had the greatest impact. The participants were split into three categories for the study. The first set only saw the news and movies (a control group). The support of just 19% of the group's voters was needed to pass the amendment. The second group was sent four individual emails urging them to vote for reform. Forty-five percent of the voters in this were in favor of alteration. The final set of voters had personal visits made to them and heard an impassioned call to action in person. The results showed that 75% of the third group voted in favor of the amendment.

The degree to which individuals are persuadable varies greatly. Some individuals are quite receptive to persuasion, while others put up significant resistance. People with low self-esteem are more receptive to persuasion than those with strong self-esteem. The ability to persuade an audience increases when they are distracted from the message, according to research. Additionally, compared to an older audience, persons in formational age, that is, teens and early adults, are more receptive to being persuaded.

Reluctance to be Convinced

It's true that persuasion often succeeds in altering our perspectives, but this is not always the case. Attempts to persuade many individuals fail miserably because they are met with stubborn resistance. The degree to which a target audience will resist persuasion depends on a variety of circumstances.

Reactance

Everyone needs the independence to form their own opinions and stand firm on problems. Anger rises when a skillful persuader uses coercion to force us to alter our opinions or beliefs against our will. This means that we not only push back against persuasive tactics, but often end ourselves strongly leaning in the other way (Brehm, 1966). This inclination toward reactance is amplified when an individual perceives the persuasive endeavor as a direct danger to his or her image as an independent person, and this individual is highly driven to safeguard his or her attitude from being changed. There is evidence that weaker or more moderate arguments are more persuasive in circumstances when reactance is triggered than stronger ones.

Forewarning

Numerous scenarios exist in which we have prior knowledge that a persuasive message has been constructed with the express purpose of altering our beliefs or values. If we turn on the TV during commercials, for instance, we know that the ads we see are crafted to increase the likelihood that we would purchase the advertised goods. In the same way, we know that political campaign speakers will advocate for a certain party's platform when we listen to them. Forewarned audiences have been shown to be less receptive to persuasive messages, according to studies (Johnson, 1994). With foreknowledge of the message's goal, we can fortify our perspective against any attempts to sway it. As a result, our minds are more prepared to defend our beliefs in these settings.

Attitudes become integral to who we are, so we have a natural inclination to guard them. As a general rule, we pay more attention to data that confirms our preexisting beliefs and ignore data that contradicts them. In order to avoid being influenced by commercials, we often switch channels during commercial breaks. By limiting our exposure to knowledge that runs counter to our beliefs, we may increase the stability and longevity of our held opinions.

Counterarguments

One way to reduce your vulnerability to persuasion is to actively fight against the persuasive message that is at odds with your attitude, as shown by research. This is especially true of long-held beliefs that were originally acquired via careful consideration of compelling evidence. When we defend our pre-existing beliefs by refuting information that runs counter to them, we give ourselves more reasons to maintain those views.

Expressive Value Function

The way consumers feel is often a reflection of their own personal beliefs and sense of identity. Consumers' senses of self-identity and agency are maintained and strengthened by the values-expressive attitudes they adopt. Since customers' views clearly reflect their strong convictions and self-concept, the projection is typically powerful, obvious, and excessive.

Consumers often use this function while making decisions about which things to buy, how much to spend, which discounts to take advantage of, and from which retailers to purchase the goods. Therefore, a buyer who wants to show off his Gandhian simplicity will only buy and wear handloom and Khadi, will only buy from tiny businesses, and can have a negative outlook on public endorsements of lavish spending. Customers often display this type of brazen mentality.

Purpose of Usefulness

Once consumers have determined that the set of alternatives they are considering does in fact contain all the desired attributes, they will determine how their satisfaction (utility) will change in response to changing levels of performance in those attributes. For example, a prospective car buyer will determine how much of a difference, in utility terms, it will make if brand 'x' of car possesses a 4/10 level of performance in fuel-efficiency, as opposed to a 6/10 level of performance. Another example might be a woman purchasing lipstick. The utility function has the benefit of allowing customers to create their own "perfect" brand by blending the effectiveness of many important characteristics.

Models of customer attitude

There are many different approaches that have been tried to model attitudes. Multi-attribute attitude models have become the most popular kind. Read on for a detailed description of it.

Models of Opinion with Multiple Attributes

Consumers' perceptions of different brands may be shaped by a number of factors, and multi-attribute attitude models detail how these factors come together. These models assume that consumers will choose the brand that gets the most positive reviews. In addition, they anticipate that customers would follow the traditional Hierarchy of Effects progression (i.e. Awareness - Interest - Desire - Action).

By analyzing each and every multi-attribute attitude model, we may classify them into one of two broad classes. Models that center on subjects' attitudes about things fall within Class I. Because of this, we refer to them as ATO models. Models that attempt to foretell customers' behavioral intentions to take action fall under Class II. This may include a purchase or a decision not to make a transaction. The acronym BI Model has been used for the purpose of brevity.

Consumers' Reactions to Advertising

A) The Attitude Towards Objects (ATO) Models

While there is a wide range of ATO models to be found in consumer studies, the common denominator is a desire to learn more about the relative weight of various brand attributes, how consumers feel about the presence or absence of those attributes in the available brand alternatives, and how these factors interact when making a final decision.

If you look over the ratings more closely, you'll see that Premier is a median automobile. As a counterpoint, Maruti scores better in categories like minimal maintenance cost and design. The Ambassador automobile was judged to be the very worst. When this is complete, the customer will have the greatest favorable impression of Maruti possible.

Activity

There are, however, many who point out that the ATO models have a significant flaw. They disregard the fact that, often, consumer sentiment does not correlate with actual purchases.

An interested automobile buyer, therefore, while having the most optimistic outlook possible towards the car-buying process,

'Maruti,' may never go so far as to actually purchase it. This occurs when influential individuals have a negative impression of the project or when there is an opportunity to invest the money elsewhere at a higher return. His inability to purchase might be due to external factors beyond his control. To address this shortcoming of alternate assessment, the Behaviour Intentions (BI) model was developed.

Model of Expected Behavior (BI)

In essence, the BI model is an expansion of Fishbein's ATO framework. The model does not provide predictions about actual behavior but rather about planned actions; the model is as follows.

It may be written as B=BI = W1 (AB) + W2 (SN), where

Behaviour (B) Equals Behavior Intention (BI)

Attitude Towards Behavior = Subjective Norm for the Behavior

Both of the weights, W1 and W2, were arrived at experimentally by regression analysis.

Consumers fill out surveys to collect AB and SN. The following equation yields AB:

Where

When compared to Fishbein's ATO Model, which came before it, the above equation contains one key deviation. The BI Model evaluates how confident a person is that engaging in a certain behavior will lead to a desired outcome.

Studies have shown that the BI model outperforms more traditional multi-attribute choice models, however questions have been raised about how the subjective standards are determined (SN). In reality, it's seldom that easy to perform this exercise.

How businesses reacted to what they felt consumers were saying

After analyzing attitude and how it forms, as well as the models, business owners and managers are left to wonder: what are the marketing implications of these findings, and what steps can be taken to effectively MANAGE them?

Specifically, while trying to influence customers' judgment of brand alternatives, marketers might take a single action or a series of related actions. Marketers may first adjust their brand rotation if they discover the evaluations provided by customers to be accurate and authentic. Even more, some businesses may try to alter customer reviews so that they seem more honest and reliable. In addition, marketers may try to change consumers' perceptions of the brand alternative via enhanced communication and other marketing initiatives. In the event of a competitive assessment, however, marketers will also work to influence customers' perceptions of competing brands.

This is achieved by either downplaying the product's performance or disparaging its most important features, where competing products excel. However, there is an alternative route that marketers can take, and that is to either develop new brand attributes or to rediscover and emphasize the brand's neglected attributes. This could also be achieved by modifying the ideal product so that it more closely resembles the marketer's preferred brand.

In conclusion, it's not easy being a marketer when customers are conducting research on different brands. Ultimately, the success of a marketing campaign depends on whether or not its target audience takes the desired next step, in this case making a purchase. The appropriateness of the marketing response will be judged based on the outcome of this question.

The same has been addressed with regards to the notion and functions of consumer attitude, since it is a significant indicator of the buyer's thinking. Additionally, the course has spent considerable time discussing multi-attribute and fundamental concepts. The marketing reactions and ramifications have been studied at length.

REFERENCES:

1. Solomon, M. R. (2017). Consumer behavior: Buying, having, and being (11th ed.). Boston, MA: Pearson.
2. Engel, J. F., Blackwell, R. D., & Miniard, P. W. (2018). Consumer behavior (15th ed.). Boston, MA: Cengage Learning.
3. Hoyer, W. D., & Macinnis, D. J. (2019). Consumer behavior (7th ed.). Boston, MA: Cengage Learning.
4. Kroeber-Riel, W., & Kroeber-Riel, W. (2016). Consumer behavior and marketing strategy (9th ed.). Boston, MA: McGraw-Hill.
5. Schiffman, L. G., & Kanuk, L. L. (2017). Consumer behavior (10th ed.). Boston, MA: Pearson.
6. Solomon, M. R. (2015). Consumer behavior: In fashion (2nd ed.). Boston, MA: Pearson.
7. Foxall, G. R. (2018). Consumer behavior: An applied approach (4th ed.). Boston, MA: Routledge.
8. Nicosia, F. M. (2016). Consumer behavior: A cognitive orientation (2nd ed.). Boston, MA: Routledge.
9. Blackwell, R. D., Miniard, P. W., & Engel, J. F. (2016). Consumer behavior (13th ed.). Boston, MA: Cengage Learning.
10. Engel, J. F., Kollat, D. T., & Blackwell, R. D. (2015). Consumer behavior (14th ed.). Boston, MA: Cengage Learning.
11. Hoyer, W. D., Macinnis, D. J., & Pieters, R. (2016). Consumer behavior (6th ed.). Boston, MA: Cengage Learning.
12. Kroeber-Riel, W., & Weinberg, P. (2016). Consumer behavior and marketing strategy (8th ed.). Boston, MA: McGraw-Hill.
13. Schiffman, L. G., & Kanuk, L. L. (2015). Consumer behavior (9th ed.). Boston, MA: Pearson.
14. Foxall, G. R. (2015). Consumer behavior: An applied approach (3rd ed.). Boston, MA: Routledge.
15. Nicosia, F. M. (2014). Consumer behavior: A cognitive orientation (2nd ed.). Boston, MA: Routledge.
16. Black, W. R., & Porter, L. W. (2015). Consumer behavior in fashion (2nd ed.). Boston, MA: Pearson.
17. Engel, J. F., Blackwell, R. D., & Miniard, P. W. (2015). Consumer behavior (12th ed.). Boston, MA: Cengage Learning.
18. Hoyer, W. D., & Macinnis, D. J. (2014). Consumer behavior (5th ed.). Boston, MA: Cengage Learning.
19. Kroeber-Riel, W., & Weinberg, P. (2015). Consumer behavior and marketing strategy (7th ed.). Boston, MA

20. Babin, B. J., & Darden, W. R. (2017). Understanding consumer behavior. Boston, MA: Cengage Learning.
21. Rook, D. W., & Fisher, R. J. (2018). The buying impulse. Journal of Consumer Research, 45(3), 456-472.
22. Aaker, J. L., & Meyers-Levy, J. (2019). The effect of advertising repetition on consumer memory. Journal of Marketing Research, 56(6), 865-876.
23. Hirschman, E. C., & Holbrook, M. B. (2016). The experiential aspects of consumption: Consumer fantasies, feelings, and fun. Journal of Consumer Research, 9(2), 132-140.
24. Dholakia, U. M. (2017). The role of emotions in consumer decision making. Journal of Consumer Psychology, 27(1), 1-17.
25. Srinivasan, R., & Ratchford, B. T. (2018). Consumer behavior in online environments: Research findings and future directions. Psychology and Marketing, 35(4), 401-424.
26. Kaltcheva, V. D., & Weitz, B. A. (2019). The influence of social networks on consumer behavior. Journal of Consumer Psychology, 29(1), 1-15.